The Challenge of Bahá'u'lláh

The
Challenge
of
Bahá'u'lláh

by

Gary L. Matthews

Bahá'í
PUBLISHING
WILMETTE, ILLINOIS

BAHÁ'Í PUBLISHING
415 LINDEN AVENUE, WILMETTE, ILLINOIS 60091-2844

05 06 07 08   4 3 2 1

Library of Congress Cataloging-in-Publication Data
Matthews, Gary L.
    The challenge of Bahá'u'lláh / by Gary L. Matthews.— Bahá'í Pub. ed.
        p. cm.
    Includes bibliographical references and index.
    ISBN 1–931847–16–9
    1. Bahá'u'lláh, 1817–1892—Prophecies. 2. Prophecy—Bahai Faith. I. Title.

BP362.2.M38 2005
297.9'3'092—dc22

                                                            2005040969

Typesetting by Stonehaven Press, Knoxville, Tennessee
Cover design by Robert A. Reddy

CONTENTS

This book is dedicated to
WINSTON G. EVANS, JR.
who awakened multitudes
to the glorious challenge of Bahá'u'lláh

PREFACE

The Challenge of Bahá'u'lláh is not primarily about "what Bahá'ís believe." It is a book about *why* Bahá'ís believe as we do—or why, at any rate, the author believes as he does. It attempts to share my admittedly personal understanding of why it makes sense, and feels right, to acknowledge the authority of Bahá'u'lláh as God's Messenger for this age.

In setting forth these grounds, it was my goal to reach the widest possible audience. This meant critiquing Bahá'u'lláh's claim from the standpoint of logic and common sense. There already are various books which seek to demonstrate His position by interpreting symbolic Bible prophecies fulfilled in His advent. This one, however, refrains from assuming the reader to be of any particular prior religious belief. It bases its appeal squarely on universal "first principles"—premises I find both logically and intuitively compelling, and which I dare hope may prove similarly satisfying to others.

Whether it succeeds is something only the reader can judge. I had little way of knowing, in advance, whether the information in *Challenge* would help others as it has helped me. I therefore feel immense gratitude to the many people who already have assured me that it does. In the acknowledgments I name specific individuals who helped in the writing and publication of this book. But more generally, I must here confess my debt to those readers who, by their letters, phone calls, and personal conversations validated its admittedly novel approach. The strength of that response far surpassed my expectations.

My thanks go especially to the numerous readers who welcomed chapter 5. This chapter correlates Bahá'í prophetic insights with recent developments in science, including relativity and quantum mechanics. Several advisers had urged me to omit such details, which they argued would be over the heads of most readers. I did not agree: Not only did I see this material as serving an important purpose, I also believed that a general audience does possess both the interest and the aptitude to follow a discussion of scientific principles. Though some findings of modern science may make one dizzy, they can be explained in nontechnical language accessible to the average reader. Were it otherwise, I could hardly write about them myself, since I am not a scientist but a journalist.

It is now clear that my confidence in the readership was fully justified. Of all the book's sections, those which relate to science have evoked the most consistently positive feedback. (Let me add, however, that anyone who prefers to skip them may do so without losing the main thread.)

A heartfelt welcome goes also to the many Christians who, through this book, have discovered in Bahá'u'lláh the fulfillment of Christianity's highest hopes. This pleases me because *Challenge,* though written for people of every religion and no religion, is meant to be completely consonant with biblical principles. Since my own roots are deeply Christian, it brings me great satisfaction to learn that the book strikes a chord with my Christian brothers and sisters. Their warm response prompted me to write a sequel and companion volume called *He Cometh with Clouds: A Bahá'í View of Christ's Return* (George Ronald, 1996). Though covering some of the same ground, *Clouds* approaches Bahá'í proofs from a biblical perspective, addressing in more detail the theological concerns of Christian believers.

Challenge is the first book, so far as I know, to correlate findings of modern physics with Bahá'í teachings concerning "luminiferous ether"—that hypothetical electromagnetic substance once believed to pervade all of space, but now, in its classical form, discredited. That part of chapter 5 is herewith expanded to include additional facts. Since first reporting my own findings, I've learned that they echo conclusions reached independently in papers written under the auspices of the Australian Association for Bahá'í Studies. Though I haven't yet seen these unpublished documents, they now are on file at the Bahá'í World Center. The Research Department of the Universal House of Justice kindly shared with me a summary of their contents.

While this edition incorporates significant new material, one section stands unchanged from past editions. That is chapter 6, which concerns Bahá'í expectations for the near-term future and events-in-process. Among topics covered in this chapter are the "Lesser Peace" and its relationship to the twentieth century. Originally written in 1989, this section remains intact, so that the future may reveal how well it stands the test of time.

Source references are numbered consecutively throughout the entire text—a departure from the usual practice of starting anew the sequence of numbers with the beginning of each chapter. This makes it simpler, in my opinion, to find a particular reference when turning to the end of the book.

The term "billion" means one thing in American English, another in British English. To avoid this ambiguity, I have at certain points used the expression "thousand million," which may sound awkward to some readers from the United States. It was a case of sacrificing familiarity for precision.

In the spelling of unfamiliar Persian and Arabic names and words, this book follows the standard phonetic system advocated by Shoghi Effendi, the Guardian of the Bahá'í Faith. In cases, however, where there exists a common anglicized spelling (Tehran, Baghdad, and so forth), I have used the familiar form to avoid confusion.

Whenever I have felt it necessary to clarify terms used in quotations from other sources, I have used [brackets] to identify my insertions. Unless specified otherwise, however, all instances of *italics* or (parentheses) in quotations are those of the writer being quoted.

Contacting the Author

I want very much to know your reaction to this book. If you have comments or questions, please share them with me. If I do not have answers, I will do my best to find someone who does.

Letters may be sent to me at the following address:

Gary L. Matthews
c/o U.S. Bahá'í Publishing Trust
415 Linden Avenue
Wilmette, IL 60091-2844

I can also be contacted by means of electronic mail: <bpt@usbnc.org>.

ACKNOWLEDGMENTS

The Challenge of Bahá'u'lláh encapsulates thirty-five years of research and reflection. Its original writing spanned 1989 through 1992. The book's first edition appeared in 1993, and it has since been updated twice—once for a 1999 second edition, and again for this new release. The first two editions were from George Ronald, Publisher (Oxford, England). This current version, though technically the third edition, is the first from Bahá'í Publishing (Wilmette, Illinois). Words can never express my gratitude to the staffs of these two wonderful companies, who worked together on the project with exemplary professionalism.

Nor could the book even have been written without the assistance of many other outstanding individuals. Foremost among these is my wife and best friend, Cheri Wallace Matthews. Always my most helpful critic, she cautions me when I am too brash, urges me on when I am too cautious, and pins me down when I am too vague or obscure. Beyond contributing many substantive ideas and insights, she spent four years rearranging her life to facilitate my often awkward schedule of research and writing.

A particularly central collaborator was the late Marzieh Gail, whose loving spirit lights these pages. It was she who encouraged me, as a student, to become a writer, who set me on many of the trails explored in this book, and who, through steady correspondence, helped sort out clues and questions that cropped up along the way. When the manuscript was complete, she was kind enough to give it a thorough polishing. This was among the last acts of her remarkable life, the earthly phase of which ended 16 October 1993, the very day this book first was published.

Also invaluable was the help of Sam G. McClellan (who, like Marzieh, no longer is physically with us), Vahid Alavian, Charles Coffey, and Kenneth Kalantar. Each kindly proofread the draft manuscript and offered many suggestions for improving it. The book's final form owes much to the expert advice and constructive criticism of these dear friends, who all gave generously of their valuable and extremely limited time.

The National Spiritual Assembly of the Bahá'ís of Grenada, West Indies, allowed me to make extensive use of its national library. The Research Department of the Universal House of Justice in Haifa, Israel, provided invaluable information concerning Bahá'í teachings on the Lesser Peace, ether, and other topics. Dr. Joel Brunson of the St. George's University School of Medicine in Grenada furnished voluminous copies of articles and textbook chapters documenting research into the genesis of cancer.

The two publishing companies cited above owe their excellence to the individuals of whom they consist. I particularly wish to thank Lee Minnerly and Terry Cassiday at Bahá'í Publishing, and May Ballerio, Wendi Momen, and Erica Leith at George Ronald.

Various other assists came from David Ruhe, Erica Toussaint, Michael Kafes, and Trip Barthel. To these dear friends, as well as to other persons and agencies too numerous to mention, I am deeply grateful.

INTRODUCTION

Religion is a system of belief, but it is also much more: It is voluntary submission to a Higher Power. This remains true whether we interpret that power as a living God, an impersonal cosmic force, or simply some noble purpose. Religion means joyous surrender, a giving of ourselves to something greater than ourselves.

No one was ever argued into such a commitment any more than anyone was ever argued into falling in love. It is not enough for religion to make sense intellectually; it must also feel right and ring true in the very depth of one's being. Beyond that, it requires deliberate choice, an act of courage and humility that must spring as much from the heart as from the head. Sometimes linear thought plays only a minor role: Persons with sharp insight may embrace a religion—knowing exactly why they choose to do so—long before they can explain or justify the logic of their decision to anyone else. Instinctively, they simply know.

Just the same, we can recognize these facts and still agree with Bertrand Russell: "What is wanted is not the will to believe, but the wish to find out, which is the exact opposite." There is deep satisfaction in thinking clearly and rationally about religion and exchanging ideas with other people. Without the illumination of spiritual intuition, reason is sterile; but without the discipline of reason, intuition can be hard to distinguish from blind emotionalism—or, worse yet, from blind imitation.

The sacred writings of the Bahá'í Faith clearly define the role of reason in attaining spiritual insight. These teachings advise a seeker to "apply thyself to rational and authoritative arguments. For arguments are a guide to the path and by this the heart will be turned unto the Sun of Truth. And when the heart is turned unto the Sun, then the eye will be opened and will recognize the Sun through the Sun itself. Then man will be in no need of arguments. . . ."[1] "In divine questions we must not depend entirely upon the heritage of tradition and former human experience; nay, rather, we must exercise reason, analyze and logically examine the facts presented so that confidence will be inspired and faith attained."[2]

This book is the fruit of one person's struggle to understand and fulfill these admonitions. It seeks to present, in rational terms, the basis for my belief that the Bahá'í Revelation is divine in origin, and to explain why I see its claim as posing a challenge of critical importance to humanity. Since religious conviction has roots that go far deeper than words or logic, it would be presumptuous to call this book a complete statement of my reasons for being a Bahá'í. Those reasons that I can explain in print constitute only one aspect (and not necessarily the most important aspect) of the experiences and promptings that have helped shape my belief. Nevertheless, I share them in the hope that they will prove useful or stimulating.

I have written primarily for two large groups of people: (1) those interested in the Bahá'í Faith but not committed to it; and (2) those already committed to the Faith who want to know more about the evidence upon which its claims rest. However, some readers may be hearing of the Bahá'í Faith for the first time. For them I have tried to provide, as the discussion unfolds, whatever background information is needed for an understanding of the points raised.

Chapter 1

A TURNING POINT IN HISTORY

The major advances in civilization are processes which all
but wreck the societies in which they occur.
—*Alfred North Whitehead*

. . . we must rise above the storm, the chaos of surface detail,
and from a higher vantage-point look for the outline of
some great and significant phenomenon. To rise up so as
to see clearly is what I have tried to do, and it has led me
to accept, however improbable they may appear, the reality
and the consequences of the major cosmic process which . . .
I have called "human planetization."
—*Pierre Teilhard de Chardin*

Humanity clearly is passing through a crisis of transition. But
a transition to what? It is easy to see turbulent changes wherever we look; easier still to see we all have a stake in those
changes. It is not so easy to see what they mean, where they
are taking us, or how we can respond constructively. Millions
of people, sensing the importance of such questions, are
earnestly seeking answers.

I believe those answers will elude us until we come to grips
with an issue the world has evaded for more than a century:

Who was Bahá'u'lláh?

It may sound unlikely that the identity of this Persian
nobleman Who lived from 1817 to 1892 can shed any light
on the upheavals that fill modern headlines. A "Who's Who"-
style biographical sketch would tell us little—merely that He
founded the Bahá'í Faith and spent forty years in prison and
exile for proclaiming a message of peace and love. Marginally

1

useful information, perhaps, in studying for a trivia quiz; but hardly crucial to an understanding of current events.

This being so, we must clarify the deeper sense in which it is important to ask who Bahá'u'lláh really was. First, however, some historical observations may make it easier to see the modern relevance of this question.

It is an intriguing fact that each major world religion—Hinduism, Judaism, Zoroastrianism, Buddhism, Christianity, and Islam—has given birth to a great civilization. These historic civilizations all have certain things in common. Each, in its turn, became the highest and most advanced culture the world had known until that time. Each, at its height, absorbed and unified hundreds of warring ethnic groups into a spiritual brotherhood. Each later declined and decayed to become more a source of conflict than of cooperation.

This cyclic rise and fall of civilizations—deriving their initial impulse from religion—has largely shaped the modern world. For example, the Hebrew culture derived from Judaism fertilized the philosophy of ancient Greece and left a code of law that became the basis for every modern legal system. When the Roman Empire collapsed, Christianity rose from its rubble, founded the new world of the West, and institutionalized a spirit of charity and philanthropy that still survives. As Western Europe sank into the Dark Ages, Islam molded primitive Arab tribes into an empire more vast than that of Rome at its peak, adorned its cities with flourishing universities and libraries, invented soap, algebra, Arabic numerals, and hundreds of other modern conveniences, and (during its centuries in Spain) indirectly triggered Europe's Renaissance. Moreover, it was Islam that introduced nationalism in the modern sense—a concept that, whatever its limitations, has spurred social and economic development throughout the world. Similar comments could be made about the magnificent civilizations engendered by Hinduism, Buddhism, and Zoroastrianism.

Each of these religious systems arose from the teachings of a single remarkable individual. Thus Moses became the central figure of Judaism, Jesus of Christianity, Muḥammad of Islam, Krishna of Hinduism, Buddha of Buddhism, and Zoroaster of Zoroastrianism. These spiritual guides are easily the most influential figures in history, for it is they who shaped and inspired the civilizations that followed them. Their lives and teachings display uncanny similarities. Each claimed to derive His influence and authority directly from God. Each was known for saintly character and vast intuitive knowledge. Each was bitterly opposed by the civil and religious authorities of His time. Each attracted a small community of followers who (often after centuries of struggle) triumphed over persecution to establish the given faith as a major force in society. Each taught the same basic spiritual concepts regarding belief in God, life after death, prayer, self-discipline, ethical principles such as the Golden Rule, and the like. Each, however, modified the previous religion's social laws and regulations according to the needs of the changed time. Each reaffirmed the divine origin of previous religions, and each promised that God would send future messengers with new and fuller revelations.

The most remarkable parallel among these religions is found in their prophecies concerning the "last days." Each faith anticipates a culmination of human history when the earth, as a result of fiery tribulations, will be transformed into paradise. Cataclysmic changes will produce the "Kingdom of God on earth"[3] in which the nations "shall beat their swords into plowshares, and their spears into pruninghooks: nation shall not lift up sword against nation, neither shall they learn war any more."[4] The various religions will be gathered under "one fold and one shepherd"[5] and "the earth shall be full of the knowledge of the Lord, as the waters cover the sea."[6] Substantially identical prophecies abound not only in the Old and New Testaments but also in the scriptures of all the world's historic faiths.

These same prophecies, with one voice, foretell the appearance of a World Reformer or Divine Teacher destined to initiate the promised changes. The central hope of every world faith revolves around the coming of such a spiritual leader, often identified as the "return" of the founder of the religion embodying the prophecy. In Judaism this Promised One is known as the Lord of Hosts; in Christianity, as the Second Coming of Christ; in Islam, as the Mihdí or Twelfth Imám; in Hinduism, as the return of Krishna; in Buddhism, as the Fifth Buddha; and in Zoroastrianism, as the promised Sháh-Bahrám.

Simply stated, the histories, teachings, and prophecies of these religions offer parallels far too numerous and too remarkable to be explained as mere coincidence. How can this seemingly arbitrary pattern repeat itself, age after age, in movements so widely separated by time, geography, and culture? Does this not suggest the possibility that all of them (not merely one or two) are truly divine in origin, that their founders were each inspired by a merciful God as agents of one vast civilizing process guiding humanity towards maturity? Would it not follow that their latter-day prophecies, foreshadowing the radical trans-formation of society through the influence of a promised redeemer, all point to the same mysterious Figure?

Bahá'ís believe that such is indeed the case. The hallmark of their faith is acceptance of Bahá'u'lláh's claim that He Himself is the Promised One of *all* religions—the long-awaited Peace-bringer whose revelation, as foretold in earlier scriptures, will bring into being a worldwide divine civilization.

"The Revelation which, from time immemorial, hath been acclaimed as the Purpose and Promise of all the Prophets of God, and the most cherished Desire of His Messengers, hath now . . . been revealed unto men," writes Bahá'u'lláh. "The advent of such a Revelation hath been heralded in all the sacred Scriptures. Behold how, notwithstanding such an announcement, mankind hath strayed from its path and shut out itself from its glory."[7]

If this claim is true—and if we can confirm or substantiate it by objective investigation—then clearly it marks the most important turning point in human history. Bahá'u'lláh says the upheavals and convulsions of today are those foretold in the sacred books of all past religions, that they are preparing the world for the promised era of peace and justice, and that His revelation has set in motion the forces that will gradually bring it about. He has also given to the world approximately one hundred volumes of guidance on how individuals and institutions can best meet the challenges of this time, hastening the Golden Age that must follow.

In deciding whether Bahá'u'lláh's claim merits investigation, we must bear in mind two points. The first is that He does not ask anyone to accept a literal interpretation of ancient prophecy. According to Bahá'u'lláh, most prophecies of past religions have important meanings that are to be understood symbolically, not literally. For example, He teaches that the "end of the world"—a recurring theme of scripture—means not the physical destruction of the planet, but rather the end of civilization as we know it through its transformation into a higher, global civilization "with a fullness of life such as the world has never seen nor can as yet conceive."[8] This process is viewed not as something magical or instantaneous, but as the result of an unfolding, divinely ordained process of social evolution.

Further examples illustrate this same first point. For instance, Bahá'u'lláh interprets the "return of Christ" (or Buddha, Krishna, or any other Divine Messenger) not as the return of the physical individual but as the mystic return of the Voice of God that spoke through Him. It is, He teaches, the return of the light rather than the lamp, the reappearance in a new human temple of the perfections, power, and authority vested in Christ and the other Divine Educators. Bahá'u'lláh expounds other prophetic themes—resurrection, judgment, and the like—in a similar allegorical manner.

The second, and more important, point is that Bahá'u'lláh does not ask anyone to accept His claim without supporting evidence. Faith is often misunderstood to mean blind acceptance of authority. Bahá'u'lláh denounces this pseudo-faith as "blind imitation" and places the independent investigation of truth in the forefront of His moral principles. Real faith is defined in His teachings to mean conscious knowledge expressed in action.[9] Although Bahá'u'lláh asks us to take His word for many things, He upholds the right and responsibility of each individual to verify independently His Faith's central premise—namely, that "This thing is not from Me, but from One Who is Almighty and All-Knowing."[10] He marshals a host of compelling reasons—both logical and intuitive—to support this claim, inviting seekers to "consider His clear evidence"[11] and to "gaze, with an open and unbiased mind, on the signs of His Revelation, the proofs of His Mission, and the tokens of His glory."[12] ". . . the evidences of His effulgent glory," He writes, "are now actually manifest. It behoveth you to ascertain whether or not such a light hath appeared."[13]

My purpose in this book is to "consider His clear evidence" by which we can "ascertain whether or not such a light hath appeared." The details of Bahá'u'lláh's life, the history of His Faith, and the specifics of His teachings will be examined primarily for the light they shed on the central issue: *Who was Bahá'u'lláh?* In other words, was He—as He claimed—the promised World Redeemer foretold in the sacred books of past ages, and is His message a genuine revelation from God?

If the correct answer is "Yes," then clearly it is vital that we know it. Bahá'u'lláh's revelation, if genuine, would enable us to understand the changes shaking the world today, to foresee the results they will produce, and to make the most of the challenges and opportunities they offer.

The second chapter of this book will provide a brief summary of Bahá'í history and of Bahá'u'lláh's major teachings; the third will suggest a few of the many ways an inquirer can test His claim. The remaining chapters will present the actual evidence that supports my own belief as a Bahá'í. Whether my personal reasons seem convincing to others is less important to me than whether they stimulate independent investigation. That, of course, will be for the reader to decide.

Chapter 2

DIVINE SPRINGTIME

We spend our lives trying to unlock the mystery of the universe, but there was a Turkish prisoner, Bahá'u'lláh in 'Akká, Palestine, who had the key.
—*Leo Tolstoy*

Once to every man and nation
    comes the moment to decide,
        Some great Cause, God's new Messiah . . .
            —*James Russell Lowell*

This chapter consists of three parts: (1) an outline of Bahá'u'-lláh's major teachings, (2) a capsule history of His Faith, and (3) further details about the nature of His claim. I will refrain, both in this chapter and the next, from offering any arguments or evidence to support that claim; these will come later. For the moment, my purpose is simply to familiarize the reader with the events and concepts to which any such discussion must refer.

BAHÁ'Í TEACHINGS

Bahá'u'lláh's fundamental teaching is that all human beings are children of one God, Who, by successively revealing His will in each of the world's historic faiths, has patiently guided humanity towards spiritual and social maturity. Having passed through infancy and adolescence, humanity is now coming of age. Its collective life is undergoing a profound transformation, akin to that of a caterpillar turning into a butterfly. The product of this metamorphosis must and will be the world's first truly global society.

This pivotal concept—planetary unification as the fruit of humankind's dawning maturity—is the principle Bahá'ís call the "oneness of humanity." As formulated by Bahá'u'lláh in the latter half of the nineteenth century, this principle is much more than a vague platitude. It incorporates a bold and detailed plan for world reconstruction, involving an "organic change" in the very nature of society. When Bahá'u'lláh says "The earth is but one country, and mankind its citizens,"[14] He means it in every sense of the phrase: political, economic, social, institutional—even military.

All of Bahá'u'lláh's other teachings revolve around the oneness of humanity, as spokes revolve around the hub of a wheel. To support and implement this overriding goal, He calls for widespread application of the following principles:

Independent investigation of truth: Each human being is born with the right and obligation to investigate reality—especially the reality of religion—without undue influence from others. ". . . see with thine own eyes and not through the eyes of others," writes Bahá'u'lláh, "and . . . know of thine own knowledge and not through the knowledge of thy neighbor."[15] "The essence of all that We have revealed for thee is Justice, is for man to free himself from idle fancy and imitation . . . and look into all things with a searching eye."[16]

Acceptance of the divine origin of all world religions: The time has come, Bahá'u'lláh says, for the world's contending faiths to recognize one another as different stages of one ever-evolving religion of God. In every age, God speaks through a chosen mediator, adapting His teaching to the specialized needs of the time and the growing capacity of humanity. Bahá'u'lláh states that despite these outward differences (compounded by many centuries of human misunderstanding and prejudice): "Every true Prophet hath regarded His Message as fundamentally the same as the Revelation of every other Prophet gone before Him."[17]

Eradication of prejudice in all its forms: Bahá'u'lláh demands vigorous effort, through individual action as well as education and public policy, to abolish the root causes of prejudice. Bahá'ís therefore cherish unity in diversity, cultivating an integrated community life wherein members socialize, work together, and even intermarry across barriers of color, nationality, religion, and social status.

Equal rights and opportunities for men and women: The two sexes are likened in the Bahá'í teachings to two wings that must be balanced before the bird of humanity can soar aloft. In particular, Bahá'u'lláh identifies equal participation by women in government decision-making as a vital key to world peace.

Reconciliation of science and religion: Both disciplines, according to Bahá'u'lláh, are different paths to a single truth. Rightly understood, science and religion are therefore in complete harmony, for truth can never contradict itself. 'Abdu'l-Bahá states, "Should a man try to fly with the wing of religion alone he would quickly fall into the quagmire of superstition, whilst on the other hand, with the wing of science alone he would also make no progress, but fall into the despairing slough of materialism." He continues, "When religion, shorn of its superstitions, traditions, and unintelligent dogmas, shows its conformity with science, then will there be a great unifying, cleansing force in the world which will sweep before it all wars, disagreements, discords and struggles. . . ."[18]

World peace through collective security: Bahá'u'lláh urges all nations to limit armaments and, by joining in a global federation, unitedly to resist aggression from any member-state. His plan goes far beyond current United Nations activities: He envisages a world constitution, a world parliament, a world court with binding authority to settle disputes among nations, and a world executive to carry out decisions of the parliament and court. While safeguarding the rights and freedoms of all members, such a system—representative self-government on a planetary scale—would empower humanity as a whole to implement its collective will peacefully through international law.

Adoption of a universal auxiliary language: He calls upon the nations to choose, by mutual consent, a single language to be taught in schools throughout the globe in addition to each country's mother tongue. This would provide a powerful tool for international understanding and cooperation while respecting the cultural heritage of all.

Universal compulsory education: This principle is one that Bahá'u'lláh forcefully enunciated long before it became routine policy in most of today's developed nations. Its importance remains tragically underestimated throughout much of the world.

Elimination of extremes of wealth and poverty: Public policy, according to Bahá'u'lláh, must limit dire poverty on the one hand and gross accumulation of excessive wealth on the other. The intent of this principle is to preserve degrees of wealth, which are necessary, while abolishing extremes, which are not. Bahá'u'lláh encourages private initiative while condemning as unjust and unworkable all attempts to impose complete economic equality.

Recognition of love and unity as the central purpose of religion: Bahá'u'lláh categorically forbids not only religious violence but all forms of religious conflict and contention as alien to the true spirit of faith. He states that God's purpose in sending His Messengers has always been to unite human hearts; if religion has the opposite effect, we would be better off without it.

While these themes accurately reflect the spirit of the Bahá'í Faith, they in no way exhaust its teachings. Bahá'u'lláh touches on literally thousands of vital issues, ancient and modern, disclosing in the process a comprehensive blueprint for a unified world society. No summary can capture so vast a panorama of ideas; it can only hint at their scope and direction.

Bahá'u'lláh's teachings emphasize, moreover, that "ideas and principles are helpless without a divine power to put them into effect."[19] The primary function of divine revelation, He explains, is not to introduce new teachings (important though these are), but to provide such a power. Here is part of what He says about this all-important topic.

The Messengers of God, according to Bahá'u'lláh, are far more than great teachers or reformers. They are Spiritual Suns through Whom God floods the world with divine energy. This intangible yet dynamic influence—traditionally called the Holy Spirit—is the power by which God stirs the Divine Messenger and, through Him, all humanity. The Messenger from God is "luminous in Himself," while all other souls must borrow His light;[20] and His recurring appearance affects human society much as springtime affects the physical world. Whenever a new Messenger "shines upon the worlds of spirits, of thoughts and of hearts, then the spiritual spring and new life appear, the power of the wonderful springtime becomes visible, and marvelous benefits are apparent."[21] New thoughts, new trends, and new movements surface everywhere (even among those unaware of their source in the new revelation), and a universal fermentation sweeps away obsolete ideas and institutions. As the mystical impulse generated by the new Messenger gradually penetrates society, it attracts ever-increasing numbers to rally around Him and recognize His divine authority. Sooner or later it culminates in the birth of a new social order based on the newly revealed laws and teachings.

Bahá'ís believe it is this divine impulse that has enabled every past revelation to create a new and higher civilization; it is this, they believe, that ensures the eventual emergence of a world commonwealth based on Bahá'u'lláh's social principles, and the continued growth and development of that commonwealth under the influence of future Messengers from God. Bahá'u'lláh indicates, however, that while this divinely ordained process is both irresistible and inevitable, it is not automatic. The social transformation that follows the appearance of a Messenger from God may be relatively quick and benign; it may be exceedingly long and painful; or it may fall somewhere between these extremes. How easily humanity navigates the transition is determined primarily by the readiness of individuals to investigate and accept the new Messenger's divine mandate. Our response also determines the extent to which we as individuals benefit spiritually from the new revelation.

Our expectations concerning the feasibility of Bahá'u'lláh's social reforms will depend greatly on whether we accept the reality of this mystical animating power—the power from which (Bahá'ís believe) the teachings derive their spiritual force. Most of His principles by now command widespread acceptance as desirable goals. Something many people still question, however, is whether such goals can ever be translated into practice. It should be clear that if the Bahá'í program is truly a divine revelation, its aims are attainable because "the power of the Kingdom of God will aid and assist in their realization."[22]

Another question often raised about the Bahá'í Faith is whether it offers anything really new. The answer is a resounding "Yes." Bahá'u'lláh's broad social principles are, of course, no longer new in the sense of being unfamiliar to the general public (although they were radically new and unfamiliar when He first propounded them in the nineteenth century). They certainly are new, however, in the sense that they are not explicit in the sacred books of any previous religion. When we move beyond broad principles to detailed specifics, we can easily identify many elements of the Faith that are new both in the sense of being still unknown to the public and in that of being unparalleled in previous religions. Bahá'u'lláh set forth detailed new laws and ordinances covering marriage and divorce, burial and inheritance, prayer and fasting, personal conduct and countless other matters; created a revolutionary new type of administrative order designed to implement His laws and principles throughout the world and serve as a pattern for future society; and provided vast amounts of never-before-revealed information concerning God's purpose for humankind, the nature of life after death and how to prepare for it, and many similar topics. His followers believe that this astonishing system of laws, institutions, and doctrines, being of divine rather than human origin, is destined to uplift and regenerate society. Be that as it may, one can hardly deny either the novelty or the originality of the overall structure.

The admitted importance of these two questions—"Is the Bahá'í program really practical?" and "Does it offer anything really new?"—is reflected in the fact that they are frequently asked by persons investigating the religion. For the reasons stated above, I believe the answer, in each case, hinges on a deeper, logically more fundamental issue: *Who was Bahá'u'lláh?* If He was the bearer of a genuine revelation from God, then that revelation must contain much that is both new and practical. To doubt that it does so is to doubt that Bahá'u'lláh Himself is Who He claims to be.

That is why this book will keep the spotlight on the crucial question of Bahá'u'lláh's identity. One must, of course, know something of His teachings in order to gauge the truth or falsity of His claim, and the book will discuss these teachings extensively in connection with that central issue. It also will provide an extensive bibliography for those seeking more information. The point I wish to stress, however, is that one cannot logically investigate the Bahá'í message without reference to the Messenger.

THE HISTORICAL BACKGROUND

Persia (currently called Iran) was in biblical times the heart of a fabulous empire. By the mid-nineteenth century, however, it had entirely lost its ancient glory and was regarded throughout most of the world as backward and insignificant. A reactionary monarchy held absolute sway over a mostly superstitious and apathetic populace; government and people alike were subject, in turn, to the pervasive influence of a fanatical Muslim priesthood. The prevailing religion was the Shí'ih sect of Islam. It was a closed—one might say locked—society, hostile to all progressive ideas and particularly those of the "satanic" West.

It was in this darkened corner of the world that the Bahá'í Faith began in 1844. Its destiny was shaped by the lives of three Central Figures—the Báb, Bahá'u'lláh, and 'Abdu'l-Bahá.

The Báb (1819–50)

On 23 May 1844, Siyyid 'Alí-Muḥammad, a twenty-four-year-old merchant from the Persian city of Shíráz, declared that He was a Messenger from God and the Herald of a still greater Messenger soon to follow. He took the title of the Báb, meaning "Gate," indicating that His mission was to pave the way for the imminent appearance of the Promised One foretold in the holy books of all religions.

The Báb's teaching stirred Persia to its depths, igniting violent opposition from both government and clergy. He was arrested, tortured, imprisoned, and eventually executed by firing squad in Tabríz on 9 July 1850. More than twenty thousand of His followers (known as Bábís) perished in a subsequent bloodbath initiated by authorities in their effort to exterminate His Faith.

The Báb's riddled remains were dumped on the ground outside the city's moat, in the hope they would be eaten by wild animals. His followers, however, risked their lives to rescue His body surreptitiously from careless guards and move it to a safe hiding place. Today it rests in a golden-domed shrine, surrounded by magnificent gardens, on Mount Carmel, at Haifa, Israel.

Bahá'u'lláh (1817–92)

Among the Báb's early followers was Mírzá Ḥusayn-'Alí, later known as Bahá'u'lláh ("the Glory of God"), a title by which the Báb addressed Him. A descendant of Persian royalty and son of a high government official, He inherited great wealth, which He might easily have augmented by taking a position at court. However, He raised many eyebrows by turning away from the halls of power, devoting Himself and His fortune instead to humanitarian service. Upon learning of the Báb's message, Bahá'u'lláh became the movement's most effective and articulate spokesman.

As a highly visible leader of the Bábí community, He was a natural target for the persecution that followed the Báb's martyrdom. In 1852 Bahá'u'lláh was chained, beaten, imprisoned, stripped of His wealth, and marked for death. However, at the last moment, the authorities, fearing awkward repercussions from the slaying of so prominent a figure, decided instead to deport Him and His family to Baghdad, Iraq. (Iraq at that time was part of the Turkish Empire, also known as the Ottoman Empire.)

For a while, the government and clergy felt they had extinguished the Faith of the Báb. Their relief was short-lived, however, as the movement again surged forward under Bahá'u'lláh's now-distant but vigorous leadership. Seeking to remove Him even farther from their borders, Persia prevailed upon the Ottoman government to banish Him again. Bahá'u'lláh and His family were therefore "invited" to Constantinople, capital of the Turkish Empire, where authorities assumed they could watch and control His activities with relative ease.

On the eve of this transfer, in April 1863, Bahá'u'lláh declared to His companions that He was the promised Messenger Whose coming it had been the Báb's mission to announce. Almost all of the Bábís eventually accepted this claim, thereafter becoming known as Bahá'ís.

Bahá'u'lláh's removal to the Ottoman capital, far from silencing Him, had the opposite effect. A cosmopolitan trade-center, Constantinople was a frequent stopover for visiting Persians and other travelers, who carried His teachings far and wide. Moreover, leaders of thought residing in Constantinople itself gravitated increasingly towards Bahá'u'lláh. Though He and His followers shunned political pursuits, Bahá'u'lláh's growing spiritual influence eventually alarmed Turkish officials, already under pressure from the government of Persia to send Him still farther away. Once again He was uprooted and banished, this time to distant Adrianople—the Turkish equivalent of Siberia. This latest countermeasure, however, proved to be simply another exercise in futility; its chief result was to amplify the proclamation of Bahá'u'lláh's message and fan the flames of His Cause. In 1868 His dismayed adversaries responded by locking Him and His retinue in the remote Turkish fortress-prison of 'Akká, now a city in Israel, though at that time within the Ottoman Empire. This punishment was intended as a death sentence, conditions in 'Akká being so foul and inhumane that the hardiest prisoner seldom survived more than a year. Many of Bahá'u'lláh's companions, including His beloved youngest son, Mírzá Mihdí, did perish in the prison; He Himself was strictly confined within the fortress walls for no less than nine years.

Throughout this grim incarceration, Bahá'u'lláh continued guiding His movement to new victories and adding to the already vast collection of His writings. From 'Akká He proclaimed His mission in letters to the kings and rulers of the world, urging them to compose their differences and create a global federation to secure a just and lasting peace. "Had they hearkened unto Me," He later wrote, "they would have beheld the earth another earth."[23] Nevertheless, He vowed that God would ensure victory for the Bahá'í Cause, with or without assistance from any king.

The harsh confinement eventually was relaxed as Bahá'u'lláh's character and personality won the friendship of His jailers. Towards the end of His life, though still nominally a prisoner, He was allowed to move about as He pleased, continue His writing, and meet with the many pilgrims and visiting dignitaries who sought His presence.

When He passed away on 29 May 1892, the news reached the Turkish government in a cable opening with the words "the Sun of Bahá has set."[24] His earthly remains are interred near 'Akká in a shrine at Bahjí (Delight), across the Bay of Haifa from Mount Carmel.

'Abdu'l-Bahá (1844–1921)

Bahá'u'lláh's eldest son, 'Abbás Effendi, was born 23 May 1844—the night of the Báb's declaration. As He grew to manhood He shared fully in the persecutions that rained upon Bahá'u'lláh, becoming His father's ablest supporter and assistant. Known to Bahá'ís as "the Master," He preferred the title He Himself chose—'Abdu'l-Bahá, "servant of the Glory." Bahá'u'lláh's last will and testament named 'Abdu'l-Bahá the head and interpreter of the Faith and made His word equal in authority, though not in rank, to Bahá'u'lláh's own.

While still a prisoner in 1898, 'Abdu'l-Bahá greeted the first Western Bahá'í pilgrims to 'Akká. After His release in 1908 He undertook a series of journeys that brought Him in 1911–13 to Europe and America. Here He expounded Bahá'u'lláh's message before large audiences in churches, auditoriums, and private homes; drew extensive press coverage; and met with many leaders of thought.

Returning to Palestine, 'Abdu'l-Bahá received a knighthood from the British Crown for His relief work during World War I, supervised preliminary construction of the Shrine of the Báb, began implementing the Administrative Order envisioned in the writings of Bahá'u'lláh, and designed a long-range teaching plan to carry the Bahá'í Faith throughout the earth.

'Abdu'l-Bahá passed away in 1921 and is interred in a northern room of the Shrine of the Báb in Haifa.

The Bahá'í Administrative Order

Bahá'u'lláh and 'Abdu'l-Bahá provided for continuing leadership of the Faith through two institutions: the Guardianship, a hereditary office holding the exclusive right to interpret authoritatively the Bahá'í teachings; and the Universal House of Justice, a democratically elected body of men empowered to legislate on all questions not covered in the sacred texts.

'Abdu'l-Bahá's will and testament named His grandson Shoghi Effendi the first Guardian of the Cause. Shoghi Ef-

fendi worked tirelessly towards the establishment of the
Universal House of Justice, which was first elected in 1963.
He also produced masterful translations of the Bahá'í sacred
writings, wrote extensively on the administration, history, and
goals of the Faith, completed construction of the Shrine of the
Báb, vigorously assisted with the construction of America's first
Bahá'í House of Worship, and launched the successive teaching campaigns planned by 'Abdu'l-Bahá. When he died in
1957 at the age of sixty-one, he had no children and was
unable to appoint a successor under the terms of 'Abdu'l-
Bahá's will; there is thus no incumbent to the Guardianship.
Although this development came as a shock to the Bahá'ís, it
had been envisioned and provided for in Bahá'u'lláh's book
of laws, the Kitáb-i-Aqdas (Most Holy Book).[25] The Universal
House of Justice, in keeping with those provisions, today
directs the Faith from the Bahá'í World Center in Haifa.

Local and national Bahá'í affairs are administered by a net-
work of Spiritual Assemblies, each consisting of nine believers
elected without regard to gender, race, class, or other social
or economic distinction. Elections are by secret ballot, with
no campaigns or nominations; and the religion has no clergy,
paid or otherwise. Financial support is accepted only from
declared believers, all contributions being both voluntary and
confidential.

As part of their global teaching effort, Bahá'ís have sought
consistently to disperse throughout the world. As a result,
though there are relatively few large concentrations of Bahá'ís,
the Faith has become the second most widely spread religion
on earth, with a significant following in more countries than
any other except Christianity. (The *Encyclopaedia Britannica*
yearbook, in successive editions beginning with 1988, lists
Christianity as first with 254 countries, the Bahá'í Faith as
second with 205, and Islam as third with 172.[26]) Moreover,
the Faith exhibits extraordinary cultural and ethnic diversity
and rapidly accelerating growth. Its broadly based unity has
made it an effective champion of such causes as international

peace, women's rights, social and economic development, environmental conservation, and literacy training.

THE MANIFESTATION OF GOD

Only by clearly understanding Bahá'u'lláh's claim can we decide how best to evaluate it. To better grasp the specifics of that claim, let us now consider what Bahá'u'lláh says about the nature of God and His Messengers.

Bahá'u'lláh teaches that there are three distinct planes of existence or levels of reality: the world of God, the world of humanity, and the world of the Messengers (or "Manifestations") Who mediate between God and humanity. A few comments are in order about each of these worlds.

Regarding the highest plane of existence, Bahá'u'lláh "proclaims unequivocally the existence and oneness of a personal God, unknowable, inaccessible, the source of all Revelation, eternal, omniscient, omnipresent and almighty."[27] The God thus described "is a God Who is conscious of His creation, Who has a Mind, a Will, a Purpose, and not, as many scientists and materialists believe, an unconscious and determined force operating in the universe. . . . To say that God is a personal Reality does not mean that He has a physical form, or does in any way resemble a human being. To entertain such belief would be sheer blasphemy."[28] Bahá'u'lláh writes that God is "immeasurably exalted beyond every human attribute such as corporeal existence, ascent and descent, egress and regress. . . . He is, and hath ever been, veiled in the ancient eternity of His Essence, and will remain in His Reality everlastingly hidden from the sight of men."[29]

At the other end of the spectrum is the human world. Bahá'u'lláh states that God created all humanity "to know Him and to love Him"[30] and "to carry forward an ever-advancing civilization."[31] Moreover, every human being is created in "the image and likeness of God" (cf. Genesis 1:25–6)—not in any physical sense (for God has no physical form), but in the sense of being able to express God's attributes such as knowledge, love, mercy, justice, kindness, will, loftiness, and countless others.

However, finite man cannot conceive or comprehend the Infinite Creator, nor can he reflect God's attributes except within the limits of his own capacity. He is able, at best, to make continual progress towards perfection without ever actually achieving it. Moreover, he cannot do even this much by his own unaided effort, since he has no direct access to the knowledge of God or His will. God therefore intervenes periodically in history, at intervals typically varying from five hundred to one thousand years, providing humankind with guidance through a chosen Christ-figure or Manifestation.

Bahá'u'lláh teaches that "this subtle, this mysterious and ethereal Being,"[32] the Manifestation of God, has two aspects—one human, the other divine. His human personality is "in the uttermost state of servitude, a servitude the like of which no man can possibly attain."[33] His inner reality, however, manifests the infinite perfections of God as a polished mirror reflects the image of the sun. He is a relay station linking the world of God with that of man. This unique capacity is a divine gift that cannot be acquired by study or effort: "However far the disciples might progress, they could never become Christ."[34] The Divine Manifestation belongs to a different sphere altogether.

Elaborating this theme, Bahá'u'lláh writes that God

> hath manifested unto men the Day Stars of His divine guidance . . . and hath ordained the knowledge of these sanctified Beings to be identical with the knowledge of His own Self. . . . Every one of them is the Way of God that connecteth this world with the realms above, and the Standard of His Truth unto every one in the kingdoms of earth and heaven.[35]

> These sanctified Mirrors, these Day Springs of ancient glory are, one and all, the Exponents on earth of Him Who is the central Orb of the universe, its Essence and ultimate Purpose. From Him proceed their knowledge and power; from Him is derived their sovereignty. . . . These Taberna-

cles of Holiness, these Primal Mirrors which reflect the light of unfading glory, are but expressions of Him Who is the Invisible of the Invisibles. . . . these illuminated Souls . . . have, each and every one of them, been endowed with all the attributes of God, such as sovereignty, dominion, and the like, even though to outward seeming they be shorn of all earthly majesty.[36]

In saying the Manifestations are "endowed with all the attributes of God," Bahá'u'lláh means just that. God is the All-Knowing; the Manifestations are therefore "omniscient at will."[37] God is the All-Powerful; for the Manifestations, therefore, "any difficult or impracticable thing is possible and easy . . . for They have all power."[38] God is infallible; consequently, "whatever proceeds from them is identical with the truth, and conformable to reality."[39] God is love; He is the source of all goodness and perfection; the Manifestations are therefore "the supreme embodiment of all that is lovable."[40] These divine qualities notwithstanding, the Messengers of God also are fully human—a duality often reflected in Their utterances. Sometimes the Manifestation speaks from His human position, evincing complete humility and self-effacement. At other times, His human personality fades into the background, leaving only "the Voice of Divinity, the Call of God Himself."[41] These two modes of speech may alternate within a single discourse, or even engage in dialogue with each other. In one of His prayers Bahá'u'lláh expresses this delightful paradox:

When I contemplate, O my God, the relationship that bindeth me to Thee, I am moved to proclaim to all created things "verily I am God!"; and when I consider my own self, lo, I find it coarser than clay![42]

Bahá'u'lláh's claim to fulfill prophecies of Christ, Buddha, and other Divine Messengers in no way exalts Him above His predecessors. Though Their revelations vary according to the receptivity of the age, no Manifestation is intrinsically superior to another. So perfect is their inward spiritual unity that they may be "regarded as one soul and the same person. . . . They all abide in the same tabernacle, soar in the same heaven, are seated upon the same throne, utter the same speech, and proclaim the same Faith."[43]

Moreover, the Bahá'í Faith "emphatically repudiates the claim to be regarded as the final revelation of God's will and purpose for mankind."[44] Bahá'u'lláh specifically affirms:

> God hath sent down His Messengers to succeed to Moses and Jesus, and He will continue to do so till "the end that hath no end"; so that His grace may, from the heaven of Divine bounty, be continually vouchsafed to mankind.[45]

He does state, however, that a period of at least one thousand years must separate His revelation from the one to follow.[46]

From these and many similar statements, we can see that there is nothing vague or ambiguous about the claim of Bahá'u'lláh. It is simple in concept, detailed and specific in its implications, and awesome in its magnitude.

We turn now to the problem of evaluating that claim. What kind of evidence might have a bearing on its truth? What credentials could a Manifestation offer that would vindicate His mission, and how might we verify them? These are, of course, subtle and intricate questions—yet they lie directly in our path. Before discussing any specific evidence in connection with Bahá'u'lláh's claim, let us try in the next chapter to map out a strategy for collecting such evidence and testing its validity.

Chapter 3

LIFE'S LABORATORY

. . . the years of searching in the dark for a truth that one feels, but cannot express; the intense desire and the alternations of confidence and misgiving, until one breaks through to clarity and understanding, are only known to him who has himself experienced them.
—*Albert Einstein*

Faith . . . plucks at a twig of evidence.
—*Emily Dickinson*

We cannot logically justify a claim of authority by invoking the very authority in question. Such an approach would commit the fallacy of circular reasoning. On the other hand, it would be pointless for an invisible Deity to reveal His will through a human envoy unless He also furnished clues or indications enabling us to recognize that envoy.

Bahá'u'lláh assures us that God can and does provide such signs. He states that it would be "far from the grace of the All-Bountiful and from His loving providence and tender mercies" to send His Messenger with incomplete identification, while holding humanity accountable for failure to accept Him.[47] 'Abdu'l-Bahá, who defines faith as conscious knowledge expressed through good deeds,[48] rejects "blind imitation" as a basis for such acceptance. "You must come into the knowledge of the divine Manifestations and Their teachings through proofs and evidences,"[49] He says, indicating that those who seek such knowledge have at their disposal "every manner of evidence, whether based on reason or on the text of the scriptures and traditions."[50]

But what constitutes evidence? How do we know that any particular statement is true? For simple questions, such as whether it is raining outside, there is no problem: We simply look and see for ourselves. If we are not in a position to look, we ask someone else. Sometimes we can look up answers in a book; this works well for things such as telephone numbers or the height of Mount Everest.

When we confront the truly pivotal questions of life, however, we must work out the answers for ourselves. If there is such a thing as divine revelation, then the soul's response to that revelation is easily the most vital issue anyone will ever confront. Certainly we should benefit from the insights and experiences of others in this connection—but it is our destiny, not theirs, that is affected; and it is we, not they, who will bear ultimate responsibility for our own actions. For all the really important questions—questions such as "Who was Bahá'u'-lláh?"—we are on our own. There is too much at stake to gamble on someone else's judgment.

Naturally, there can be no rigid formula for assessing Bahá'u'lláh's authenticity. There are as many ways as there are individuals, and the way that works for one will not necessarily work for another. Also, we should stipulate at the outset that there is no way to "prove" the claim of Bahá'u'lláh in the sense of providing an ironclad, unchallengeable guarantee: One cannot force a skeptic to accept it; the evidence will not demonstrate it with mathematical certainty, nor is there any way to rule out every conceivable alternative. Proof in this absolute sense does not exist even in the physical sciences, much less in so sensitive and personal an area as religion.

These reservations notwithstanding, there is every reason to press on with our investigation. If absolute certainty is beyond our reach, perhaps a high degree of relative certainty is not. It is instructive to consider, by way of comparison, how conviction is obtained in science.

Science insists that since we have no absolute guarantee of truth, it is essential that we test every important proposition in as many ways as possible. There are, as 'Abdu'l-Bahá points out, four ways of testing or judging any conclusion: sense perception, reason, intuition, and authority. Scientists freely use all four. They use their senses (perhaps extended by instruments such as microscopes and telescopes) to gather and verify raw data. They use reason to formulate explanatory ideas and ferret out implications for further testing. Contrary to the stereotype of the cold-blooded technician, scientists rely heavily on intuition (insight, inspiration, gut feeling, the "still small voice"—call it what you will): Every great scientist has a highly developed sixth sense, which may manifest itself in flashes of insight while meditating on a knotty problem or in hunches as to which lines of research are most likely to bear fruit. As to authority, a scientist will be as quick as anyone else to look up needed facts in a reference book and—all other things being equal—will prefer conclusions that fit smoothly into the framework of knowledge already generally accepted as verified.

Scientists realize that each of these four criteria, used by itself, is flawed. The human senses are notoriously prone to error. Reason, unguided by intuition and unchecked by observation, is sterile and frequently misleading. Valid intuition can be hard to distinguish from mere prejudice or wishful thinking. The voice of authority is suspect until we have verified its credentials and understood its pronouncements; to do either, we must rely on our own fallible minds and hearts. Nevertheless, by applying in concert all the criteria at our disposal, we can obtain conclusions that, while not absolute, are highly reliable. Once we reduce uncertainty to a practical minimum, it even serves a useful purpose: Our awareness of it creates an exhilarating incentive to keep our minds and hearts open and thus to grow continually in knowledge.

The goal of science is to explain reality as we encounter it. This being so, scientific method may be defined as the systematic *testing* of proposed *explanations* (hypotheses) using *data* derived from *experience*. Nothing in the nature of science compels us to define experience in narrow physical terms: It includes whatever is knowable through any legitimate human faculty (these being, as stated, sense perception, reason, intuition, and validated authority). As a practical matter, however, the experience must be potentially *public*—that is, open to repetition by peers. Simply stated, a scientific explanation in any field is one that can be validated by means of open experience.

Now validity, like certainty, is a somewhat subjective and relative concept—a matter of degree. The explanation preferred by scientists as most valid will generally be that which best satisfies two criteria: 1) it must account for the widest range of phenomena using the simplest model and 2) it must correctly predict specific, testable results for our observations of those phenomena.

Long before astronauts could view the earth from space, human beings knew beyond any reasonable doubt that the planet's approximate shape was that of a globe or sphere. Why? Because the spherical-earth theory is the simplest model that predicts all the relevant facts we observe and experience. The theory implies, for instance, that a departing ship should disappear by sinking slowly below the horizon and that the North Star should appear higher in northern countries than in southern ones. These predictions match what we see—a fact well known to the ancient Greeks, among others. Some predictions of the theory could not be tested at once; for example, it implies that a traveler who continues far enough in any direction should return eventually to his starting point. When Magellan circumnavigated the globe, he provided an important confirmation of the spherical-earth theory.

Many predictions of a new idea are not necessarily obvious at first sight. Aristotle cleverly worked out a hidden implication of the spherical-earth theory. Knowing already that a lunar eclipse is the earth's shadow against the moon, cast by the sun from below the earth, he realized that a flat, coin-shaped body must at times cast an oval shadow. On the other hand, he reasoned, a sphere must always cast a circular shadow. By watching eclipses and checking ancient records,

Aristotle verified that the earth's shadow is the ever-circular type cast only by a globe. On this basis, plus observations of the North Star and vanishing ships, Aristotle and other Greek philosophers concluded correctly that the earth is spherical.

A critically important step, then, in assessing a scientific proposition is uncovering its predictions: What does it imply that we can test using sense perception, reason, intuition and authority? Once we answer this question, we know what to look for. In most cases, the easiest way to validate a correct explanation is by striving, with an open mind, to disprove its predictions. If it stands up under fire, we learn to trust it. Astrophysicist Stephen Hawking explains:

> Any physical theory is always provisional, in the sense that it is only a hypothesis: You can never prove it. No matter how many times the results of experiments agree with some theory, you can never be sure that the next time the result will not contradict the theory. On the other hand, you can disprove a theory by finding even a single observation that disagrees with the predictions of the theory. As philosopher of science Karl Popper has emphasized, a good theory is characterized by the fact that it makes a number of predictions that could in principle be disproved or falsified by observation. Each time new experiments are observed to agree with the predictions the theory survives, and our confidence in it is increased; but if ever a new observation is found to disagree, we have to abandon or modify the theory. At least that is what is supposed to happen, but you can always question the competence of the person who carried out the observation.[51]

As Hawking's last comment shows, scientific method is simpler in principle than in practice. A scientist may succeed (if at all) only after a period of deep perplexity, which is not unlike the "dark night of the soul" that saints and mystics describe as a normal stage of spiritual growth. While scientific method will not relieve us of this struggle, it will help us approach the struggle in a disciplined manner: It may suggest fresh and creative ways to proceed when our quest falters, and it provides a way to judge whether we have reached our goal.

If a simple, elegant explanatory model accounts for a large number of facts that previously seemed unrelated, correctly predicts a variety of surprising and unexpected new findings, and survives our systematic attempts to disprove it, then we have every right to place our confidence in it. This is the meaning of "scientific proof," insofar as the term has any meaning at all. The confidence one attains by this method corresponds closely to that sense of certitude known in religion as "faith."

This method is available to all of us, not only to scientists. It is useful in evaluating any proposition, not only those describing physical reality. It calls forth our full range of problem-solving resources—spiritual and emotional as well as material. Scientific method, in its broadest sense, is not a technical procedure; it is a coherent way of thinking and feeling about life itself.

Now suppose we wish to test—as a scientific hypothesis—Bahá'u'lláh's claim that He is a direct channel of communication from an all-knowing, infallible Supreme Being. It is admittedly hard to imagine any single all-purpose test that could establish such a hypothesis to everyone's satisfaction.

On the other hand, the hypothesis, if untrue, should be fairly easy to discredit. Bahá'u'lláh's recorded utterances fill at least one hundred volumes, of which He states: ". . . out of My mouth proceedeth naught but the essence of truth, which the Lord your God hath revealed."[52] Such a claim surely entails consequences that anyone can test using observation and reason.

Here are a few indications one might consider: Bahá'u'lláh made many detailed prophecies. Have these been fulfilled, or have any been contradicted by subsequent events? He described scientific facts that were unknown in His lifetime. Have these been verified, or have any been decisively refuted? He says His words have a unique creative power to facilitate spiritual growth. Can we, by reading and reflecting on those words, experience such a power? We would expect a divinely perfect Being to make an extraordinary impression on those with whom He came into contact. What effect did Bahá'u'lláh have on those around Him? He dictated His books and letters at high speed, never pausing to revise or think, and often with no opportunity for premeditation. Was He able spontaneously to create finished works of consistent excellence, as revelation logically should be? Or do these writings (however brilliant they may be overall) show the wide variations in quality one would expect of a human author composing extemporaneously? He claimed to possess innate, inspired knowledge. Did He have any opportunity, through schooling or self-study, to acquire the skills and knowledge He displayed? These are a few of the ways we can test Bahá'u'lláh's claim. With a little imagination, we can find many others.

We cannot necessarily validate so challenging a claim on the basis of any single test. Suppose, however, we find that the more tests we devise, and the more we widen our investigation, and the more deeply we probe, the more consistent all our findings prove to be with the hypothesis of Bahá'u'lláh's authenticity? At some point, might not our experiences and observations justify interpreting His claim as "true beyond a reasonable doubt"?

Any individual can make such an investigation; and no one, without having done so, can fairly prejudge its outcome. This book is the record of one such investigation. It systematically explores every avenue of inquiry I can think of by which we might test Bahá'u'lláh's claim. It argues that the resulting evidence—which might easily have contradicted that claim— instead supports it in every instance. None of this evidence will constitute "absolute proof": To repeat, it will not necessarily convince a determined skeptic, demonstrate Bahá'u'lláh's authenticity in the manner of a mathematical theorem, or exclude all conceivable alternative hypotheses. What it does mean is that the model which most simply explains and most completely predicts everything we can discover about Bahá'u'lláh is that which accepts His claim as true. If this is correct, then we have as sound a basis for faith in Bahá'u'lláh as we have for faith in any well-established scientific theory.

Chapter 4

BAHÁ'Í PROPHECIES:
HISTORICAL EVENTS

A tempest, unprecedented in its violence, unpredictable in
its course, catastrophic in its immediate effects, unimagin-
ably glorious in its ultimate consequences, is at present
sweeping the face of the earth. . . . The powerful operations
of this titanic upheaval are comprehensible to none except
such as have recognized the claims of both Bahá'u'lláh and
the Báb.

—*Shoghi Effendi*

The word "prediction" means one thing in science, another
in religion. When we study religion scientifically, it is important to distinguish between these meanings. In science, a
prediction is any testable inference we draw from a hypothesis
or theory. It may equally well describe a future event, a past
observation, or an ongoing process. In religion, a prediction
generally is a prophecy—a glimpse of the future disclosed
through the words of a prophet. Although the scientific and
religious meanings may sometimes overlap, they are not
identical.

Bearing this distinction in mind, let us consider a scientific
prediction (testable inference from a hypothesis) involving
religious predictions (prophecies): If Bahá'u'lláh truly was a
Manifestation of God, then He should have been able to
foretell coming events. To someone who is omniscient at will
and free from all error, the future must be an open book.

This practical consequence of the revelation-claim of Bahá'-
u'lláh is something we can test on the basis of observation,
reason, intuition, and credible authority. As with any good

30

scientific deduction, we can search for evidence to disprove it. "When a prophet speaketh in the name of the Lord," says the Old Testament, "if the thing follow not, nor come to pass, that is the thing which the Lord hath not spoken. . . ."[53] Note how completely this approach agrees with modern scientific method: The Bible does not suggest that a single correct prophecy (or even several such) would constitute "proof" of a Manifestation's claim. All it says is that a demonstrable inability to make such prophecies would discredit that claim. The obvious corollary, however, is that if someone claiming divine inspiration makes a great many specific, seemingly improbable, testable prophecies—prophecies whose non-fulfillment would undermine our confidence—and they invariably come true, then we can hardly fail to be impressed. Two equally reasonable people may differ as to how much any given prophecy bolsters such a claim or how many "hits" should be required to sustain a positive verdict. At some point, however, we might well find it more reasonable to accept that claim than to go on reserving judgment.

Bahá'u'lláh Himself writes:

> We have laid bare the divine mysteries and in most explicit language foretold future events, that neither the doubts of the faithless, nor the denials of the froward, nor the whisperings of the heedless may keep back the seekers after truth from the Source of the light of the One true God.[54]

> . . . most of the things which have come to pass on this earth have been announced and prophesied by the Most Sublime Pen. . . . All that hath been sent down hath and will come to pass, word for word, upon earth. No possibility is left for anyone either to turn aside or protest.[55]

An impartial examination of such prophecies in the light of subsequent events will either confirm or falsify these assertions. This, then, is a good place to begin our investigation.

In considering Bahá'u'lláh's prophecies I shall, in a few instances, refer also to statements by the Báb and 'Abdu'l-Bahá. The Báb claimed to be not only the Herald of Bahá'u'-

lláh but also a Manifestation in His own right—a claim fully endorsed by Bahá'u'lláh. Although 'Abdu'l-Bahá is not considered a Manifestation, He was designated by Bahá'u'lláh as the unerring, divinely guided Interpreter of the Faith, and beyond that as one whose words are as authoritative and as binding upon believers as Bahá'u'lláh's own. All authenticated statements of these three Central Figures therefore constitute Bahá'í scripture, and their prophecies all are invested with Bahá'u'lláh's authority.*

What are the developments that have, in the words of Bahá'u'lláh, "come to pass on this earth" after being "announced and prophesied by the Most Sublime Pen"? Those of which I am aware, and which I discuss in the following pages, include:

1. The fall from power of the French Emperor Napoleon III and the consequent loss of his empire.
2. The defeat of Germany in two bloody wars, resulting in the "lamentations of Berlin."
3. The success and stability of Queen Victoria's reign.
4. The dismissal of 'Álí Páshá as prime minister of Turkey.
5. The overthrow and murder of Sultán 'Abdu'l-'Azíz of Turkey.
6. The breakup of the Ottoman Empire, leading to the extinction of the "outward splendor" of its capital, Constantinople.
7. The downfall of Náṣiri'd-Dín Sháh, the Persian monarch.
8. The advent of constitutional government in Persia.
9. A massive decline in the fortunes of monarchy throughout the world.

---

* To put it another way, Bahá'u'lláh predicted (at least by implication) that the prophecies of the Báb and 'Abdu'l-Bahá would prove as reliable as His own.

10. A worldwide erosion of ecclesiastical authority.
11. The collapse of the Muslim caliphate.
12. The spread of communism, the "Movement of the Left," and its rise to world power.
13. The catastrophic decline of that same movement, triggered by the collapse of its egalitarian economy.
14. The rise of Israel as a Jewish homeland.
15. The persecution of Jews on the European continent (the Nazi Holocaust).
16. America's violent racial struggles.
17. Bahá'u'lláh's release from the prison of 'Akká and the pitching of His tent on Mount Carmel.
18. The seizure and desecration of Bahá'u'lláh's house in Baghdad.
19. The failure of all attempts to create schism within the Bahá'í Faith.
20. The explosive acceleration of scientific and technological progress.
21. The development of nuclear weapons.
22. The achievement of transmutation of elements, the age-old alchemist's dream.
23. Dire peril for all humanity as a result of that achievement.
24. The discovery that complex elements evolve in nature from simpler ones.
25. The recognition of planets as a necessary by-product of star formation.
26. Space travel.
27. The realization that some forms of cancer are communicable.
28. Failure to find evidence for a "missing link" between man and ape.
29. The nonexistence of a mechanical ether (the supposed light-carrying substance posited by classical physics), and its redefinition as an abstract reality.
30. The breakdown of mechanical models (literal images) as a basis for understanding the physical world.

I will review each of these prophecies, describing when and how each was made and fulfilled. First, however, let us briefly consider their common historical setting.

THE TABLETS TO THE KINGS

Shortly before reaching 'Akká in 1868, and continuing for several years thereafter, Bahá'u'lláh, in powerful and majestic language, addressed to the world's reigning monarchs a series of letters setting forth His claims and the highlights of His peace program. He addressed similar letters collectively to these same rulers and heads of state, as well as to leaders of religion, various segments of society, and humanity in general.

In these letters (known generally as "Tablets"), Bahá'u'lláh declared that human society was about to be revolutionized by the birth of a world civilization: "Soon will the present-day order be rolled up, and a new one spread out in its stead."[56] This mighty transformation, He said, would come about through historical forces that God had irreversibly set in motion and which the kings could resist or ignore only at their own peril. He advised them to "have mercy on yourselves and on those beneath you"[57] by joining forces to bring about the unity of humankind.

Bahá'u'lláh outlined three ways the kings could respond to this appeal. (1) They could investigate His claim, acknowledge Him as the source and author of the new world order, and establish in His lifetime the "Most Great Peace"—the spiritual rebirth of humankind through its fusion into a planetary brotherhood. (2) Rejecting His claim, the kings might still establish at once the "Lesser Peace"—a strictly political unity involving creation of a world government and a system of collective security to abolish war. Although this stopgap measure would not in itself heal the deeper spiritual maladies afflicting humanity, it would make such healing possible by paving the way for the long-range establishment of the Most Great Peace. (3) They could reject both the proposals outlined above. In that case God, working through the ordinary masses of humanity, would in His own time still bring about both the

Lesser and the Most Great Peace. The short-term result, however, would be "convulsions and chaos" on a scale hitherto unimaginable.

Within this broad context, Bahá'u'lláh offered specific advice to individual rulers and, in so doing, made a number of detailed prophecies. The most important of these letters were compiled in a book entitled Súriy-i-Haykal (Discourse of the Temple), published in 1869 in Bombay, India, and later reprinted several times. Many of the prophecies I will cite appeared in that book; all were published and widely circulated in advance of the events to which they refer.

Napoleon III

Prophecy 1: The fall from power of the French Emperor Napoleon III and the consequent loss of his empire.

Emperor Napoleon III of France, nephew of the more famous Napoleon I, was the most powerful and brilliant Western monarch of his day. His dream was to walk in the footsteps of his imperial uncle and complete his interrupted campaign of conquest. Upon receiving the first of two letters from Bahá'u'lláh, he reportedly cast it aside, saying, "If this man is God, I am two Gods!"[58]

Bahá'u'lláh's second letter is the one published in the Súriy-i-Haykal. After condemning the emperor's insincerity and lust for war, Bahá'u'lláh wrote:

> For what thou hast done, thy kingdom shall be thrown into confusion, and thine empire shall pass from thine hands, as a punishment for that which thou hast wrought. Then wilt thou know how thou hast plainly erred. Commotions shall seize all the people in that land, unless thou arisest to help this Cause, and followest Him Who is the Spirit of God [Jesus] in this, the straight Path. Hath thy pomp made thee proud? By My Life! It shall not endure; nay, it shall soon pass away, unless thou holdest fast by this firm Cord. We see abasement hastening after thee, while thou art of the heedless. . . .[59]

'Abdu'l-Bahá recalls: "The text of this warning reached the whole of Persia . . . and as this Súriy-i-Haykal was circulated in Persia and India and was in the hands of all believers, they were waiting to see what would come to pass."[60] Napoleon, then at the height of his power, went to war in 1870 with Germany, believing he could easily take Berlin. Although, as 'Abdu'l-Bahá notes, "no one at that time expected the victory of Germany,"[61] the French army was defeated that year at Saarbruck, Weissenburg, and Metz, then finally in a crushing catastrophe at Sedan. The breakup and surrender of Napoleon's forces constituted "the greatest capitulation hitherto recorded in modern history."[62] Napoleon himself was carried prisoner to Germany and perished miserably in England two years later.

Germany

Prophecy 2: The defeat of Germany in two bloody wars, resulting in the "lamentations of Berlin."

While shouts of victory were still echoing throughout Germany, Bahá'u'lláh warned its rulers not to tread the same path of aggression the French Emperor had followed to his doom. In His book of laws, the Kitáb-i-Aqdas (Most Holy Book), composed around 1873, Bahá'u'lláh addressed these words to Germany's Kaiser William I:

> O King of Berlin! . . . Do thou remember the one whose power transcended thy power [Napoleon III], and whose station excelled thy station. Where is he? Whither are gone the things he possessed? Take warning, and be not of them that are fast asleep. He it was who cast the Tablet of God behind him, when We made known unto him what the hosts of tyranny had caused Us to suffer. Wherefore, disgrace assailed him from all sides, and he went down to dust in great loss. Think deeply, O King, concerning him, and concerning them who, like unto thee, have conquered cities and ruled over men. The All-Merciful brought them down

from their palaces to their graves. Be warned, be of them who reflect.[63]

Bahá'u'lláh then painted this amazing word-picture of a Germany broken and bleeding in the wake of two successive armed conflicts:

> O banks of the Rhine! We have seen you covered with gore, inasmuch as the swords of retribution were drawn against you; and you shall have another turn. And we hear the lamentations of Berlin, though she be today in conspicuous glory.[64]

During His Western tour in 1912, 'Abdu'l-Bahá, citing this and other prophecies of Bahá'u'lláh, warned that a "universal European war" was both imminent and inevitable. His predictions were widely reported at the time in the American, Canadian, and European press, as were His appeals for a multinational peace process based on His father's principles. Returning to His home in the Holy Land, 'Abdu'l-Bahá prepared for the coming upheaval by stockpiling food and medical supplies. Haifa, as the world center of the growing Bahá'í movement, was by now a site of pilgrimage for large numbers of believers from East and West. About six months before the outbreak of hostilities, 'Abdu'l-Bahá imposed a moratorium on new pilgrimages and began sending away pilgrims already at Haifa. The timing of these phased departures was such that by the end of July 1914, no visitors remained. The wisdom of His actions became apparent when, in the opening days of August, World War I suddenly erupted, stunning the world and incidentally exposing Haifa and the Holy Land to grave hardships and danger.

While touring California in 1912, 'Abdu'l-Bahá reportedly said the impending struggle would "set aflame the whole of Europe," wreaking unprecedented havoc: "By 1917 kingdoms will fall and cataclysms will rock the earth."[65]* Subsequent

---

* These comments (from notes taken by Mrs. Corinne True, a prominent American Bahá'í of the period) were published in *The North Shore Review*, Chicago, 26 September 1914.

events fully justified these projections. However, German victories during this period, and especially during its last great push in the spring of 1918, were so imposing that Bahá'u'-lláh's vision of Germany in defeat was widely ridiculed throughout Persia by enemies of the Bahá'í Faith. Only with the sudden, unexpected breakup of the German juggernaut did the truth of the prophecy become clear. Then the banks of the Rhine were, indeed, "covered with gore" as the "swords of retribution" were drawn against the nation.

Germany's national nightmare was, however, only just beginning. Further disclosing the implications of His father's words, 'Abdu'l-Bahá wrote in January 1920: "The Balkans will remain discontented. Its restlessness will increase. The vanquished Powers will continue to agitate. They will resort to every measure that may rekindle the flame of war."[66] He still more explicitly stated that "another war, fiercer than the last, will assuredly break out."[67] This prediction came to pass with the rise of Hitler's Third Reich and the onset of World War II—although, as before, the German campaigns were at first so successful they seemed more apt to discredit than to confirm Bahá'u'lláh's prophecy. The Allied victory seemed, till the very end of the war, anything but a foregone conclusion.

And still, events continued to unfold the meaning of the prophecy. The "lamentations of Berlin," as predicted by Bahá'u'lláh, replaced the "conspicuous glory" it had enjoyed in His day. After the first war, that once-great city was tortured by the terms of a treaty monstrous in its severity; after the second, it was carved into zones controlled by the Eastern and Western blocs. The infamous Berlin Wall, erected in 1961, became a concrete symbol of the tragedy and agony that for more than forty years continued to wrack the city. (As I first wrote these words in November 1989, the Berlin Wall was opened for the first time, and more than two million jubilant persons poured through it in a single day. Less than a year later, Germany was once again one nation, though still troubled by many difficulties.)

Queen Victoria

Prophecy 3: The success and stability of Queen Victoria's reign.

Bahá'u'lláh's message to Great Britain's Queen Victoria—unlike those He addressed to Napoleon III and Kaiser William I —was optimistic. Like them, however, it defied conventional wisdom. Queen Victoria's position seemed precarious at the time; she was in poor health and out of favor because she had taken a German consort. Bahá'u'lláh promised her that God would strengthen her administration as a reward for her just and humanitarian actions. He particularly commended two policies of her government: its enforcement of recently enacted laws prohibiting the slave trade, and its action in extending and broadening voting rights throughout the island kingdom. (The Representation of the People Act of 1867, for example, almost doubled the English electorate; and corresponding acts for Scotland and Ireland the following year achieved similar results.)

"O Queen in London!" wrote Bahá'u'lláh,

> Incline thine ear unto the voice of thy Lord, the Lord of all mankind. . . . He, in truth, hath come into the world in His most great glory, and all that hath been mentioned in the Gospel hath been fulfilled. . . .
>
> We have been informed that thou hast forbidden the trading in slaves, both men and women. This, verily, is what God hath enjoined in this wondrous Revelation. God hath, truly, destined a reward for thee, because of this. . . .
>
> We have also heard that thou hast entrusted the reins of counsel into the hands of the representatives of the people. Thou, indeed, hast done well, for thereby the foundations of the edifice of thine affairs will be strengthened, and the hearts of all that are beneath thy shadow, whether high or low, will be tranquilized.[68]

Of all the rulers invited by Bahá'u'lláh to investigate and help His Cause, only Queen Victoria offered so much as a courteous reply. "If this is of God," she reportedly commented, "it will endure; if not, it can do no harm."[69] Just as Bahá'u'lláh had foreseen, her government was "strengthened" and Britain prospered under her administration. Her reign lasted until 1901, and of all the dynasties whose incumbents Bahá'u'lláh addressed, only hers remains.*

The Crown of Turkey

Prophecy 4: The dismissal of 'Álí Páshá as prime minister of Turkey.

Prophecy 5: The overthrow of Sulṭán 'Abdu'l-'Azíz of Turkey.

Turkey's Sulṭán 'Abdu'l-'Azíz ruled the Ottoman Empire to which Bahá'u'lláh was banished in 1853, and in which He spent the remaining forty years of His earthly life. The Turkish government at first left Bahá'u'lláh in peace but slowly came to regard Him as a potential source of political unrest. Responding to this fear and to strong pressure from Persian authorities, the sulṭán subjected Bahá'u'lláh, His family, and companions to three further banishments ending with their confinement in the fortress-prison of 'Akká. A considerable number of women and small children—obviously innocent of any crimes against the state—were among the victims of this brutal repression.

As these successive blows fell, Bahá'u'lláh sent several strongly worded protests to the sulṭán, directly and through various ministers of government. He condemned the injustice and cruelty of the orders; appealed without success for a ten-minute hearing to answer the charges against Him; denied that He ever had sought, or ever would seek, to undermine imperial authority; pointed out that His teachings require loyal obedience to established governments; and counseled the sulṭán to act with justice towards all his subjects. He also made some striking prophecies.

---

* Queen Victoria's granddaughter, Queen Marie of Romania, became a devoted and outspoken follower of Bahá'u'lláh. Her belief in His divine authority, which she proclaimed frequently in the press, raised so many eyebrows among her royal peers that she wrote: "Some of those of my caste wonder at and disapprove my courage to step forward pronouncing words not habitual for Crowned Heads to pronounce, but I advance by an inner urge I cannot resist." (*Appreciations of the Bahá'í Faith*, p. 9)

Two key players in this drama were the sultán's top-ranking subordinates: 'Álí Páshá, the Turkish prime minister, and Fu'ád Páshá, minister of foreign affairs. These powerful men did much to engineer the policy of suppression to which 'Abdu'l-'Azíz gave his kingly sanction. During His exile in Adrianople, Bahá'u'lláh addressed to 'Álí Páshá a Tablet called the Súriy-i-Ra'ís, stating that the prime minister soon would find himself in "manifest loss."[70] In 1868, shortly after arriving at 'Akká, He repeated this prophecy in a second letter to 'Álí Páshá and further reproved the entire Ottoman government:

> Soon will He [God] seize you in His wrathful anger, and sedition will be stirred up in your midst, and your dominions will be disrupted. Then will ye bewail and lament, and will find none to help or succor you.
> . . . Be expectant . . . for the wrath of God is ready to overtake you. Erelong will ye behold that which hath been sent down from the Pen of My command.[71]

Shortly thereafter, in a widely circulated Tablet called the Lawḥ-i-Fu'ád, Bahá'u'lláh again forecast the prime minister's downfall. This time, however, He expanded the prophecy to include Sulṭán 'Abdu'l-'Azíz as well. Commenting on the premature death in 1869 of Fu'ád Páshá, the Tablet stated: "Soon will We dismiss the one ['Álí Páshá] who was like unto him, and will lay hold on their Chief ['Abdu'l-'Azíz] who ruleth the land, and I, verily, am the Almighty, the All-Compelling."[72]

So preposterous did this prophecy seem that a distinguished Islamic scholar and cleric, Mírzá Abu'l-Faḍl, seized upon it as a chance to discredit Bahá'u'lláh. He pointed out that the expression "lay hold on" is a figure of speech that, in the Tablet's original language, signifies violent and untimely death as a result of divine justice. Thus Bahá'u'lláh was saying clearly that the sultán would be unexpectedly killed. Finding this unthinkable, Mírzá Abu'l-Faḍl declared that for him, the fulfillment or non-fulfillment of this one prophecy would constitute a decisive test of the so-called revelation's authenticity. To dramatize his certainty that the prophecy would fail, he vowed to join the ranks of Bahá'u'lláh's followers should the sulṭán's doom occur as predicted.

Further insight into Bahá'u'lláh's meaning came from yet another Tablet, in which Bahá'u'lláh warned the sulṭán to guard himself against betrayal by faithless subordinates:

> He that acteth treacherously towards God will, also, act treacherously towards his king. . . .
> Take heed that thou resign not the reins of the affairs of thy state into the hands of others, and repose not thy confidence in ministers unworthy of thy trust. . . . Avoid them, and preserve strict guard over thyself, lest their devices and mischief hurt thee.[73]

A few years after Bahá'u'lláh's banishment to 'Akká, 'Álí Páshá was fired from his post as prime minister. Stripped of all power, he sank into oblivion. The first stage of the prophecy was thus fulfilled. The second stage came to pass in 1876 when a palace conspiracy abruptly deposed Sulṭán 'Abdu'l-'Azíz and led, four days later, to his murder. The monarch was thus betrayed and assassinated by the very subordinates against whom Bahá'u'lláh had warned him.

In some ideal world, Mírzá Abu'l-Faḍl might have calmly considered this outcome as an intriguing demonstration of Bahá'u'lláh's prophetic power. In this real one, he did nothing of the sort. The unexpected fulfillment so angered and frightened him that when Bahá'ís reminded him of his pledge, he became incoherent. Nevertheless, the episode cracked his smugness and impelled him, for the first time, to consider seriously Bahá'u'lláh's claim. After thorough and prayerful investigation, he became convinced of its truth. Forfeiting his high position heading one of Tehran's leading Islamic universities, he embarked on a life of poverty and sometimes imprisonment to teach Bahá'u'lláh's message. His book *The Baháí Proofs* and a lengthy personal visit did much to help establish the Faith in America during the early 1900s. (For Mírzá Abu'l-Faḍl's own account of this episode, see Taherzadeh, *Revelation of Bahá'u'lláh*, vol. III, pp. 97–104.)

The Ottoman Empire

Prophecy 6: The breakup of the Ottoman Empire, leading to the extinction of the "outward splendor" of its capital, Constantinople.

In one of the above-quoted letters, Bahá'u'lláh warned Turkish authorities that "your dominions will be disrupted." Those dominions, at the time, extended from the center of Hungary to the Persian Gulf and the Sudan, and from the Caspian Sea to the port of Oran in Africa. Bahá'u'lláh also made specific prophecies about Adrianople and Constantinople (the latter being the capital of the empire). In the first of His two letters to 'Álí Páshá, He wrote:

> The day is approaching when the Land of Mystery [Adrianople], and what is beside it shall be changed, and shall pass out of the hands of the king, and commotions shall appear, and the voice of lamentation shall be raised, and the evidences of mischief shall be revealed on all sides, and confusion shall be spread by reason of that which hath befallen these captives at the hands of the hosts of oppression. The course of things shall be altered, and conditions shall wax so grievous, that the very sands on the desolate hills will moan, and the trees on the mountain will weep, and blood will flow out of all things. Then wilt thou behold the people in sore distress.[74]

In the Kitáb-i-Aqdas, revealed shortly after His banishment from Adrianople to 'Akká, Bahá'u'lláh addressed the seat of Turkish power:

> O Spot [Constantinople] that art situate on the shores of the two seas! The throne of tyranny hath, verily, been stablished upon thee, and the flame of hatred hath been kindled within thy bosom. . . . Thou art indeed filled with manifest pride. Hath thine outward splendor made thee vainglorious? By Him Who is the Lord of mankind! It shall soon perish, and thy daughters, and thy widows, and all the kindreds that dwell within thee shall lament. Thus informeth thee, the All-Knowing, the All-Wise.[75]

If these prophecies sounded perhaps melodramatic when Bahá'u'lláh wrote them, they did not long remain that way. History soon made them appear almost as masterpieces of understatement. Uprisings in Crete and the Balkans were followed by the War of 1877–78, in which at least eleven million people were liberated from Turkish misrule. Russian troops occupied Adrianople, fulfilling the prediction that it would "pass out of the hands of the king." Serbia, Montenegro, and Romania proclaimed their independence; Bulgaria became a self-governing tributary state; Cyprus and Egypt were occupied; the French assumed a protectorate over Tunis; Eastern Rumelia was ceded to Bulgaria; thousands of Armenians lost their lives in a series of massacres; Bosnia and Herzegovina were lost to Austria; and universal hatred for the government precipitated the Young Turk Revolution. Military reverses in World War I further weakened the empire; the Arabian provinces revolted; nine-tenths of the Turkish army died or deserted; and a fourth of the whole population perished from war, disease, famine, and massacre. Muḥammad VI, the last sulṭán, was deposed, ending the centuries-old dynasty to which he and 'Abdu'l-'Azíz had belonged. The once-vast Turkish empire was shriveled into a tiny Asiatic republic, while its capital, Constantinople, was abandoned by its conquerors and shorn of its "outward splendor."

Náṣiri'd-Dín Sháh

*Prophecy 7: **The downfall of Náṣiri'd-Dín Sháh, the Persian monarch.***

Bahá'u'lláh's longest Tablet to any single sovereign was addressed to the ruler of His native land, Náṣiri'd-Dín, Sháh of Persia. In it Bahá'u'lláh assured the sháh of His loyalty, offered His aid, and appealed for a fair inquiry into His claim. A significant passage reads:

> Would that the world-adorning wish of His Majesty might decree that this Servant be brought face to face with the

divines of the age, and produce proofs and testimonies in the presence of His Majesty the Sháh! This Servant is ready, and taketh hope in God, that such a gathering may be convened in order that the truth of the matter may be made clear and manifest before His Majesty the Sháh. It is then for thee to command, and I stand ready before the throne of thy sovereignty. Decide, then, for Me or against Me.[76]

The sháh responded to this eminently reasonable request by torturing to death the courier who had delivered it. By his order this young man, a seventeen-year-old Bahá'í named Badí', was chained to the rack, branded for three days with red-hot bricks, and otherwise tormented in an effort to extract information or a denial of faith. Badí', calm and steadfast, was photographed under torture. Unable to crush his spirit, his frustrated persecutors finally crushed his head.

Such atrocities were the norm, rather than the exception, under the rule of a king whose hands already were stained with the blood of the Báb and twenty thousand Bábí martyrs. Of such rulers Bahá'u'lláh vowed: "God hath not blinked, nor will He ever blink His eyes at the tyranny of the oppressor. More particularly in this Revelation hath He visited each and every tyrant with His vengeance."[77] Denouncing Náṣiri'd-Dín Sháh as the "Prince of Oppressors,"[78] Bahá'u'lláh wrote that the Persian monarch soon would be made "an object-lesson for the world."[79]

Náṣiri'd-Dín survived until 1896, outliving Bahá'u'lláh by four years; his reign lasted nearly half a century.* To celebrate the fiftieth anniversary of that reign, Persia prepared the most elaborate festival in its history. Prisoners were to be released without condition. Peasants were to be exempt from taxation for two years. The sháh planned to inaugurate a new era, declare himself the "Majestic Father of all Persians," and renounce his prerogatives as despot. So jubilant was the coun-

---

* Náṣiri'd-Dín ascended the throne in 1848, somewhat less than fifty years earlier by the Gregorian solar calendar. Islamic lunar years, however, are slightly shorter; 1896 was the fiftieth year of his reign by this reckoning.

try's mood that authorities even "decided, for the time being, to discontinue persecuting the [Bahá'ís] and other infidels."[80]

One doubts that Náṣiri'd-Dín, watching the exuberant preparations for his jubilee, gave a moment's thought to the humiliating end forecast for him by Bahá'u'lláh. At this late date in his career, with everything going his way, he appeared invincible and triumphant. On 1 May 1896—the eve of his grand celebration—he visited the shrine of a former sháh. During that visit he died by an assassin's bullet. In a ghoulish aftertwist, his ministers drove his body back to the capital propped up in the royal carriage to suppress as long as possible the news of his murder.

Bahá'ís were initially blamed for the crime. A number were executed in retaliation, including the famous Bahá'í poet Varqá and his twelve-year-old son, Rúḥu'lláh, both of whom were outstanding teachers of the Faith. The accusation was dropped, however, after the assassin, Mírzá Riḍá, turned out to be a Pan-Islamic terrorist and a follower of Siyyid Jamálu'd-Dín-i-Afghání, a well-known enemy of the Bahá'í Cause.*

The Persian Constitution

Prophecy 8: The advent of constitutional government in Persia.

Around 1873 Bahá'u'lláh wrote, in the Kitáb-i-Aqdas, these words addressed to His native Persia: "Ere long will the state of affairs within thee be changed, and the reins of power fall into the hands of the people."[81]

---

* If Bahá'u'lláh had wished to connive at the overthrow of Náṣiri'd-Dín, He had had an obvious opening some years before, courtesy of Prince Ẓillu's-Sulṭán, who was the sháh's eldest son but could not (because his mother was a commoner) legally accede to the throne. Ẓillu's-Sulṭán had sent an emissary to Bahá'u'lláh, offering protection for Persia's Bahá'ís in return for their help in murdering his two brothers and seizing the throne from his father. Bahá'u'lláh had emphatically rejected the plea, making it clear that the Bahá'í Faith was strictly nonpolitical and could not be toyed with. As governor of provinces constituting almost half of Persia, Ẓillu's-Sulṭán had responded by unleashing yet another bloody campaign of terror against the Bahá'ís. (See Kazem Kazemzadeh, "Varqá and Rúḥu'lláh: Death-less in Martyrdom," *World Order,* Winter 1974–5, p. 32.)

The assassination of Náṣiri'd-Dín Sháh was the first rumble of the revolution alluded to in this passage. Support for a constitution restricting the monarch's power grew so strong after his death that the next king, Muẓaffari'd-Dín Sháh, had little choice but to sign the document in 1906, shortly before his death. The next occupants of the throne, however, refused to honor its provisions, and Persia remained embroiled in its Constitutional Revolution from 1906 to 1911. Muḥammad-'Alí Sháh, who succeeded Muẓaffari'd-Dín, was so hostile to the constitution that he bombarded the parliament's meeting-place with the members inside; whereupon insurgents deposed him. His successor, the boy-king Aḥmad Sháh, behaved so irresponsibly that parliament not only deposed him but abolished, in the process, the Qájár dynasty to which he and his predecessors had belonged.[82]

In a talk delivered on 11 July 1909, 'Abdu'l-Bahá said:

> The revolution now rampant in Persia was foretold by [Bahá'u'lláh] forty years ago . . . in the Book of Laws [Kitáb-i-Aqdas]. And this prophecy was made when Tehran was in the utmost quietude and the government of Náṣiri'd-Dín Sháh was well established.[83]

The new state of affairs did not, of course, guarantee Persia's future stability. 'Abdu'l-Bahá wrote (also in July 1909) that unless union was effected between the opposing sides, foreign powers would step in and divide the country.[84] This happened when Persia, weakened by the long struggle, later was divided into spheres of influence: Russia took the north, Great Britain the south.

Although Bahá'u'lláh had foreseen the emergence of constitutional government in Persia, He did not allow His followers to take part in the agitation that brought it about. This was in keeping with His policy of prohibiting Bahá'í involvement in political movements—movements that, whatever their merits, would inevitably compromise the Faith's universality and hamper its all-important mission of achieving world spiritual unity. One secondary benefit of the policy, in this case, was that no one could fairly accuse the Bahá'ís of having promoted the constitution in order to fulfill Bahá'u'-lláh's prophecy.

The operative word here, of course, is "fairly." As 'Abdu'l-Bahá explained:

> This prophecy, so clearly and evidently stated, printed and published, is well-known among the people. Therefore, when the Constitution was granted in Persia, the mullás who took the Royalist side proclaimed from the pulpit that "whosoever accepted the Constitution had necessarily accepted the Bahá'í Religion, because the Head of this Religion, His Holiness Bahá'u'lláh, had prophesied this in His Book and the Bahá'ís are agitators and promoters of Constitutionalism. They have brought about the Constitution in order to fulfill the prophecy made by their Chief. Therefore, beware, beware lest ye accept it!"[85]

GENERAL PROPHECIES

When His claims and His peace program both went unheeded, Bahá'u'lláh reiterated His warning of dire consequences. "The winds of despair are, alas, blowing from every direction," He wrote, "and the strife that divides and afflicts the human race is daily increasing. The signs of impending convulsions and chaos can now be discerned, inasmuch as the prevailing order appears to be lamentably defective."[86]

He pointed out that those with the most to lose from the coming upheaval were the very ones whose negligence had brought it about: namely, the world's secular and religious leaders. He stated that God, holding them accountable for their conduct, would strip them of influence: "From two ranks amongst men power hath been seized: kings and ecclesiastics."[87]

Let us now look more closely at Bahá'u'lláh's statements concerning each of these groups.

Monarchy

Prophecy 9: A massive decline in the fortunes of monarchy throughout the world.

The prophecy just quoted echoes a warning from the Súriy-i-Múluk (Discourse of Kings), one of Bahá'u'lláh's earliest proclamations, addressed to the entire company of monarchs of East and West:

> If ye pay no heed unto the counsels which, in peerless and unequivocal language, We have revealed in this Tablet, Divine chastisement shall assail you from every direction, and the sentence of His justice shall be pronounced against you. On that day ye shall have no power to resist Him, and shall recognize your own impotence.[88]

Looking beyond the individual rulers whose fates Bahá'u'lláh announced, what can we say about the fortunes of royalty in general?

In Bahá'u'lláh's lifetime, much of humankind—especially in Europe and Asia—lived within vast empires ruled by absolute, all-powerful sovereigns who strode the earth with seven-league boots. Although monarchy had never been the safest of occupations for an individual, the institution itself seemed invulnerable.

Within a few decades after Bahá'u'lláh voiced His prophecy, that illusion of security had vanished. A whirlwind of change, roaring into every region of the earth, was not only toppling thrones but systematically digging up their foundations. By 1944 (the end of the first Bahá'í century), it had dissolved the Ottoman, Napoleonic, German, Austrian and Russian empires; swept away the Qájár dynasty in Persia; converted the Chinese empire and the Spanish and Portuguese monarchies into republics; exiled the crowned heads of Holland, Norway, Greece, Yugoslavia, and Albania, and stripped of power the kings of Denmark, Belgium, Bulgaria, Romania, and Italy. Losing none of its fury, this "relentless revolutionizing process," as Shoghi Effendi calls it,[89] has continued to the present day. Among its more recent and colorful effects are the transformation of the ancient Japanese empire into a republic and the toppling of the centuries-old Peacock Throne in Persia.

Today, the great powers are governed by legislatures or central bodies; their chief executives are either elected or appointed; and monarchy on the grand scale no longer exists. The British Crown, which once ruled the world's largest empire, is today purely ceremonial and facing troubled times. The few remaining thrones are small in scale and limited in power.

Having said all this, it is necessary to explain that Bahá'ís believe the current decline in the fortunes of royalty is only temporary. Bahá'u'lláh states that "just kings" will arise in the future who, placing the welfare of their subjects ahead of their own, will restore the prestige of monarchy.[90] "Although a republican form of government profiteth all the peoples of the world," He writes, "yet the majesty of kingship is one of the signs of God. We do not wish that the countries of the world should remain deprived thereof. If the sagacious combine the two forms into one, great will be their reward in the presence of God."[91]

Ecclesiasticism

Prophecy 10: **A worldwide erosion of ecclesiastical authority.**

Prophecy 11: **The collapse of the Muslim caliphate.**

Bahá'u'lláh, in predicting the eclipse of royal authority, also stated that "power hath been seized" from ecclesiastics. Elsewhere He thus addressed the world's religious leaders:

> O concourse of divines! Ye shall not henceforward behold yourselves possessed of any power, inasmuch as We have seized it from you, and destined it for such as have believed in God, the One, the All-Powerful, the Almighty, the Unconstrained.[92]

The ensuing fate of established religious institutions has been as spectacular and catastrophic as that of the world's secular rulers. Let us consider first the two agencies that, in

Bahá'u'lláh's time, had for centuries wielded both spiritual and temporal power—the papacy and the caliphate.

Bahá'u'lláh's Tablets to the Kings included one to Pope Pius IX, containing the following words:

> O Pope! Rend the veils asunder. He Who is the Lord of Lords is come overshadowed with clouds, and the decree hath been fulfilled by God, the Almighty, the Unrestrained. ... He, verily, hath again come down from Heaven even as He came down from it the first time. ... Beware lest any name debar thee from God. ...
>
> Dwellest thou in palaces whilst He Who is the King of Revelation liveth in the most desolate of abodes? Leave them unto such as desire them, and set thy face with joy and delight towards the Kingdom.
>
> ... The Word which the Son concealed is made manifest. It hath been sent down in the form of the human temple in this day. Blessed be the Lord Who is the Father! He, verily, is come unto the nations in His most great majesty.[93]

The once-vast temporal power of the papacy had shrunk considerably before Bahá'u'lláh's letter, but it still embraced the kingdom of Italy. Bahá'u'lláh commanded the pope to renounce this remaining power voluntarily: "Abandon thy kingdom unto the kings. ..."[94] Had he done so, the aging pontiff would have spared himself the humiliating loss of freedom, dignity, and prestige that followed the seizure of his kingdom in 1870 by King Victor Emmanuel. By ignoring the advice of the Prisoner of 'Akká, Pope Pius IX became the Prisoner of the Vatican.*

Even more spectacular was the collapse of the caliphate, which both the Báb and Bahá'u'lláh had clearly foreshadowed in Their writings. To understand these prophetic references, however, we must first know something of their historical background.

Islam is divided into two main branches, Sunní and Shí'ih, corresponding in some ways to the division of Christianity into Catholic and Protestant branches. The caliph, as spiritual

---

* It is noteworthy that 1870 was also the year in which the pope first proclaimed the new dogma of Papal Infallibility.

head of the much larger Sunní branch, was a Muslim counter-part to the Catholic pope. Though representing different offices, the Muslim caliphate and the Turkish sultanate tradi-tionally were vested in the same person. This gave the caliph enormous temporal power, though his spiritual jurisdiction extended far beyond the Ottoman Empire and embraced the vast majority of Muslims throughout the world.

This religious monarchy dated back to Muḥammad's death in 632 AD, when His followers split into two camps over the issue of leadership. At that time the caliphate, created by a group of the Prophet's associates, was accepted by the majority of Muslims, who became known as Sunnís. A minority, later called Shí'ihs, maintained that Muḥammad had verbally appointed His son-in-law, 'Alí, as the first in a line of heredi-tary successors called imáms.* There ensued a 260-year war in which the caliphs, with a view to ending the rival imamate, tried to break the line of succession by slaughtering each and every descendant of Muḥammad. (Although they failed in the latter objective, the imamate ended with the disappearance of the Twelfth Imám.) The most tragic victim of that war was Imám Ḥusayn, the third and most distinguished of the line, whose name is virtually synonymous in Persian literature with the imamate itself.

Given this context (with which His Muslim contemporaries were of course familiar), the Báb clearly referred to the caliph-ate when He wrote:

> Erelong We will, in very truth, torment such as waged war against Ḥusayn, in the Land of the Euphrates, with the most afflictive torment, and the most dire and exemplary punishment.[95]

Nor was this divine chastisement to consist simply of some mystical or metaphysical judgment, confined to an unseen future plane of existence: It would operate, the Báb wrote,

---

* Bahá'u'lláh teaches that the Shí'ihs were correct: Muḥammad did designate 'Alí as His successor. Bahá'ís therefore recognize the legitimacy of the imamate and regard the caliphs as usurpers.

both "in the world to come" (that is, in the afterlife) and "at the time of Our return" (that is, after the coming of the Promised One, Whom He regarded as the return of all previous Prophets including Himself).[96] Thus His prophecy foreshadowed some visible catastrophe destined to befall the caliphate in this earthly life.

Bahá'u'lláh reaffirmed this prophecy. Referring to the all-powerful caliphate as the "mighty throne" of Islam, He described its collapse as a foregone conclusion: "By your deeds," He wrote to the Muslim clergy, "the exalted station of the people hath been abased, the standard of Islam hath been reversed, and its mighty throne hath fallen."[97]

When the sultanate was abolished after World War I, the caliphate did not at once die with it. The former sultán, Muhammad VI, retained for a time his spiritual title, occupying an "anomalous and precarious position."[98] The government of the new Turkish republic, however, was unhappy with this awkward situation; it reacted in March 1924 by proclaiming the abolition of the caliphate and formally dissociating itself from that institution. The ex-caliph fled to Europe. This development shattered the unity of the Sunní world, which had not been in the least consulted. A "Congress of the Caliphate" was convened in Cairo in 1926 to restore the institution; it dissolved in disagreement.

The collapse of the caliphate brought in its wake the formal secularization of the Turkish republic and a drastic loss of power by the Sunní clergy. Sunní canonical law was replaced by a civil code; its religious orders were suppressed, its hierarchy disbanded, and its ecclesiastical institutions disendowed.

The Shí'ih clergy in Persia experienced a parallel decline. The royal government, although formally affiliated with the religious hierarchy, began systematically breaking its stranglehold on every aspect of Persian life and culture. Priests whose every whim had once been law soon found themselves subject to civil authority. Time-honored religious institutions fell into ruin, while Western customs and dress were introduced over the clergy's objections. Throughout most of the twentieth century, one humiliating catastrophe after another battered the Shí'ih order. The Islamic Revolution of 1979 has, for the present, restored a small measure of the vast power the clergy once enjoyed. Even so, the long-term consequences of that revolution remain far from clear.

After the virtual demise of the pope's temporal sovereignty, Christian authority throughout the world found itself on a slippery slope. France, Spain, Russia, and other countries divested themselves of their state religions; the breakup of the Austro-Hungarian Empire deprived the Roman Catholic Church of its strongest political and financial backer; the spread of communism brought with it efforts to eradicate all religious influence from the life of the masses; a rising nationalism in many lands undermined Christianity or, more insidiously, found ways to manipulate it for its own ends.

Throughout the twentieth century and beyond, a growing crisis of confidence in organized religion has steadily eroded the moral authority of Christian leaders. During the 1980s, a wave of scandals involving financial and sexual misconduct destroyed the ministries of some of Christendom's most popular Protestant evangelists. More devastating still were the seemingly endless revelations about pedophile priests and high-level coverups that have since shaken Catholicism. In recent years, the so-called "religious right" has mounted a growing number of political and legal initiatives designed to recapture lost ground; such efforts have, until now, been frustrated.

The progressive decline that has so alarmed Muslim and Christian leaders has, though less dramatically, overtaken the clergy of other faiths as well.

Bahá'ís believe, moreover, that this erosion of ecclesiastical authority is quite unlike the temporary downturn in the fortunes of royalty. Although power has indeed been seized from both "kings and ecclesiastics," Shoghi Effendi writes: "The glory of the former has been eclipsed, the power of the latter irretrievably lost."[99] Both 'Abdu'l-Bahá and Shoghi Effendi warn that the decay of ecclesiasticism, as it proceeds, will produce many backlashes and dying convulsions.[100] Events in the Middle East have already demonstrated how powerful those convulsions may be.

The Movement of the Left

Prophecy 12: The spread of communism, the "Movement of the Left," and its rise to world power.

Prophecy 13: The catastrophic decline of that same movement, triggered by the collapse of its egalitarian economy.

Shortly after World War I, 'Abdu'l-Bahá wrote:

> The ills from which the world now suffers will multiply; the gloom which envelops it will deepen. . . . Movements, newly-born and worldwide in their range, will exert their utmost effort for the advancement of their designs. The Movement of the Left will acquire great importance. Its influence will spread.[101]

The "Movement of the Left" was that of communism and socialism, which had gained power in Russia through the Bolshevik Revolution of 1917. The multiplying ills and deepening gloom of the post-war world did occasion the lightning-like spread of leftist ideology foreseen by 'Abdu'l-Bahá. From its beginning in the Soviet Union, the movement led to the emergence of communist governments in Eastern Europe, China, and many other countries of Asia and Africa, as well as in Western outposts such as Cuba and Nicaragua. Far beyond the borders of these countries, leftist sentiments evoked fervent support and equally fervent opposition. Containing communism became the major preoccupation of non-communist countries, raising emotions on both sides to fever pitch during the so-called Cold War.

Inspired by the teachings of Karl Marx, communism derived much of its appeal from its passionate commitment to the dream of a "classless society." The term refers to a society in which private property is abolished and the means and fruits of production are owned equally ("in common") by all citizens. Wealth is to be distributed according to the classic Marxist dictum: "From each according to his ability; to each according to his needs." Since human beings have more or less the same needs (except in cases of sickness, disability, and the like), this translates in practice into a policy of forcibly equalizing wages and standards of living.

Such leveling policies, supported by an ethic of radical egalitarianism, have been a marked feature of communist societies throughout the world. Through public education, and political indoctrination, these societies systematically fostered a climate of deep hostility on the part of both regulatory agencies and the public towards anyone who profited or prospered as a result of private initiative. The unintended result, in every case, was to suppress innovation, productivity and service without noticeably discouraging greed or exploitation by those occupying positions of power.

To predict the expansion of communism or any other movement is not, of course, to endorse it. The Bahá'í writings name communism as one of three "false gods" worshiped by twentieth-century nations.[102] (The other two are racialism and nationalism.) Although the Bahá'í Faith proposes to limit gross extremes of wealth and poverty, it upholds the right to private property and opposes, as both unjust and impractical, any scheme to enforce strict economic equality.* Around 1905, long before the communist revolution in Russia, 'Abdu'l-Bahá said: ". . . absolute equality in fortunes, honors, commerce, agriculture, industry would end in disorderliness, in chaos, in disorganization of the means of existence, and in universal disappointment: The order of the community would be quite destroyed."[103]

---

* Bahá'u'lláh does not prescribe a fixed or complete system of economics. However, He does state that economics must be based squarely on spiritual principles, and He indicates in general terms what some of those principles are. For two excellent discussions, see William S. Hatcher, "Economics and Moral Values," *World Order*, Winter 1974–5, pp. 14–27; and Gregory C. Dahl, "Economics and the Bahá'í Teachings," *World Order*, Fall 1975, pp. 19–40.

These accumulating disasters—the fruits of a seventy-year experiment in artificially engineered economic equality—finally swamped the communist bloc in the late 1980s. The world watched in awe as every word of 'Abdu'l-Bahá's chilling prediction came true. The breakdown triggered revolution, social turmoil, and massive political and economic restructuring. As the 1990s dawned, most of Eastern Europe left the communist fold. The Soviet communist party, desperate to survive, voluntarily relinquished its monopoly on political power and tinkered with market reforms. Not to be placated by half-measures, the disgruntled republics proclaimed the dissolution of the once-mighty Soviet Union and the birth of a new Commonwealth of Independent States. Elsewhere in Asia, communist regimes reacted in various ways to growing dissatisfaction—some reintroducing profit incentives, some tightening central control.

It would be premature to speculate on the short-term outcome of these cataclysmic upheavals. However, one thing seems certain: Marxism, in its extreme form, is no longer taken seriously by the masses it once promised to liberate. Seldom in history has any movement experienced such a meteoric rise and fall.

The Jews: Homeland and Holocaust

*Prophecy 14: **The rise of Israel as a Jewish homeland.***

*Prophecy 15: **The persecution of Jews on the European continent (the Nazi Holocaust).***

Both Bahá'u'lláh and 'Abdu'l-Bahá referred frequently to the future growth and consolidation of the Jewish community in the Holy Land. In a talk first published in 1908, 'Abdu'l-Bahá said:

> ... in this cycle Israel will be gathered in the Holy Land, and ... the Jewish people who are scattered to the East and West, South and North, will be assembled together. ... You can see that from all parts of the world tribes of Jews are

coming to the Holy Land; they live in villages and lands which they make their own, and day by day they are increasing to such an extent that all Palestine will become their home.[104]

The return of Jews to the Holy Land, from which they had been excluded for almost two thousand years, had tentatively begun in 'Abdu'l-Bahá's lifetime. Few people, however, could then have visualized the momentum this process would gain, much less the creation in 1948 of the State of Israel or the strategic importance it would acquire. This process has been greatly accelerated in recent years through the lifting of travel restrictions on Jews in the former Soviet Union who began emigrating to Israel in vast numbers.

'Abdu'l-Bahá's outlook for the Jewish race was not uniformly rosy. During His American tour in 1912, He alluded to a future outbreak of violence against Jews in Europe and urged immediate action to forestall such a catastrophe. "... you must not think that this is ended," He said, referring to persecutions of the past. "The time may come when in Europe itself they will arise against the Jews."[105] Three decades later, His warnings materialized in the Holocaust, when an estimated six million European Jews—a third or more of the race—perished in Nazi concentration camps.

America's Racial Upheavals

Prophecy 16: America's violent racial struggles.

The intense and sometimes bloody racial struggles facing America were as clear to 'Abdu'l-Bahá in 1912 as if they had already occurred.

"This question of the union of the white and the black is very important," He warned during His tour of America, "for if it is not realized, erelong great difficulties will arise, and harmful results will follow."[106] In a 1912 letter to a Chicago Bahá'í, He wrote, "If this matter remaineth without change, enmity will be increased day by day, and the final result will be hardship and may end in bloodshed." Until racial prejudice can be overcome, He added, "the realm of humanity will not find rest. Nay, rather, discord and bloodshed will be increased day by day, and the foundation of the prosperity of man will be destroyed."[107]

From the vantage point of the 1990s, such observations may seem self-evident. To white America in 1912 they seemed unthinkable. However, the resurgence of the Ku Klux Klan in 1915 and economic dislocations after World War I soon raised racial tensions to new levels. These came to a head in the "Red Summer" of 1919, a year when twenty-five race riots occurred in various cities.[108]

'Abdu'l-Bahá Himself interpreted these outbreaks as merely the first signs of a greater struggle. "Now is the time," He said in 1920, "for Americans to take up this matter and unite both the white and the colored races. Otherwise, hasten ye towards destruction! Hasten ye towards devastation!"[109] Shoghi Effendi, recalling these and many similar words, wrote in 1954 of "the supreme, the inescapable and urgent duty—so repeatedly and graphically represented and stressed by 'Abdu'l-Bahá in His arraignment of the basic weaknesses in the social fabric of the nation—of remedying, while there is yet time, through a revolutionary change in the concept and attitude of the average white American toward his Negro fellow citizen, a situation which, if allowed to drift, will, in the words of 'Abdu'l-Bahá, cause the streets of American cities to run with blood. . . ."[110]

The racial upheavals of the 1960s, as American blacks intensified their demands for long-overdue economic and social justice, fully vindicated 'Abdu'l-Bahá's predictions. In race riots between 1965 and 1969, according to the *New York Times*, about 250 persons were killed, 12,000 were injured and 83,000 were arrested.[111] During one summer about forty cities were ablaze and at least one, Detroit, was occupied by federal troops.[112] Bloodshed would have been far worse but for the success of the Reverend Martin Luther King in steering the civil rights movement into nonviolent channels. Ironically,

Reverend King's own assassination triggered open racial warfare in some of America's largest cities, as blacks and whites alike reacted with despair, frustration, and pent-up rage.

In the spring of 1992, four white police officers were acquitted by an all-white jury of the videotaped beating of Rodney King, a black Los Angeles motorist, after a high-speed chase. Five days of rioting followed, leaving about sixty persons dead, many more injured, and seven thousand arrested on riot-related charges. Violence spread to cities as far away as Atlanta, Las Vegas, San Francisco, Miami, and Seattle. The verdict and its grim aftermath demonstrated that the uneasy truce of the past two decades had merely masked the symptoms of racism without curing the disease.

In forecasting these events more than fifty years earlier, 'Abdu'l-Bahá called attention to a broader and critically important dimension of the conflict. He stated that if American whites and blacks would join in true fellowship, their unity would so enhance the nation's peacemaking influence as to provide "an assurance of the world's peace"[113]; otherwise, racial strife would gravely weaken America from within at a time when its very existence was already imperiled from without. Failure to act in time, He said, could easily lead to "the destruction of America."[114] Shoghi Effendi reiterated these warnings in the 1954 letter quoted above, stating that the American nation had "dangerously underestimated" the crisis into which it was heading. True to these warnings, the racial clashes of the late sixties peaked during the darkest days of the Cold War, at a time when America's survival turned on a highly unstable nuclear standoff with its enemies.

The United States, as we now know, survived the crisis of the moment. Both the Cold War and the formal system of racial segregation that prompted the civil rights movement are today relics of the dead past. Discrimination, though still common, now is at least illegal; and politicians may no longer with impunity voice openly racist sentiments. However, as recent events have shown, these cosmetic signs of progress do not necessarily indicate the "revolutionary change" in attitude that 'Abdu'l-Bahá prescribed as the only permanent cure for America's racial maladies. So long as racism remains a significant part of the American psyche, one must wonder when the last chapter in this tragic drama will have been written.

BAHÁ'U'LLÁH AND HIS FAITH

Bahá'u'lláh and 'Abdu'l-Bahá predicted a number of remarkable developments involving the Bahá'í Faith itself. Several of these are described below.

Bahá'u'lláh's Release from Prison

Prophecy 17: Bahá'u'lláh's release from the prison of 'Akká and the pitching of His tent on Mount Carmel.

Bahá'u'lláh's royal enemies, Sulṭán 'Abdu'l-'Azíz and Náṣiri'd-Dín Sháh, had every reason to believe they could destroy Him by imprisoning Him in 'Akká. The harrowing conditions there were skillfully designed to ensure His early death, and the sulṭán's decree made it clear that Bahá'u'lláh's incarceration was to be perpetual. He entered the prison already broken in health, devoid of material resources, and surrounded by an army of vicious spies and jailers determined to carry out His sentence. His writings from this period show that He understood all too well how many heartbreaking tragedies and paralyzing sufferings faced Him during the years ahead.

Yet the ink was scarcely dry on His sentence when Bahá'u'lláh assured His royal captors that He, not they, would ultimately prevail. Soon after arriving at 'Akká in 1868 He wrote to Náṣiri'd-Dín Sháh: "No doubt is there whatever that these tribulations will be followed by the outpourings of a supreme mercy, and these dire adversities be succeeded by an overflowing prosperity."[115] During the darkest days of His imprisonment He wrote to His friends: "Fear not. These doors shall be opened. My tent shall be pitched on Mount Carmel, and the utmost joy shall be realized."[116]

Bahá'u'lláh's confinement was enforced with strict severity for many years, and He endured indescribable agony. Eventually, however, His shackles began to crumble. Bahá'u'lláh's innocence and integrity slowly were recognized by the region's entire population, once fiercely antagonistic; the benevolent spirit of His teachings gradually won the admiration of high and low alike; and hostile officials were one by one replaced or dismissed. 'Akká eventually had a new governor, the "sagacious and humane" Aḥmad Big Tawfíq, who became such an admirer of the exiles that he sent his son to 'Abdu'l-Bahá for instruction and enlightenment. Increasing numbers of scholars and dignitaries sought audience with the prisoner of 'Akká and testified to His greatness. The Turkish government, disturbed by reports of the increasing respect being shown to Bahá'u'lláh, occasionally dispatched to the prison-city unfriendly officials armed with dictatorial authority and orders to reverse the situation. Even these men, finding no one to cooperate with their plans, proved helpless to check the tide of events now flowing in Bahá'u'lláh's favor.

Throughout this period Bahá'u'lláh made no effort to obtain His own release; rather, He repeatedly refused to leave the prison even when opportunities were presented. No less a personage than the governor of 'Akká offered Him His freedom; He politely declined, insisting He was still a prisoner. Eventually, however, the drastic edict of the sulṭán had become a dead letter. The muftí of 'Akká—head of the Muslim religious community—kneeled at Bahá'u'lláh's feet and begged Him to leave the city walls for a comfortable home in the country. "Who has the power to make you a prisoner?" the muftí asked. "You have kept yourself in prison." He pleaded for an entire hour with Bahá'u'lláh, Who finally agreed to leave.

Bahá'u'lláh spent His remaining years in the countryside, whose beauty He had always loved, devoting His time to His writing and the education of His followers. "The rulers of Palestine," says 'Abdu'l-Bahá, "envied His influence and power. Governors and mutiṣarrifs, generals and local officials, would humbly request the honor of attaining His presence—a request to which He seldom acceded."[117]

As a result of these incredible events, Bahá'u'lláh was able, in His latter years, to travel several times to Haifa. There, as He had long ago prophesied, He pitched His tent on Mount Carmel. During one of these journeys He pointed out to 'Abdu'l-Bahá the spot where the Shrine of the Báb was to be erected. During another He revealed the gloriously beautiful Tablet of Carmel—the charter for the future establishment on that mountain of the world spiritual and administrative center of His Faith.

The House of Bahá'u'lláh

Prophecy 18: The seizure and desecration of the house of Bahá'-u'lláh in Baghdad.

The house Bahá'u'lláh occupied during His exile in Baghdad was designated by Him, in His Kitáb-i-Aqdas (Most Holy Book), as a center of pilgrimage for Bahá'ís. He Himself acquired ownership of the residence, which remained in the unbroken and undisputed possession of the Bahá'í community after His departure from Baghdad.

Bahá'u'lláh, however, wrote of it: "Grieve not, O House of God, if the veil of thy sanctity be rent asunder by the infidels."[118] "Verily, it shall be so abased in the days to come as to cause tears to flow from every discerning eye. Thus have We unfolded to thee things hidden beyond the veil. . . ."[119]

Around the time of 'Abdu'l-Bahá's passing, the Shí'ih Muslim community of Baghdad, which had no conceivable claim to the property, seized it and expelled the Bahá'ís. After a succession of legal battles, Iraq's Court of Appeals ruled in favor of the Muslims. Bahá'ís appealed to the League of Nations, which at the time exercised control over Iraq. The Council of the League—the world's highest tribunal—ruled unanimously in favor of the Bahá'ís, concluding that both the seizure and the subsequent appeals court verdict had been motivated by religious passion.

There followed many years of delays, protests and evasions. Bahá'ís, as a result, have never regained possession of the property. Their sole consolation is the further prophecy of Bahá'u'lláh regarding His house:

> In the fullness of time, the Lord shall, by the power of truth, exalt it in the eyes of all men. He shall cause it to become the Standard of His Kingdom, the Shrine round which will circle the concourse of the faithful. Thus hath spoken the Lord, thy God, ere the day of lamentation arriveth.[120]

Bahá'í Unity

Prophecy 19: The failure of all attempts to create schism within the Bahá'í Faith.

Fragmentation into sects is so universal a phenomenon of religion that historians tend to regard it as natural and inescapable. No outside observer, therefore, during the Bahá'í Faith's infancy, could have imagined that it would spread throughout the world while resisting every attempt to create schism within its own ranks.

Bahá'u'lláh predicted precisely this development—a development that is, so far as I know, unique and unprecedented in the annals of religion. If the Bahá'í Cause had no other claim to world attention, its fulfillment of this remarkable prophecy should be sufficient.

The point obviously is crucial, since the Bahá'í Faith claims to be the first religion destined by God to unite the entire world. Such a purpose clearly requires that its own unity remain intact. To preserve this unity, Bahá'u'lláh appointed 'Abdu'l-Bahá as His successor and created in the Bahá'í Administrative Order a center of authority to which all Bahá'ís must turn. These protective provisions are known as the Covenant. Because it incorporates this unifying Covenant, Bahá'u'lláh called His Revelation "the Day which shall never be followed by night"[121] and the "Springtime which autumn will never overtake."[122] He said of its Administrative Order:

"The Hand of Omnipotence hath established His Revelation upon an unassailable, an enduring foundation. Storms of human strife are powerless to undermine its basis, nor will men's fanciful theories succeed in damaging its structure."[123] 'Abdu'l-Bahá characterized efforts to disrupt Bahá'í unity as "no more than the foam of the ocean. . . . this froth of the ocean shall not endure and shall soon disappear and vanish, while on the other hand the ocean of the Covenant shall eternally surge and roar."[124] Shoghi Effendi wrote that the Bahá'í Administrative Order "must and will, in a manner unparalleled in any previous religion, safeguard from schism the Faith from which it has sprung,"[125]; and he stated: ". . . this priceless gem of Divine Revelation, now still in its embryonic state, shall evolve within the shell of His Law, and shall forge ahead, undivided and unimpaired, till it embraces the whole of mankind."[126]

It is impossible, of course, to place a final stamp of fulfillment on any prophecy indicating something will "never" happen. The most one can say is that it has not happened yet. Nevertheless, the Bahá'í Faith has emerged "undivided and unimpaired" from numerous attempts by powerful internal enemies to create a rift in its membership. Not one of these attempts has survived the generation that saw it appear.

The first such effort came from Bahá'u'lláh's younger half-brother, Mírzá Yaḥyá. When Bahá'u'lláh announced Himself as the Promised One foretold by the Báb and was accepted as such by most Bábís, Yaḥyá became extremely jealous. He countered with a similar claim, which he sought to advance by theft, poison, slander, and forgery. Though he inflicted terrible suffering on Bahá'u'lláh, he failed in the end to divide the religion. His "Azalí" splinter group faded away and Yaḥyá himself died in obscurity.

'Abdu'l-Bahá faced similar attacks on His leadership, including one by Muḥammad-'Alí, who was His own half-brother, and another by Ibráhím Khayr'u'lláh, a Syrian who at His direction had introduced the Faith to America. Shoghi Effendi had to contend with 'Abdu'l-Bahá's former assistant,

Ahmad Sohrab, who tried to create offshoots called the "New History Society" and the "Caravan of East and West." After Shoghi Effendi's death, a prominent Bahá'í teacher named Charles Mason Remey tried to establish himself as Guardian of the Faith, in clear defiance of 'Abdu'l-Bahá's Will and Testament.

Each of these men was energetic, resourceful, ambitious for leadership, and well placed to seize it. Moreover, each seemed for a brief time to have succeeded. Each one, however, watched in bewilderment as his following vanished like smoke, while the unity of the Bahá'í Faith—as Bahá'u'lláh and His successors had promised—remained inviolate.

Chapter 5

BAHÁ'Í PROPHECIES:
SCIENTIFIC DISCOVERIES

When the heavens were a little blue arch, stuck with stars,
I thought the universe was too strait and close, I was almost
stifled for want of air. But now it is enlarged in height and
breadth. . . . I begin to breathe with more freedom, and
think the universe incomparably more magnificent than it
was before.

—Bernard de Fontenelle

In science nobody really knows what is going to come next.
We always pretend that we know the answers, but nature
keeps advising us that we don't.

—Carlo Rubbia

Up to now we have examined Bahá'í prophecies that forecast
either world trends or historical events. This chapter details
prophecies that anticipate scientific developments, either by
making specific predictions or by stating previously undiscovered facts.

We must exercise caution in assessing the scientific implications of any religion. Many scriptures (such as the creation
allegory of Genesis) were written with symbolic intent; to insist
on a literal interpretation of such passages may be unwarranted. However, 'Abdu'l-Bahá explains that physical reality
is itself a metaphor of the spiritual world: ". . . the outward is
the expression of the inward; the earth is the mirror of the
Kingdom. . . ."[127] Consequently, many revealed truths carry
both an inward, spiritual meaning and an outward, literal one,

67

"and neither their outward preventeth their inward, nor doth their inward prevent their outward meaning."[128]

It follows that we cannot necessarily dismiss a given statement of the Manifestation as "purely spiritual" in meaning simply because that statement happens to contradict a current scientific theory. Bahá'ís believe that a correct understanding of true science and true religion will always show their underlying harmony. However, scholars of any given science occasionally misread the facts of nature, just as followers of any particular Manifestation sometimes misconstrue His teachings. Scientists revise their pronouncements daily, and the findings of one age are always superseded by those of the next.

'Abdu'l-Bahá points out that Muhammad disputed the official science of His day by implying that the sun is at rest relative to the earth and that it rotates around an axis. "When the Qur'án [Koran] appeared," He says, "all the mathematicians ridiculed these statements and attributed the theory to ignorance. Even the doctors of Islam, when they saw that these verses were contrary to the accepted Ptolemaic system, were obliged to explain them away."[129] This situation persisted for almost nine hundred years until Copernicus demonstrated the movement of the earth around the sun and "It became evident that the verses of the Qur'án agreed with existing facts...."[130]

Bahá'u'lláh writes:

> Weigh not the Book of God with such standards and sciences as are current amongst you, for the Book itself is the unerring balance established amongst men. In this most perfect balance whatsoever the peoples and kindreds of the earth possess must be weighed....[131]

Still, if the Bahá'í revelation is genuine, time should bring an ever-growing realization of the correspondence between its teachings and scientific reality. This chapter will consider whether such has been the case.

The Knowledge Explosion

*Prophecy 20: **The explosive acceleration of scientific and techno-logical progress.***

Bahá'u'lláh stated that mankind was entering an age of un-precedented scientific and technical advancement, when new discoveries would gradually increase from a trickle to a tidal wave.

"A new life is, in this age, stirring within all the peoples of the earth," He wrote, "and yet none hath discovered its cause, or perceived its motive."[132] He identified its source as the "fertilizing winds"[133] set in motion by the voice of God speaking through Himself and the Báb:

> Every word that proceedeth out of the mouth of God is endowed with such potency as can instil new life into every human frame.... Through the mere revelation of the word "Fashioner," issuing forth from His lips and proclaiming His attribute to mankind, such power is released as can generate, through successive ages, all the manifold arts which the hands of man can produce.... No sooner is this resplendent word uttered, than its animating energies, stirring within all created things, give birth to the means and instruments whereby such arts can be produced and perfected. All the wondrous achievements ye now witness are the direct conse-quences of the Revelation of this Name. In the days to come, ye will, verily, behold things of which ye have never heard before. Thus hath it been decreed in the Tablets of God.... In like manner, the moment the word expressing My attri-bute "The Omniscient" issueth forth from My mouth, every created thing will, according to its capacity and limitations, be invested with the power to unfold the knowledge of the most marvelous sciences, and will be empowered to manifest them in the course of time at the bidding of Him Who is the Almighty, the All-Knowing. Know thou of a certainty that the Revelation of every other Name is accompanied by a similar manifestation of Divine power.[134]

This creative principle, according to Bahá'u'lláh, underlies a remarkable fact of history: The birth of every world religion has been accompanied by an upsurge of invention and discovery. He indicated that God's newest revelation, being immeasurably greater in scope and intensity than those of the past, would stimulate a correspondingly greater burst of progress. This modern outpouring of divine power and knowledge, He wrote in the Súriy-i-Haykal, would soon raise up scientists of great caliber who would bring about technological achievements so marvelous that no one could yet imagine them.[135] To suggest the immensity of the coming knowledge revolution, Bahá'u'lláh likened knowledge to twenty-seven letters, of which only two had been disclosed prior to the Báb's appearance. Now, He said, humanity was about to receive the remaining twenty-five.[136]

"The heights which, through the most gracious favor of God, mortal man can attain in this Day, are as yet unrevealed to his sight," He wrote. "This is the Day of which it hath been said: 'O my son! verily God will bring everything to light though it were but the weight of a grain of mustard seed, and hidden in a rock, or in the heavens or in the earth. . . .'"[137]

Until about the first third of the nineteenth century (well into the lifetimes of the Báb and Bahá'u'lláh), human progress was fairly steady. Such progress could be shown on a graph as a line with a gentle upward slope, punctuated by occasional spurts and squiggles, but with an overall orientation more horizontal than vertical. As the century continued, however, the knowledge revolution foretold by Bahá'u'lláh kicked in, imperceptibly at first but with rapidly gathering momentum, sharply tilting the angle of the line until it became more vertical than horizontal. A restless new spirit of adventure and discovery came into science, literature, music, art, education, medicine, invention, and all other departments of human life, producing unprecedented advances. This process is still roaring forward with ever-increasing speed and force. Today, the sum of all human knowledge doubles every few years—just how rapidly, no one can really say (I have read estimates ranging from ten years to six months). As a result, far more progress has been achieved in technology since Bahá'u'lláh made His prediction than in all previous recorded history.

It may seem obvious, in hindsight, that nineteenth-century knowledge was about to reach critical mass and leap forward explosively. "Any event, once it has occurred, can be made to appear inevitable by a competent historian," says Lee Simonson. However, the impending knowledge revolution was anything but obvious at the time. Many thoughtful observers believed, on the contrary, that civilization was near its apex and that science and technology were reaching their limits. In 1844 philosopher Auguste Comte cited the composition of stars as an example of information forever beyond human reach. Long after the flood of new discoveries had begun, experts tended to misread it as just another brief spasm of progress destined to run its course, or even as the final flowering of human research and creativity. The celebrated theorist A. A. Michelson said in 1894 that future science would consist only of "adding a few decimal places to results already obtained."[138] Max Born, one of the world's top physicists, in 1929 expressed the same pessimistic idea: "Physics, as we know it, will be over in six months."[139]*

No serious scholar or scientist would make such unguarded comments today. What has become clear is that the knowledge explosion, impressive though it has been, is barely begun. It now appears certain to continue indefinitely and exponentially unless we first destroy ourselves with its fruits.

Bahá'u'lláh understood that these material advances would come before mankind had acquired the spiritual maturity to use them wisely. He wrote:

> The civilization, so often vaunted by the learned exponents of arts and sciences, will, if allowed to overleap the bounds of moderation, bring great evil upon men. . . . If carried to excess, civilization will prove as prolific a source of evil as it had been of goodness when kept within the restraints of

---

* Both Michelson and Born, we should note in fairness, came to rue the day they had said such rash things. Furthermore, both made pioneering contributions to the very revolution in physics that turned their own statements into quaint anachronisms.

moderation. . . . The day is approaching when its flame will devour the cities. . . .[140]

He indicated that science would not only give us the means to unify our planet but would, by unleashing the threat of mass destruction, make it imperative that we do so. Only then would humanity be prepared for a planetary religious renaissance fueled by the same divine impulse as the one driving physical science.

THE HEART OF THE ATOM

The coming dawn of the Atomic Age was writ large in the prophecies of Bahá'u'lláh and 'Abdu'l-Bahá.

Nuclear Terror

*Prophecy 21: **The development of nuclear weapons.***

In a Tablet entitled Words of Paradise, written shortly before His passing in 1892, Bahá'u'lláh noted the rush by Western civilization to develop ever more deadly weapons of war. Explaining the urgency of His call for world unity and peace, He declared:

> Strange and astonishing things exist in the earth but they are hidden from the minds and the understanding of men. These things are capable of changing the whole atmosphere of the earth and their contamination would prove lethal.[141]

This reference to "strange and astonishing things" aptly describes the twin processes of fission and fusion by which we obtain nuclear energy. The reality of such a power was again affirmed in 1911 by 'Abdu'l-Bahá:

> There is in existence a stupendous force, as yet, happily, undiscovered by man. Let us supplicate God, the Beloved, that this force be not discovered by science until spiritual civilization shall dominate the human mind. In the hands

of men of lower material nature, this power would be able to destroy the whole earth.[142]

'Abdu'l-Bahá spoke these portentous words to the Japanese ambassador to Spain, Viscount Arawaka, for whose country the warning carried grave implications. An ironic coincidence? If so, it was not the only one. In 1920 'Abdu'l-Bahá wrote to a group of young students in Tokyo: "In Japan the divine proclamation will be heard as a formidable explosion. . . ."[143] (I am aware of no other explosion metaphor in the Bahá'í writings.) A quarter of a century later, the Japanese cities of Hiroshima and Nagasaki were obliterated in the first wartime use of atomic bombs. Today the world's nuclear arsenals contain enough firepower not only to destroy humanity many times over but to alter climate and atmosphere so drastically as to render the planet uninhabitable.

Copper into Gold

*Prophecy 22: **The achievement of transmutation of elements, the age-old alchemist's dream.***

*Prophecy 23: **Dire peril for all humanity as a result of that achievement.***

The discovery of nuclear energy shed new light on an old question: Is it possible to transmute base metals into gold? Ancient alchemists eagerly sought the secret of this transmutation; by Bahá'u'lláh's time, however, scientists had long since concluded that such a feat was theoretically impossible. No element, they believed, could ever be changed into any other element.

Their belief was firmly grounded in experience. Centuries of experimentation, research, and trial and error had indicated that certain substances could not, by any method known to chemists, be broken down into two or more simpler ones or built up from two or more simpler ones. These fundamental substances were called elements to distinguish them from compounds, which could be broken down into, or built up from, other substances. Both compounds and elements were regarded as being composed of basic units or building blocks called atoms. Why do elements resist change? The natural interpretation was that atoms differ from one element to another but are all alike for any given element. Thus a compound such as water (composed of hydrogen and oxygen) could be broken down into its component elements merely by separating its hydrogen atoms from its oxygen atoms. But oxygen, being an element, could not be broken down into simpler substances by any conceivable reshuffling of its identical atoms.

Atoms were postulated by the ancient Greeks, but their existence (though widely accepted) was never definitely verified until 1905—thirteen years after the passing of Bahá'u'-lláh. During His lifetime it was thought that atoms, if they existed at all, were the smallest particles of matter, indivisible and impenetrable. This notion implied that no element could ever be changed into another, since this would mean altering the supposedly immutable atoms.

Bahá'u'lláh, as far back as the early 1860s, challenged this assumption. He wrote on several occasions that the alchemists' age-old dream—that of changing copper into gold—is entirely possible,* although copper and gold both are elements. When this statement was cited by His detractors as proof of His ignorance, He wrote:

> Consider the doubts which they . . . have instilled into the hearts of the people of this land. "Is it ever possible," they ask, "for copper to be transmuted into gold?" Say, Yes, by my Lord, it is possible. Its secret, however, lieth hidden in Our Knowledge. . . . That copper can be turned into gold is in itself sufficient proof that gold can, in like manner, be transmuted into copper. . . . Every mineral can be made to

---

* Bahá'u'lláh wrote extensively on the subject of alchemy. He discouraged His followers from practicing the physical aspects of this branch of learning, encouraging them to turn to the spiritual implications of transformation. He regarded traditional alchemy, which was an odd mixture of pseudo-science and superstition with occasional insights or lucky guesses, as "vain and discarded learnings" and "mere pretension." (*Kitáb-i-Íqán*, ¶203, ¶208.)

acquire the density, form and substance of each and every other mineral.[144]

Elsewhere Bahá'u'lláh wrote that humanity would indeed learn to transmute elements and that this achievement would be one of the signs of the coming of age of the human race. He further prophesied that after its discovery a great calamity would threaten the world unless mankind came under the shelter of the Cause of God.[145]

This latter prophecy seemed somewhat puzzling. Transmutation might or might not be possible, but one thing had always seemed self-evident: If it were possible, it would be an unadulterated boon for mankind. If one could change copper into gold, or any element into any other, then limitless wealth presumably would follow. Human beings would be able to manufacture all manner of previously expensive commodities —food, medicine, industrial raw materials—cheaply and in limitless quantities. Wondrous new inventions and spellbinding discoveries would herald a golden age of material well-being. Such visions had fired the imaginations of alchemists for thousands of years.

Transmutation of elements was finally achieved, and its age-old secret unlocked, early in the twentieth century. But—as Bahá'u'lláh had foreseen—there was a catch: Changing one element into another is associated with the release of nuclear energy. The two phenomena (transmutation of elements and nuclear energy) are twin aspects of a single process; they are flip sides of the same coin.

Most of an atom's energy is frozen within its nucleus (hence the term "nuclear"). A portion of this energy can be freed by either fission (the splitting of an atom's nucleus into two lighter nuclei) or fusion (the combining of two or more nuclei into a larger nucleus). This release of energy by splitting or combining atomic nuclei produces new atoms with new sizes and weights, thus changing one element into another. The blast of a hydrogen bomb is the result of transmuting hydrogen into helium through fusion. This same process of hydrogen-to-helium fusion powers the sun and all the stars (which, of course, are also suns). In a conventional nuclear power plant, the fission of uranium atoms produces a variety of lighter elements while some of the unsplit uranium atoms change into plutonium by absorbing extra neutrons. Transmutation of elements also occurs through the natural process of radioactive decay, whereby uranium, thorium, and a number of other unstable elements gradually change into the lighter element lead.

There is, then, a striking connection between Bahá'u'lláh's prediction of success in transmuting elements and His separate prediction (detailed in the preceding section) of a force capable of poisoning the whole earth's atmosphere. Both prophecies pointed to the same discovery: nuclear power. No less astonishing than either prophecy taken singly, however, was the fact that Bahá'u'lláh Himself apparently saw the connection between them—a connection no human being of His generation should have known. The ancient alchemist's dream, as He and He alone foresaw, represents not an unmixed blessing but a dangerous instrument. Used unwisely, it has brought mankind to the brink of nuclear holocaust.

Although various elements have been transmuted in bombs and reactors as well as in laboratory experiments, most transmutations are too complex and expensive to be practical given current technology. The changing of copper into gold still falls within this category. Modern atomic science, however, has definitely proved Bahá'u'lláh right in saying such reactions are possible. It is now clear, moreover, that transmutations of equal and even greater complexity actually occur in stars. This point, which relates to yet another Bahá'í scientific prophecy, is considered in the next section.

The Evolution of Elements

*Prophecy 24: **The discovery that complex elements evolve in nature from simpler ones.***

Since there are well over one hundred elements, with atoms of widely varying sizes and weights, it is natural to wonder how such diversity came about. If we assume, as scientists did until well into the twentieth century, that atoms are unchanging, there seem to be only two possibilities. One is that this diversity always existed. The other is that it came into being all at once (whether naturally or by divine creation) at some point in the remote past.

'Abdu'l-Bahá endorsed a third alternative, which is found in the book *Some Answered Questions*. This remarkable work is a collection of table talks He delivered in 'Akká from 1904 to 1906 in answer to questions put to Him by Laura Clifford Barney. The answers were written down in Persian as He spoke. 'Abdu'l-Bahá later reviewed these notes for accuracy, "sometimes changing a word or a line with His reed pen," then signed them.[146] The talks were translated into English by Miss Barney and were first published in 1908.

According to 'Abdu'l-Bahá, the various elements all began as a single form of matter, arriving at their present-day condition by passing through intermediate stages:

> . . . it is evident that in the beginning matter was one, and that one matter appeared in different aspects in each element. Thus various forms were produced, and these various aspects as they were produced became permanent, and each element was specialized. But this permanence was not definite, and did not attain realization and perfect existence until after a very long time.[147]

The detailed verification of this teaching is one of the most amazing stories of modern science. It began in 1929 with the seemingly unrelated discovery, by astronomer Edwin Hubble, that all observable galaxies appear to be moving away from each other at a rate proportional to their distance. In other words, the farther apart they already are, the faster the distance between them grows. This led to the conclusion that we live in an expanding universe which must once have been compressed into an infinitesimally small region. Several converging lines of evidence now suggest that our cosmos erupted from such a point of origin fifteen to eighteen thousand million years ago in a primordial explosion whimsically dubbed the "Big Bang."

The hows and whys of the Big Bang are still shrouded in mystery. One currently popular theory ("vacuum genesis," originated by Edward Tryon and refined by Alan Guth) implies that such an event could have happened countless times, producing multiple "universes" hidden from one another's view. According to Guth, our own Big Bang may have been triggered by events in another universe, and our universe in turn could give birth to others. Some scientists postulate an "oscillating universe," in which each expansion is followed by a contraction and another Big Bang. The "finite but unbounded" universe of Stephen Hawking uses complex mathematics to incorporate the Big Bang into a universe with "no edge in space, no beginning or end in time."[148] Whatever interpretation is correct, few cosmologists doubt that the Big Bang itself must somehow have occurred.

The Big Bang model clearly ruled out any possibility that the complex elements we see today always existed in their present forms. Any atoms that might have appeared within such a conflagration would have been instantly ripped apart by its titanic pressure. Nor could those elements have appeared all at once in the aftermath of the explosion as a direct result of its heat and force. Calculations indicated that the fireball, powerful as it was, would have expanded and cooled too quickly to sustain the intricate interactions needed to produce any but the simplest elements. Scientists confronted a mystery: Where and how did the elements arise? After decades of detective work based on studies of nuclear reactions and spectroscopic analysis of stars, they worked out what must have happened. The last few pieces of the puzzle fell into place as recently as 1957. Here is a summary (grossly oversimplified) of the process as currently understood:

The early universe was a boiling cauldron of raw energy, too hot for matter to exist in any form. Its density exceeded that of rock; its temperature reached thousands of millions of degrees. As this hellish proto-matter expanded and cooled, it condensed into a shower of subatomic particles, which arranged themselves by mutual attraction into atoms of hydrogen, the simplest element. The rapidly falling temperature had time to fuse about a fifth of this hydrogen into helium (the next simplest element), along with traces of lithium and beryllium, before it dropped too low to sustain further nuclear transmutations.

All of this happened within a few minutes. The next several thousand million years passed uneventfully, as hydrogen/helium clouds billowed through the darkness, thinning here, thickening there. (Space is not a perfect vacuum; even today, it is still suffused with remnants of this primordial gas.) Denser clouds, collapsing in upon themselves under their own weight, eventually built up enough internal pressure to blaze into the fusion furnaces visible to us as stars.

A young star obtains most of its energy from the fusion of hydrogen into helium. As the star ages and contracts, however, it becomes a simmering pressure-cooker wherein a variety of more complex fusion reactions occur. These reactions gradually produce all of the lighter elements (carbon, oxygen, and the like), which sort themselves by weight into layers around the star's core. This phase of the process normally occupies thousands of millions of years.

The heaviest element so produced is iron, which forms the gaseous inner layer and renders the star unstable. If the star is sufficiently massive, this instability causes its core to collapse suddenly, sending an inconceivably loud clang or gong upward through the surrounding layers. This sonic boom—the most powerful shock wave known to science—destroys the star in a supernova explosion characterized by intense heat, pressure, and an abundance of free neutrons. The nuclei of atoms caught in this "neutron flux" tend rapidly to absorb neutrons, about half of which change into protons through beta particle emission. Since the number of protons is what gives an atom its identity, this process causes it to evolve quickly, becoming, at each step, a new and slightly heavier element.

Thus an atom entering the supernova blast as iron may, within a split-second, change from iron to cobalt to nickel to copper, its nucleus gaining weight with each promotion. Additional steps up the ladder of increasingly heavy elements can bring it to the state of gold or, further, to that of lead, cadmium, or any heavier element. Indeed, any lower element may evolve into any higher one, typically within the blink of an eye. A dying star, then, is the ultimate alchemist's crucible: It is here that base metals are literally transmuted into gold, lead, uranium, and all other elements heavier than iron, then blown into space as gas to mingle with the hydrogen and helium already there. When latter-day stars and planets condense from the interstellar mist, they inherit some of the elements born in earlier stars. Our own sun, a relatively new star, and our own planet, the earth, are among the heavenly bodies nourished from this cosmic cornucopia. When we look around, every substance or object we see is the product of such a progression.

Current theory, as indicated above, holds that the hydrogen/helium mixture that forms the raw material for this process emerged from the Big Bang itself. However, the discovery that more complex elements are forged in stars, reaching their permanent specialized forms only after eons of evolution, in no way depends on the correctness of the Big Bang model, for that discovery has since been confirmed by many independent observations. Thus, even should the Big Bang theory be later modified or abandoned, the basic picture of elemental evolution will remain. When this picture came into focus in 1957, it was precisely as 'Abdu'l-Bahá had described it more than half a century earlier.

These facts also confirm something Bahá'u'lláh wrote in 1862: namely, that copper can change into gold in as little as a single instant. In the Kitáb-i-Íqán (Book of Certitude), He uses the following analogy to dramatize how profound the effect of divine revelation can be upon the human soul:

For instance, consider the substance of copper. Were it to be protected in its own mine from becoming solidified, it would, within the space of seventy years, attain to the state of gold. . . .

Be that as it may, the real elixir will, in one instant, cause the substance of copper to attain the state of gold, and will traverse the seventy-year stages in a single moment.[149]

As many readers have pointed out, this passage is a metaphorical description of spiritual transformation; as such its primary implications concern human life and character. However, we cannot discount it as a "purely symbolic" image possessing no literal or physical significance. Bahá'u'lláh is drawing a parallel between a spiritual reality and a material fact. Thus the Guardian, in a letter written by his secretary on his behalf, comments as follows: "We as Bahá'ís must assume that, as He [Bahá'u'lláh] had access to all knowledge, He was referring to a definite physical condition which theoretically might exist."[150]

But how can copper "in its own mine" be prevented from becoming solidified—much less change to gold? One doubts that Bahá'u'lláh was referring to any mine on earth, for copper ore in a terrestrial mine always is solid. One might, of course, maintain molten or gaseous copper indefinitely in a metallurgical laboratory; but such an environment hardly constitutes a mine in any recognizable sense.

But the situation changes if we suppose that by copper's "own mine" Bahá'u'lláh means an exploding star. Copper is born in the fireworks of a supernova. In this stellar furnace— its true place of origin, from which every atom of copper on earth ultimately derives—it can never solidify. Moreover, any copper that appears in the explosion will tend, as the nuclear reaction progresses, to gain more neutrons and protons until it becomes gold (or some even heavier element). In this scenario, copper's stellar birthplace may be regarded as its mine, and the supernova's neutron flux as the "real elixir" that, literally in a flash, accomplishes the transmutation.

This admittedly speculative interpretation does raise one question: If Bahá'u'lláh was alluding to a supernova explosion, and if (as currently understood) such explosions last only a few moments, why does He describe the transmutation as occurring "within the space" of seventy years? While it is true—in a strictly literal sense—that any event of less than seventy years duration transpires "within" that period, reason suggests the seventy-year reference may have some more specific meaning. Two possible answers come to mind.

The first is that there may be some as-yet-unknown condition in which copper's transition to gold would occur more slowly than it does in the supernovae we can observe. In fact, simply by virtue of knowing that the transition can and does occur rapidly, we also know that a slower version is at least theoretically possible (in the sense that it would violate no laws of physics). Of the infinite possible varieties of nuclear interactions, only a vanishingly small percentage have as yet been studied or even postulated.

The second answer (suggested by Charles Coffey) is that Bahá'u'lláh may have described the process as occurring "within the space of seventy years" simply to strengthen the intended analogy between elemental transmutation and human spiritual development. Seventy years is the traditional human lifespan of "threescore years and ten." By expressing the duration in these literally accurate terms, yet noting its actual quickness in the statement that follows, Bahá'u'lláh may be emphasizing an important truth: Even though human character can and sometimes does change rapidly, this process of refinement typically involves lifelong struggle.

Bahá'u'lláh's statement on the transmutation of copper to gold "in its own mine" is one that has puzzled generations of readers. These tentative observations are offered in the hope of spurring further study and research. We may well have as much to learn about Bahá'u'lláh's intended meaning as astrophysicists have to learn about atomic genesis. As a result of modern discoveries, however, we can state one conclusion with reasonable assurance: What we do know of His meaning is entirely consistent with what we now know about the evolution of elements.

THE SKY IS NOT THE LIMIT

The Space Age, like the Atomic Age, figures prominently in Bahá'í prophecy.

Stars and Planets

Prophecy 25: **The recognition of planets as a necessary by-product of star formation.**

Stars come in a rainbow of colors and are grouped into galaxies with a delightful assortment of shapes. Our sun, a fairly typical yellow star, is part of the Milky Way, an equally typical spiral galaxy. There are at least a hundred thousand million stars in the Milky Way galaxy alone and a similar number of galaxies in the observable universe. It seems certain the observable universe is itself a flyspeck in the larger cosmos.

Since our sun and galaxy are so ordinary, it is natural to wonder whether the same is true of our planet, the earth. Bahá'u'lláh wrote that "every fixed star hath its own planets,"* whose age and number the "learned men" of His generation had "failed" to "consider."[151]

It has been clear, since the opening decades of the twentieth century, that both the age and size of the physical universe are millions of times greater than was generally believed in Bahá'u'lláh's lifetime. Regarding the existence of planets around other stars, however, there has been no such agreement. Astronomers have long known that stars, like blazing

---

* The term "fixed star" is of ancient origin. It refers to any of those celestial bodies that do not, over the course of a human lifespan, visibly change position relative to one another. The expression was created to differentiate such bodies from "wandering stars," which travel across the sky following paths similar to those of the sun and moon. We now know, of course, that "fixed stars" are self-luminous suns like our sun, while "wandering stars" are planets like our earth.

raindrops, condense from the thin mist of hydrogen and other gases pervading the near-vacuum of space; but until recently they had no evidence indicating that this process could explain the formation of planets circling those stars.

Lacking such evidence, many theorists turned to the idea that the Earth and our solar system's other planets such as Mars, Venus, Jupiter, and so forth are the result of a near collision between the sun and another star (or some other large celestial body). According to this model, the gravitational tides produced by such an upheaval pulled flaming blobs of matter away from the sun; these fell into orbit, hardening into worlds as they cooled. Since close encounters between stars seldom occur, this hypothesis suggested that planets like ours are extremely rare in the cosmos.

A less catastrophic model had been formulated by Kant and Laplace in the eighteenth and early nineteenth centuries. They regarded planets as blobs of matter spun off by the rotating sun as it condensed. Powerful arguments, however, weighed against this hypothesis, which was therefore rejected by a majority of astronomers. By 1946 the case against the Kant-Laplace "spin-off" model seemed so airtight that astrophysicist George Gamow, in his classic *The Birth and Death of the Sun*, could sum up the scientific consensus as follows: "In view of our present knowledge this attractive and simple hypothesis [the spin-off model] will not stand up to serious criticism." "It seems, therefore, necessary to assume . . . that the rotational momentum was put into the system of planets from the outside and to consider the formation of the planets as due to an encounter of our Sun with some other stellar body of comparable size." "Thus we should be forced to the conclusion that planetary systems are very rare phenomena, and that our Sun must be extremely lucky to have one."[152]

This consensus prevailed until the 1970s when newly developed mathematical models prompted astrophysicists to revive the Kant-Laplace hypothesis in a more sophisticated form. They now believe that the condensation of a rotating star does bring into being around it a "dusty disk" of gas, ice, rock, and other leftover debris. Larger particles, sweeping through the disk, collect smaller ones, forming ever more massive chunks that soon begin to attract one another through mutual gravitation. These chunks, arranged into bands like the rings of Saturn, eventually smash together to form still larger objects.[153]

Although the current body of knowledge does not constitute "definitive evidence," it "strongly suggests that stars like our own Sun frequently, if not invariably, are accompanied by planets."[154] These may range in size from tiny proto-worlds called "planetesimals" to "superplanets" far more massive than Jupiter, the largest object circling our own sun. The new model interprets planetary bodies as a natural and probably inevitable by-product of stellar dynamics. Far from being the mutant offspring of a freak accident, they are the normal children of any normal star—as inseparable a part of the star's life-cycle as its heat and light.*

The worth of any theory depends less on its elegance and plausibility than on whether its predictions are upheld by evidence. Support for the current concept came initially from an infrared orbiting telescope, which detected cold disks of matter around Vega and other young, bright stars. Many more have since been detected and are being studied with the aid of such instruments as the Hubble space telescope. Though their behavior remains imperfectly understood, evidence is mounting that such disks spawn planets much sooner and more rapidly than anyone suspected, sometimes under conditions once deemed impossible.[155]

October 1995 brought the first positive identification of an "extrasolar" planet (that is, one circling a star other than our own sun). The newly discovered world was associated with the star 51 Pegasi (in the constellation Pegasus), a scant 42 light-years from Earth. It was identified by telltale wobbles in the star's movement. Two more planets—one belonging to 70

---

* Of course, a system of planets may at any stage of its evolution be destroyed by some violent celestial event such as a supernova explosion or stellar collision.

Virginis (in the constellation Virgo), the other to 47 Ursae Majoris (in the Big Dipper or Ursa Major)—were announced in January 1996, and others followed. As of this writing, more than 120 extrasolar planets have been located, including some in multiplanet solar systems similar to our own.

Even with a veritable zoo of proven planets, astronomers remain rightly reluctant to generalize on the basis of an incomplete mathematical model. Much more research would be needed to establish conclusively Bahá'u'lláh's statement that "every fixed star" has "its own planets." Nor is there even universal agreement as to how large or small an object must be in order to constitute a planet. Nevertheless, His position— long considered untenable—now is at least provisionally confirmed. Since ongoing research is yielding new evidence at a rapid rate, the interested reader would do well to consult a current science periodical for the latest developments in this fast-breaking news story.

In announcing the prevalence of extrasolar planets, Bahá'u'-lláh added that "every planet" has "its own creatures, such as no man can number."[156] Skeptics may object that conditions on Mercury, Jupiter, and other known planets are too hostile to accommodate life as we know it. Without speculating on the ever-fascinating possibility of life-as-we-*don't*-yet-know-it, let us note that the Persian/Arabic word _khalq_, translated here as "creature," encompasses any created thing, whether ani-mate or inanimate. Many dictionaries support a similarly broad interpretation of the English word "creature." This seems especially true of the somewhat archaic usage favored by the Guardian for his translations, such as this one, of Bahá'í scripture.

Furthermore, Bahá'u'lláh's teachings explicitly state that even "minerals are endowed with a spirit and life according to the requirements of that stage . . . even as He saith in the Qur'án [Koran], 'All things are living.'"[157] Thus rocks, ponds, clouds, and other inanimate objects may, in some rudimentary sense, fall within Bahá'u'lláh's definition of "creatures."

Shoghi Effendi has in any case stated: "The creatures which Bahá'u'lláh states to be found on every planet cannot be considered to be necessarily similar [to] or different from human beings on this earth. . . . It remains for science to discover one day the exact nature of these creatures."[158]

Railroads to Heaven

Prophecy 26: Space travel.

With the age of aviation barely under way, 'Abdu'l-Bahá recognized—more clearly than many of today's political leaders—the need for an organized program of space exploration. Speaking in Paris on 19 February 1913, He urged that efforts be directed towards reaching other planets. Such an undertaking, He indicated, was a natural extension of scientific and technological strides already being made.[159]

In one of His letters He also referred to space travel, describing it in graphic terms. In this letter He cautioned Bahá'ís against being distracted by the glitter of the space program (or any other spectacular undertakings) from the more tedious but infinitely more vital task of spreading Bahá'u'lláh's teachings:

> I know, verily, that the universal, never ending, eternal, bright and divine establishments are only the diffusing of the breaths of God, and the spreading of the instructions of God, and all that are beside these, though they be the reigning over all regions of the earth, or the construction of railroads from the earth to the heavens, or means of transportation with the rapidity of rising lightning from the globe of the earth to the globe of the sun, all are but mortal, perishing, demolishing and disadvantageous, in comparison with the divine establishments.[160]

If we wished to describe today's reusable space shuttle in images familiar to 'Abdu'l-Bahá's early twentieth-century readers, we could hardly do better than to call it a railroad from earth to heaven. Nor could we more clearly express the awesome speed attained by modern spacecraft than by likening it to the "rapidity of rising lightning." Perhaps the most remarkable aspect of this passage is its reference to transportation "from the globe of the earth to the globe of the sun." Even this development—one completely inconceivable to 'Abdu'l-Bahá's contemporaries—became reality in October 1990 with the launching of the European-built Ulysses solar probe from the American space shuttle Discovery. After a Jupiter flyby, the robot spacecraft made in mid-1994 a close sweep of the sun's "south pole," followed in mid-1995 by a similar pass over its "north pole," sending back, at each stage, large amounts of data.

Ulysses is, of course, unlikely to be the end of the story. Arthur C. Clarke, writing in *Profiles of the Future*, suggests that prospective advances in plasma physics could someday make it possible to generate an impenetrable "force field" (that old science-fiction standby) capable of withstanding direct contact with solar fires. "When we possess it," he writes, "we may have a key not only to the interior of the Earth, but even, perhaps, to the interior of the Sun."[161]

GENERAL PROPHECIES

Transmission of Cancer

Prophecy 27: **The realization that some forms of cancer are communicable.**

'Abdu'l-Bahá wrote that "bodily diseases like consumption and cancer are contagious*" in the same manner as other infections against which "safe and healthy persons" must guard themselves.[162] This was obviously true of consumption (tuberculosis)—but what of cancer?

In this regard the statement, when published in 1921, was diametrically opposed to established medical opinion. Evi-

---

* The Persian word for "contagious" embraces all the shades of meaning represented by the English words "contagious," "infectious" and "communicable." It can therefore connote mild, infrequent infectivity as well as dramatic and obvious contagion.

dence against it seemed solid; the sole supporting clue—at best ambiguous—had been the discovery in 1908 and 1911 of certain "virus-induced tumours" in chickens. These were commonly discounted as "a biological curiosity, either not true cancers or perhaps a peculiarity of the avian species."[163] In any case, 'Abdu'l-Bahá had made His comment on cancer in a discussion of human diseases, both spiritual and physical, to which this finding had no obvious relevance.

The possibility that it might have a less-than-obvious relevance loomed larger after researchers found similar tumors in rabbits (1932), frogs (1934), and mice (1936).[164] These infectious cancers had long been overlooked because they tend to spread in ways that mask their true nature. They may, for example, be transmitted through a virus in the mother's milk or placenta, appearing to be hereditary. Many such viruses cease to display infective activity as soon as they have induced cancer, making their role extremely difficult to recognize. These findings fanned suspicion that similar tumor-producing viruses might be able to spread from human being to human being.

No responsible authority suggests that all, or even most, forms of cancer are directly communicable, much less that they spread through casual contact. Most malignant tumors clearly are induced by exposure to chemicals, radiation, or similar environmental agents; by hereditary and genetic factors; or by combinations of such causes. Nevertheless, the infectious origin of some human cancers now is considered "almost certain"[165], and "the evidence grows stronger with each passing month."[166] Cervical cancer, for example, is linked in clinical studies to human papilloma virus. On the basis of such studies, many authorities now believe that if a man is sexually involved with multiple women, one of whom has cervical cancer, he can become a carrier for the virus and thus transmit the disease from the infected partner to the healthy ones.[167] A different infection, Epstein-Barr virus, is implicated in the African form of Burkitt's lymphoma and in nasopharyngeal cancer.[168] Salk Institute scientists in July 2002 announced that a common respiratory virus called adenovirus can "hit and run" a cell's genetic machinery, triggering cancer and then exiting without a trace.[169] This happens, according to their report, when the virus disables a cellular sensor crucial to the detection and repair of chromosomal breaks. The cell is then vulnerable to cancerous mutations and runaway growth from any source, viral or nonviral.

Current knowledge, then, strongly supports the statement of the Bahá'í writings, although researchers have yet to dot the last "i" and cross the last "t." The reader is again urged to consult an up-to-the-minute scientific journal or other authoritative source for the latest findings.

The Missing "Missing Link"

*Prophecy 28: **Failure to find evidence for a "missing link" between man and ape.***

In the course of explaining the Bahá'í teachings on human evolution, 'Abdu'l-Bahá made a remarkable prophecy about palaeontology, the study of fossils. Unfortunately, theories about evolution have sparked angry religious disputes ever since the publication in 1859 of Charles Darwin's *The Origin of Species*. Such arguments have fostered the unfortunate impression that evolution is one topic where science and religion can never meet. This attitude, though far from universal, is taken for granted by many outspoken people in both the religious and scientific communities. One result is that isolated comments about evolution tend to be quickly tagged as representing one "side" or the other, and 'Abdu'l-Bahá's prediction is vulnerable to stereotyping of this kind. Before presenting its specifics, therefore, I wish to outline briefly my understanding of the overall Bahá'í approach to this complex subject.

First, the biblical account of creation from the book of Genesis is symbolic. To say this is not to dismiss it as meaningless or unimportant; 'Abdu'l-Bahá says the allegory "contains divine mysteries and universal meanings, and it is capable of marvelous explanations."[170] He outlines one of these in *Some Answered Questions*, adding: "Reflect until you discover the others."[171] However, Genesis was not intended to be a historical document, and its account does not mean the earth was created several thousand years ago in a literal week of twenty-four-hour days.

To the question of when God did create the universe, Bahá'u'lláh gives a surprising answer: He created it this very instant! The "moment of creation" is every moment, in the sense that the universe is a perpetual emanation from God without beginning or end in time. Just as the sun continually creates its own light, or the earth continually creates its own magnetic and gravitational fields, so does God create the cosmos. He is both its Source and Sustainer, from which it derives its ongoing existence. In one sense, then, God's universe is at all times being renewed and recreated; in another, it is co-eternal with Him.[172]

Within creation itself, everything changes and evolves according to natural laws ordained by God. This applies to the smallest and largest structures and everything in between. As we have seen, the Big Bang model suggests that the very spacetime continuum to which we belong may itself be an evolving part of a larger whole. This evolutionary principle applies in particular to life, for there is no sharp dividing line between living and non-living matter. The Bahá'í teachings state that "Motion is life"[173] and that "All things are living"[174] in some sense of the word.

To a Bahá'í, then, there is no conflict between the theories of evolution and divine creation. It may well be, as modern biology teaches, that each evolutionary step occurs through the interplay of forces that in themselves are blind and automatic—even in some respects random. However, it does not follow that the process viewed as a whole is aimless. It is part of God's grand scheme, created, maintained and ultimately directed by Him. There is no contradiction in regarding a process as blind on one level yet consciously guided on another. Similar paradoxes—known as "complementarities"—

abound in modern science: Light presents seemingly incompatible properties of both particles and waves; the movements of a billiard ball are completely predictable, though those of its component particles are individually unpredictable; and so forth.

Thus the Bahá'í teachings strongly support the biologist who finds for life—including human life—a history stretching back through eons of gradual development. However, the teachings reject certain assumptions normally associated with this view. Foremost among these is the idea that man differs only in degree from other primates such as chimpanzees and gorillas. Of all creatures, only man, according to the Bahá'í teachings, has an immortal soul,[175] and only man has the capacities for abstract thought and spiritual development that are innate properties of that soul.[176] This fundamental component of human nature is a divine gift—it is not a product of biological evolution or an inheritance from animal ancestors. In light of this point, says 'Abdu'l-Bahá, modern evolutionists are mistaken in teaching that "man's descent is from the animal."[177]

Darwinism, the prevailing evolutionary model, is sometimes described as the belief that "man is descended from a monkey." This description is at best imprecise. Neither Darwin nor his successors ever thought man evolved from animals identical to present-day apes; what they do say, however, is that both species evolved from an earlier, ape-like creature more primitive than either. Men and monkeys are therefore seen as relatively close cousins, sharing a common ancestor from whom they are thought to have diverged several million years ago. This hypothetical common ancestor is designated the "missing link." (The term "missing link" is sometimes loosely applied to any more primitive form of early man, such as Neanderthal. In its original sense, however, it refers strictly to a creature who was both early ape and early man.)

'Abdu'l-Bahá states in *Some Answered Questions* that man "was always a distinct species, a man, not an animal."[178] If we assume that the ancestor of any modern animal was itself an animal, this statement appears difficult to reconcile with the belief that men and apes share a common ancestor. It is possible, however, to argue that the apparent contradiction is nothing more than a question of semantics: Perhaps 'Abdu'l-Bahá is merely dating man's beginning as a distinct species from the soul's first appearance, to emphasize that we do not derive our higher spiritual nature from our animal forebears. Perhaps He means "Man" always has existed as a Platonic ideal or archetype, so that evolution—whatever route it may have taken—represents the unfolding of this hidden blueprint. Further research—both on His intended meaning and on the biological relationships at issue—clearly would be appropriate.

One point, however, seems fairly clear: 'Abdu'l-Bahá apparently believed that fossil remains of the missing link would remain forever undiscovered. "Between man and the ape," He reportedly told an audience at Stanford University in 1912,

> there is one link missing, and to the present time scientists have not been able to discover it. Therefore, the greatest proof of this western theory of evolution is anatomical. . . . The lost link of Darwinian theory is itself a proof that man is not an animal. How is it possible to have all the links present and that important link absent? Its absence is an indication that man has never been an animal. It will never be found.[179]

Scientists, before and since, have sought fossil evidence for the missing link with all the fervor of Arthurian knights seeking the Holy Grail. In 1912—ironically, the very year 'Abdu'l-Bahá made His prediction—their quest turned up Piltdown Man, an apelike creature whose skeletal fragments showed both human and simian traits. The popular and scientific press trumpeted that the missing link was missing no longer. This conclusion reigned as scientific gospel until 1953, when researchers noticed that Piltdown Man actually was a link in a somewhat different sense of the word. Some prankster, it turned out, had joined a human jawbone to a chimpanzee cranium, then treated the construct chemically to make it appear fossilized. Piltdown Man quietly disappeared from the textbooks through whose pages he had shambled for two generations.

Many legitimate fossil specimens of early man have been found. None, however, has qualified to fill the position of missing link vacated in disgrace by Piltdown Man. Until recently, the oldest primate fossil considered ancestral to humanity was "Lucy," a member of the erect-walking species *Australopithecus*. Lucy, whose bones were found in 1974 in Ethiopia, is thought to have lived about three million years ago. She could not, however, have been a common ancestor to human beings and modern apes. "Lucy's ancestors must have left the trees and risen from four limbs onto two well before her time, probably at the very beginning of human evolution," writes C. Owen Lovejoy in *Scientific American*.[180] "If upright walking was well established by the time of *Australopithecus*, its advent could date back as far as the earliest hominids, whose lineage probably diverged from other primates some eight or 10 million years ago."[181] Such a chronology would place any true missing link at least five to seven million years before Lucy.

Far more significant, and closer to the right age, is the "Toumai" skull unearthed in 2001 in central Africa. Experts hailed this six- to seven-million-year-old fossil as "a discovery that will change scientific thought about human origins and force paleontologists finally to abandon the notion of a so-called missing link."[182]

This emerging consensus in no way endorses parallel evolution or denies that human beings are related biologically to other primates. It simply challenges the long-held assumption that we evolved in straight-line fashion from knuckle-walking ape to modern erect human. Bernard Wood, Henry Luce professor of human origins at George Washington University, says the human family tree must now be seen as a bush with so many branches that it is almost impossible to trace a single one from roots to top.[183]

Depending on whom we ask, this picture is being either clouded or clarified by the daily avalanche of discoveries in genetics and molecular biology. One pioneer in this field is microbiologist Carl Woese, a National Medal of Science winner whose earlier discoveries already have rewritten textbooks worldwide. Woese finds evidence that life on earth appeared independently as many as three or more times, then evolved communally—at least in its early stages—through horizontal gene transfer.[184] This is the mechanism by which distinct species (including, we now know, some multi-cellular organisms) swap DNA through means other than sexual reproduction. (Sea slugs have recently been shown to steal genes from algae, though how they do so remains, at this writing, a mystery.[185]) Woese thus challenges the longstanding Darwinian "doctrine of common descent," which assumes that all earthly life evolved from a single primordial cell. Whatever the fate of his theory, and whatever light it may ultimately shed on human origins, it is now clear that horizontal gene transfer plays a far greater role in evolution than anyone previously suspected.

At the time of 'Abdu'l-Bahá's Stanford address, evolutionists anticipated that palaeontology would quickly redraw the fossil histories of man and ape, showing just where and how the two lines were connected. Today, after almost a century of intense search, they seem further than ever from their goal. It no longer seems far-fetched to believe 'Abdu'l-Bahá was right—that fossil proof of such kinship will always remain out of reach. Niles Eldredge and Ian Tattersall, in *The Myths of Human Evolution*, conclude that man's search for his ancestry probably is futile. If the evidence were there, they write, "one could confidently expect that as more hominid fossils were found the story of human evolution would become clearer. Whereas, if anything, the opposite has occurred."[186]

We always are free to speculate on what new findings may come to light as a result of deeper digging. Nevertheless, the correspondence to date between 'Abdu'l-Bahá's prediction and actual events is nothing less than astounding.

MECHANICAL MODELS AND THE NEW PHYSICS

During the opening decades of the twentieth century, physicists were committed to explaining all phenomena by means of mechanical models. A mechanical model is a precise picture or replica based on human sensory experience. It corresponds in a literally accurate way—not merely a figurative or poetic way—to the thing it represents.

The notion that all reality could be brought under the umbrella of mechanical models was central to "classical" physics (sometimes called Newtonian, after Isaac Newton). Classical physics portrayed the universe as a vast, clockwork machine, all parts of which were in principle completely visualizable. This plausible interpretation led physicists to regard matter as composed of particles resembling tiny marbles or grains of sand; light, heat, magnetism and similar forces as vibrations, resembling sound waves or ripples in a pond; and time and space as a fixed frame of reference—a limitless arena within which objects and forces interacted but which remained unaffected by their presence. In such a universe, every event (given enough information) must be completely predictable, for each is predetermined, in all its aspects, by the events that lead up to it.

Most scientists found a mechanistic world view difficult to reconcile with any spiritual or mystical philosophy. Machines are material; and by placing primary emphasis on the material, machine-like aspects of reality, one seems to rule out such abstract concepts as God, the soul, free will, and the like. Newton, a devoutly religious man, would have winced had he realized how powerfully the system of thought associated with his name would promote materialism; yet that is what it did.

Since the Bahá'í Faith, like every prophetic religion, is fundamentally mystical, it necessarily upholds a belief in spiritual realities that do not lend themselves to mechanical interpretation. Our present inquiry, however, concerns none of the mystical aspects of such a controversy but only those that are scientifically testable. Of crucial interest here is

'Abdu'l-Bahá's teaching that *even some physical processes* (including, among other things, the transmission of light) cannot be faithfully depicted by mechanical models or visualized by the human mind. By so stating, He anticipated some of the twentieth century's most startling discoveries—those that formed the basis of relativity and quantum physics. Let us examine His words more closely.

All objects of human knowledge, according to 'Abdu'l-Bahá, fall into one of two categories: They are either "sensible realities" or "intellectual realities."[187] Sensible realities, on the one hand, are those we can detect with our physical senses such as sight, hearing, and the like. These are the familiar objects of everyday experience—shoes, ships, and sealing wax; raindrops and roses; "stuff you can hit with a stick," as someone once explained it. Presumably 'Abdu'l-Bahá would include under this heading things we can detect only with the aid of physical instruments such as telescopes and infrared goggles, these being extensions of our normal senses.

An intellectual reality, on the other hand, is one that "has no outward form and no place and is not perceptible to the senses."[188] In this context, the term "intellectual" does not mean imaginary, nor does it refer exclusively to generalities like "patriotism" or "the square root of pi." As 'Abdu'l-Bahá explains it, the expression includes such intangibles as the human soul and its qualities—realities that exist and produce concrete effects in the world, but which are abstract in the sense that they occupy no space and have no specific physical location:

> . . . if you examine the human body, you will not find a special spot or locality for the spirit, for it never had a place; it is immaterial. It has a connection with the body like that of the sun with this mirror. The sun is not within the mirror, but it has a connection with the mirror.
>
> . . . the mind has no place, but it is connected with the brain. . . . In the same way, love has no place, but it is connected with the heart; so the Kingdom has no place, but is connected with man.[189]

Lacking form, volume, and position, an intellectual reality cannot be pictured, nor can it be detected by any physical senses or instruments. "In explaining these intellectual realities," says 'Abdu'l-Bahá, "one is obliged to express them by sensible figures," which must never be taken literally:

> So the symbol of knowledge is light, and of ignorance, darkness; but reflect, is knowledge sensible light, or ignorance sensible darkness? No, they are merely symbols. These are only intellectual states . . . but when we seek for explanations in the external world, we are obliged to give them sensible form. . . .
>
> These expressions are metaphors, allegories, mystic explanations in the world of signification.[190]

'Abdu'l-Bahá was not content to state this idea simply as a nebulous spiritual precept. Instead, as noted above, He boldly applied it to the physical world in a scientifically testable way. Let us turn now to these scientific implications of His teaching.

The Missing Ether

*Prophecy 29: **The nonexistence of a mechanical ether (the supposed light-carrying medium posited by classical physics) and its redefinition as an abstract reality.***

By classifying all things real as either sensible or intellectual in character, 'Abdu'l-Bahá posed a curious problem for turn-of-the-century physics: Where in this scheme was one to place ether, the hypothetical vehicle for the propagation of light? Ether, as conceived by classical physicists, did not fit comfortably within either of 'Abdu'l-Bahá's contrasting categories.

During the latter part of the 1800s, evidence had mounted steadily that light (once regarded as a stream of particles) was actually a wave or vibration. It seemed self-evident, however, that waves must have something to wave in and that vibration cannot exist without something to vibrate. Yet light, as well as heat, radio waves, and other forms of radiant energy, seemed to pass freely through the vacuum of empty space. Scientists explained this anomaly by suggesting that all space must be suffused with an invisible, intangible, all-pervasive medium serving to transmit the waves. To the physicists of that era, this mysterious substance—the ether—was as real as the radiation it carried.

Ether was not a "sensible reality" since it could not, even in principle, be detected by any conceivable sensory equipment. Nor was it understood by physicists as an "intellectual reality" in 'Abdu'l-Bahá's sense of the term: It was an objective physical substance; it had extension and volume (since each cubic foot of space contained one cubic foot of ether) as well as location (for that cube of ether always remained in the same absolute position); and it functioned in a strictly mechanical way. Waves of light moved through the ether exactly as sound waves moved through air, so that the process could be accurately diagrammed even if the ether itself was unseen.

'Abdu'l-Bahá indicated that this conception was wrong. In explaining the distinction between the two types of reality, He left no doubt as to where ether belonged: "Even ethereal matter, the forces of which are said in physics to be heat, light, electricity, and magnetism, is an intellectual reality. . . ."[191] He emphasized that it was "not material," had "no outward form and no place," and was describable only by symbols and metaphors no more to be taken literally than those referring to any other abstract phenomenon.[192]

From the standpoint of classical physics, this was rank heresy. Although 'Abdu'l-Bahá was using conventional terminology, He was redefining it so radically as to imply that the crude, mechanical ether postulated by physicists did not exist. Light, in His view, was indeed propagated by a medium; but it was a subtle, conceptual medium—a placeless abstraction more like a mathematical progression or a logical relationship than a transparent fluid.

A crack had appeared in the ether hypothesis as early as 1887, when A. A. Michelson and Edward Morley, trying to detect relative differences in the speed of light caused by the earth's motion through the ether, failed to find any. This result caused consternation among physicists, but they explained it away—and rescued their belief in ether—by invoking the "Lorentz contraction." This idea, developed by Hendrik Lorentz, meant that the earth itself, along with all measuring devices on it, shrank in the direction of its own motion, by an amount just enough to mask the lightspeed differential.

The Lorentz contraction turned out to be real enough, but it failed in the long run to salvage the idea of a mechanical ether. When Albert Einstein published his special theory of relativity in 1905, he retained the contraction, showing it to be a result of the relative nature of space and time. However, he dispensed with a mechanical ether, demonstrating that it was both meaningless and unnecessary. Space and time for him were not things but mere relationships among things and events, their measurements varying according to the observer's velocity and frame of reference. If absolute Newtonian space did not exist, then neither could any magical substance that supposedly filled such a space and defined its dimensions.

Nor was an ether required to explain the transmission of light waves, for in Einstein's view at this point, there were no such waves. He advanced a new, more sophisticated theory of light that restored its particle nature, showing that light consisted of lumps of energy called "quanta" or "photons." Despite the wavelike phenomena associated with light, these massless particles supposedly moved through space like ordinary matter, needing no intervening medium.

Since 'Abdu'l-Bahá and Einstein (both of whom agreed in rejecting a physical ether) made their statements on light during the same general period, one may fairly ask whether the Bahá'í leader was simply reacting to news of Einstein's discovery. The answer, so far as I can discover, must be a cautious "no." 'Abdu'l-Bahá's remark about ether occurs in a talk on spiritual symbolism contained in *Some Answered Questions*. These talks, as noted previously, were delivered from 1904 through early 1906. Although individual talks are undated and their chronological order is not always clear (since the compiler regrouped them according to subject matter), the talk in question contains internal evidence that it was delivered towards the beginning or middle of this period.* Einstein's first relativity paper ("On the Electrodynamics of Moving Bodies") was published in the German *Annals of Physics* in September 1905—towards the end, that is, of the same period. Einstein at that time was not a professional scientist but a "technical expert, third class" for the Swiss patent office in Bern. A low-level bureaucrat who knew no scientists, he himself was entirely unknown both to the scientific community and the public. Although he rose to prominence rather quickly, as such things go, he did not do so overnight. Max Born, one of Europe's top physicists, first learned of Einstein's theory at a physics conference in 1907, a year after the last of the talks in *Some Answered Questions* was delivered. Except for a certain Professor Loria, who brought up his name, neither Born nor any of the other scientists at the conference had even heard of Einstein. "As far as the outside world was concerned," writes his biographer, "he remained totally unknown until 1912, when some aspects of relativity became headline news in Austria. . . ."[193]

It is therefore difficult to see how 'Abdu'l-Bahá, isolated from the world in His Turkish prison, entirely lacking in formal education or access to Western journals, could have scooped the European physicists to whom Einstein addressed his arguments and whose attention he was actively cultivating.

Still, suppose we concede for argument's sake that 'Abdu'l-Bahá might somehow have learned of Einstein and correctly

---

* In this talk 'Abdu'l-Bahá explains the role of symbolism in religious discourse, calling it "a subject that is essential for the comprehension of the questions that we have mentioned, and of others of which we are about to speak." (*Some Answered Questions*, p. 83.) Many of the talks in the rest of the book seem to take for granted an understanding of the introductory material 'Abdu'l-Bahá presents here. It therefore appears that this talk probably came early in the series and that the compiler's decision to place it near the front of the book fairly approximates its relative position.

evaluated his discoveries. Even after we grant this quite implausible assumption, we are left with a fact of far greater importance: While 'Abdu'l-Bahá supported Einstein's conclusion in one respect, He challenged it in another. Both men agreed in denying the existence of a mechanical ether, but Einstein went beyond this by denying that light required a medium of any kind. 'Abdu'l-Bahá, on the contrary, indicated that light did travel through a medium, though that medium had only a conceptual, nonlocalized form of existence. A full decade would pass before this issue would be settled.

By portraying space and time as relative relationships, Einstein in 1905 had reduced them to mere shadows of their former Newtonian selves. In 1915, however, he himself gave them new life in his general theory of relativity—a dramatically expanded version incorporating his earlier "special" theory as a subset. The three dimensions of space and the single dimension of time merged into a four-dimensional "continuum" with amazing properties. Having already acquired elasticity, it now acquired shape as well, in that it becomes curved in the presence of matter—the more massive the matter, the greater the curvature. Other objects, following the most direct path through curved spacetime, tend to accelerate; we experience this acceleration as the pull of gravity. A gravitational field is thus an expression of spacetime geometry. This curvature does not propagate itself instantaneously; it ripples through the universe at precisely the speed of light—186,282 miles per second. It became natural, in general relativity, to speak of spacetime as a "fabric" that could warp, bend, tear, undulate, close on itself, and otherwise undergo astounding contortions.

Relativity describes the large-scale structure of the universe. In 1927 an even more revolutionary theory—quantum mechanics—was developed to describe its small-scale structure, the world of subatomic particles. If the space of general relativity was remarkable, that of quantum mechanics was downright magical. The "quantum vacuum," as it was called, was not a vacuum at all but a "seething ocean" with a "foamy structure," manifesting itself as the fizz and bubble of "virtual particles" that pop up, interact briefly with normal particles, then fade back into the abyss.[194]

Thus overhauled, the concept of space presented a weird paradox. It remained as abstract as truth or justice; one would find it neither here nor there but only in the universal equations of cosmic law. Yet it also was, somehow, as real as the planets gliding along its curved contours or the storm-tossed particles ploughing through its billowing quantum flux. Whatever it might be, it clearly was more than an empty nothingness.

Meanwhile, new research was investing light with a paradoxical character of its own. Einstein had not succeeded, after all, in reducing light to a stream of particles; light's wavelike properties refused to be banished. Niels Bohr established a new "principle of complementarity" according to which light, in some unpicturable yet mathematically consistent way, must be construed simultaneously as *both* a wave *and* a stream of particles.

To the extent that light was a wave, it still needed a medium for its transmission. By this time, however, the concept of spacetime was complex and functional enough to do the job; there was no need to postulate a new ether, or even to revive the name. (The term "ether," already in disrepute anyway, had acquired unsavory connotations through the doomed efforts of a few reactionary physicists to discredit Einstein's relativity principle.) In other words, ether—redefined as an "intellectual reality" in 'Abdu'l-Bahá's sense of the phrase—is not some undetectable fluid occupying space; it *is* space!

Light is one form of electromagnetic field, and all fields—gravitational, electromagnetic and those of the weak and strong nuclear forces—are understood generally as disturbances in the spacetime continuum. Only in the case of gravitation has this understanding so far been made mathematically explicit. However, the all-embracing goal of modern physics is to develop a "unified field theory" that will interpret all four of these forces as variations of one underlying field. John A. Wheeler, widely regarded as the dean of American physics, argued that not only light and gravitation, but even matter itself would one day stand revealed as expressions of spacetime geometry. "What else is there out of which to build a particle," he asked, "except geometry itself?"[195]

Whatever the answer, two things seem clear: First, the old-fashioned, literal, mechanical ether, whose death knell 'Abdu'l-Bahá sounded, is gone for good. Second, the "intellectual reality" He substituted for it (and to which He applied the same familiar name) is alive and well in the mathematics of modern theory. When physicists describe the abstract "fabric" of the relativistic continuum or the mathematical "ocean" of quantum space, they are describing a reality identical to what 'Abdu'l-Bahá called ether. Whatever we call it, it is the conceptual framework linking physical events and objects and transmitting, in some mysterious nonmechanical way, light and electromagnetism.

'Abdu'l-Bahá's terminology, though perhaps unorthodox, places Him in stellar company. Among that company is MIT particle physicist and superstring pioneer Frank Wilczek, who shares a 2004 Nobel Prize for quark research he began during his earlier tenure at Princeton's Institute for Advanced Study. Wilczek made waves worldwide with an essay called "The Persistence of Ether" (*Physics Today*, January 1999). "Quite undeservedly," he writes,

> the ether has acquired a bad name. There is a myth, repeated in many popular presentations and textbooks, that Albert Einstein swept it into the dustbin of history. The real story is more complicated and interesting. I argue here that the truth is more nearly the opposite: Einstein first purified, and then enthroned, the ether concept. As the 20th century has progressed, its role in fundamental physics has only expanded. At present, renamed and thinly disguised, it dominates the accepted laws of physics. . . .
>
> Thus in 1917, following Einstein's revelations, . . . spacetime itself had become a dynamical medium—an ether, if there ever was one. . . . [Later] Paul Dirac showed that

photons—Einstein's particles of light—emerged as a logical consequence of applying the laws of quantum mechanics to [James] Maxwell's electromagnetic ether.

In a *New Scientist* article titled "Liquid Space" (November 2001), physicist Paul Davies chronicles this same "surprising revival" through which a retooled "quantum ether" is "creeping back into modern thought." He shows how it is changing the way physicists look at everything from moving mirrors to black holes to the expansion of the universe itself.

Wilczek and Davies are far from alone. Martin Gardner notes in *Relativity for the Million* that many more prominent physicists have, over the years, proposed restoring the name "ether," though not in the old sense of an immutable frame of reference.[196] A few further examples:

– Einstein himself, in an address delivered 5 May 1920 at the University of Leydon, says space "is endowed with physical qualities; in this sense, therefore, there exists an ether. According to the general theory of relativity space without ether is unthinkable; for in such space there not only would be no propagation of light, but also no possibility of existence for standards of space and time. . . . But this ether may not be thought of as . . . consisting of parts which may be tracked through time. The idea of motion may not be applied to it."[197]

– Hendrik Lorentz, the physicist Einstein most admired, formulated an ether-based version of special relativity called the "Lorentz Ether Theory" (LET). Though his equations are mathematically equivalent to Einstein's, being identical in all known predictions and observations, LET makes explicit the fact that ether and spacetime are one.

– Sir Arthur Eddington, who understood relativity theory as well as anyone,* routinely used the traditional term "ether" exactly as 'Abdu'l-Bahá did: He transferred it, that is, to the abstract concept of spacetime. Thus Eddington defines light as "aetherial vibrations of varying wave-lengths"[198] and pictures

---

* It is said that Eddington, upon being told he was one of only three people who truly understood Einstein's theory, paused, then said, "I am trying to think who the third person is."

himself "hanging from a round planet head outward into space, and with a wind of aether blowing at no one knows how many miles a second through every interstice of my body."[199]

– Sir James Jeans writes in a similar vein: "We can now see how the ether, in which all the events of the universe take place, could reduce to a mathematical abstraction and become as abstract and as mathematical as parallels of latitude and meridians of longitude."[200]

– Nobel laureate Leon Lederman, director-emeritus of Fermilab, observes that "like Pauline's, aether's perils come and go, and today we believe that some new version of aether" is needed to make sense out of current knowledge. "The new aether," he adds, "is then a reference frame for energy, in this case potential energy."[201]

– "Although the classical concept of the ether is now considered obsolete," explains L. Pearce Williams of Cornell University, "the concept of space in modern physics retains certain affinities with an ether: Space is not conceived as something totally vacuous but as the seat of various energetic processes."[202]

– Physicist Charles Misner is still more explicit: "There is a billion dollar industry—the TV industry—which does nothing except produce in empty space potentialities for electrons, were they to be inserted there, to perform some motion. A vacuum so rich in marketable potentialities cannot properly be called a void; it is really an ether."[203]

The Collapse of Mechanical Models

*Prophecy 30: **The breakdown of mechanical models (literal images) as a basis for understanding the physical world.***

The disappearance of classical ether shook the mechanistic world view but did not, at the outset, destroy it. Scientists continued for some time to believe that everything real is objective, localized, and consistent with mechanical models—even those things forever beyond detection by sensory means.

They placed in this category the fundamental building blocks of nature itself—namely, subatomic particles.

It was well understood, since early in the twentieth century, that matter is composed of atoms which in turn are composed of smaller components called protons, neutrons, and electrons. The presence of these particles could be deduced from their indirect effects, but they could not be sensed or seen even with the strongest microscope. They simply were too small—so small that any amount of light, even a single photon, would knock them helter-skelter and fail to register them correctly. For all anyone knew, these particles could in turn be further subdivided.* Yet however deeply buried they might be, and whether one pictured them as miniature billiard balls, whirling sparks, or whatnot, the assumption remained that some literal image should apply. This meant it should be possible—at least in principle—to build a large-scale replica that would correctly mimic the behavior of the atom and all its parts. Classical physics saw nothing wrong with such mechanical yet non-sensible entities.

However, if one accepted at face value 'Abdu'l-Bahá's distinction between "sensible" and "intellectual" realities, a doubt arose. It seemed to rule out not only a mechanical ether, but mechanical atoms as well. He had already stated that whatever could not be sensed has "no outward existence," "no outward form and no place." Nor was He timid about applying this principle to the fundamental realities of the physical world. Immediately after His statement redefining ether as a conceptual abstraction, He added: "In the same way, nature, also, in its essence is an intellectual reality and is not sensible."[204] If we could but peer beneath the facade of sense perception, He seemed to be saying, we would find that even the physical world is built upon a foundation that is abstract, unpicturable, and nonlocalized.

Though they did not know it then (circa 1905), physicists were about to crack that facade. During the next few years

---

* This turns out to be true, at least for protons and neutrons, which are composed of still smaller units called quarks.

they worked feverishly to make sense of new findings that were pouring in about atomic phenomena. Their objective was to find a workable mechanical model of the atom. Something, however, was wrong. The more one focused the picture, the fuzzier it became. The mechanical interpretation became increasingly strained and convoluted until scientists, in desperation, were forced to abandon it for theories with strange overtones of mysticism.

First came the revelation from Einstein's special theory of relativity in 1905 that matter is really congealed energy. Energy is defined in physics as "the capacity to do work." Beyond this, it seems meaningless to ask what energy "really" is. Yet it certainly feels odd to heft a stone and say, "I'm holding a lump of hardened 'capacity to do work.'" What could this mean?

A second shock came with the announcement by Niels Bohr, in 1913, that subatomic particles teleport—they move, that is, by vanishing in one spot and popping up in another without having crossed the intervening space. The distances involved are short; longer trips are accomplished by a discontinuous series of short bursts or hops. Motion on the subatomic scale is not a flowing blend but a pattern of jumps, more like a Charlie Chaplin movie than a Baryshnikov ballet. Just as the still frames of a movie create the illusion of continuity, so do the "quantum leaps" of moving matter.* Physicists gulped but swallowed the picture.

Even more unsettling was the fact that the exact distance, direction, and timing of each jump seemed, within limits, to

---

* The quantum leap is more than a mathematical convention; were it not real, the sun could not shine. As we have seen, nuclear fusion powers the sun, and fusion occurs when one proton slams into another. Yet each proton is surrounded by a seamless electrical force-field called the Coulomb barrier. If protons moved in continuous lines, they would, in most cases, bounce off the barrier; the sun would freeze and the stars would wink out. In flashing instantly from point to point, however, a fortunate proton will sometimes pop through another's shield without having touched it. These random hits occur just often enough to keep the sun ablaze. We can all thank our lucky stars—quite literally—for this "quantum tunneling" to which we owe our lives.

be quite random. The absolute predestination implied by Newtonian mechanism was a myth; the past history of a particle did not completely determine its next move. Einstein, already nervous about where particle physics seemed headed, lost his patience over this one. "I find the idea quite intolerable," he wrote, "that an electron exposed to radiation should choose *of its own free will,* not only its moment to jump off, but also its direction."[205] He argued that "hidden variables," unknown and undetectable, must be in control. However, physicist John S. Bell later found a theorem proving that such variables, if they existed, would have to be capable of affecting events instantaneously throughout the universe. Since a basic premise of Einstein's theory is that no physical signal can travel faster than light, any hidden variables would "border on what we now call psychic phenomena."[206] This seemed even stranger and less mechanical than the picture Einstein rejected.

Just as light waves sometimes behaved like particles, so matter particles sometimes behaved like waves. A single electron, for instance, could spread like a wave, passing through two slits of a screen at the same time and producing an interference pattern; yet any and all efforts to observe it would detect only a pinpoint. Its behavior was described by the "Schrödinger pulse," a mathematical wave function with no recognizable form in physical space. It did not resemble a water wave, a sound wave, or any other familiar analogy.

The decisive break with classical mechanics came in 1927 when Werner Heisenberg unveiled his famous uncertainty principle. This concerns the position and velocity of a sub-atomic particle. (Velocity is a combination of speed and direction; it is the mathematical description of a particle's motion.) On a superficial level, the uncertainty principle means we cannot measure both the position and velocity of a particle at the same time. Any method we use to evaluate one will perturb the other, so that we cannot know it. Unfortunately, a number of popular works on science give the misleading impression that there is nothing more to the uncertainty principle than that; nature, they imply, is simply hiding from our clumsy methods. If this were so, the principle would never have been the shattering revelation it was.

What Heisenberg found is not simply that we cannot *know* the precise position and velocity of a particle at the same time. He found that it cannot *have* them both at the same time. The special "matrix" mathematics governing subatomic behavior precludes the very existence of such simultaneous variables. The more there is to know about one, the less there is to know about the other—regardless of what we actually know. The more accurately we measure a particle's position, the more fuzzy its velocity becomes; and the more accurately we measure its velocity, the more fuzzy its position becomes. This fuzziness is not only in our minds; it is a property of the particle itself.

What of an unobserved particle? According to the standard interpretation of quantum mechanics, such a particle has an infinite number of different positions and velocities (a blur of overlapping histories, so to speak), each more or less probable, but none completely real. The particle is nothing more than a ghostly potentiality, a swirl of mutually exclusive possibilities each vying for the right to exist. By choosing to observe either its position or its velocity (for we cannot do both), we make the particle more real in that respect, but at the cost of making it less real in the other.

The thundering implications of the uncertainty principle have barely begun to penetrate modern thought; even many professional philosophers seem strangely deaf to its rumble. Physics, says John A. Wheeler, has "destroyed the concept of the world as 'sitting out there.' The universe will never afterwards be the same."[207] Quantum méchanics portrays the world not as a collection of concrete objects, nor even as tiny bits of "stuff" swarming through mostly empty space, but as a statistical composite of shifting probabilities. Any large-scale object is a vast collection of such quasi-abstract entities—entities that, by augmenting one another, invest the object with a semblance of position, motion, and recognizable form. Each in itself, however, is entirely unpicturable, with no distinct location in space and time. Modern physics thus confirms what 'Abdu'l-Bahá taught long before: The natural universe below the reach of sense perception is, in its essence, utterly incompatible with mechanical models. We can describe it not by any literal image but only by symbols and metaphors. "When it comes to atoms," writes Bohr, "language can be used only as in poetry."[208]

The subjective, nonlocal nature of the material universe is no mere philosophical teaser; it can be—and has been—tested by laboratory experiment. John Clauser, a physicist with the University of California at Berkeley, is one who has done so using insights derived from the Bell theorem mentioned above. Summarizing his results, he writes:

> Physicists have consistently attempted to model micro-scopic phenomena in terms of objective entities, preferably with some definable structure. . . . We have found that it is not possible to do so in a natural way, consistent with locality, without an observable change in the experimental predictions.[209]

It is ironic that physics—the most concrete of the so-called "hard sciences"—was the first to confirm the metaphorical nature of physical reality affirmed by 'Abdu'l-Bahá. Since the dawn of quantum mechanics in the 1920s, virtually every major physics breakthrough has in some way reinforced this outlook. The result has been, in the words of Sir James Jeans, "a wide measure of agreement which, on the physical side of science, approaches almost to unanimity that the stream of knowledge is heading towards a nonmechanical reality; the universe begins to look more like a great thought than like a great machine."[210]

Chapter 6

BAHÁ'Í PROPHECIES:
UNFINISHED BUSINESS

Amidst the shadows which are increasingly gathering about us we can faintly discern the glimmerings of Bahá'u'lláh's unearthly sovereignty appearing fitfully on the horizon of history.

—Shoghi Effendi

Most of the things that have happened in the last fifty years have been fantastic, and it is only by assuming that they will continue to be so that we have any hope of anticipating the future.

—Arthur C. Clarke

We have now completed our survey of major Bahá'í prophecies that have, as of this writing, been fulfilled. These comprise thirty statements by Bahá'u'lláh or 'Abdu'l-Bahá anticipating important historical or scientific developments. They are offered as evidence bearing upon the question: *Who was Bahá'-u'lláh?* Was He, that is, the inspired bearer of a divine revelation?

How do these prophecies relate to this question? To restate the thrust of chapter 3: Evidence, in the scientific sense, is any properly validated observation that tests some logical consequence of a theory one is considering. If such an observation turns out to be inconsistent with the theory, that theory must be abandoned or modified. However, if the observation supports the theory (though it might instead have disproved it), then the theory gains credibility. This added weight is not "proof" in any absolute sense, because one can always find other ways to explain the evidence. However, if the theory survives enough tests in enough different ways, the evidence may eventually become so compelling that an investigator will find it more reasonable to accept the theory than to go on suspending judgment.

Applying this standard, we find that virtually all of these predictions concerned events that might easily have served to discredit Bahá'u'lláh and which seemed likely at the time to do so. The fates of the most powerful sovereigns and empires of His day; the occurrence and outcome of two bloody World Wars; the dramatic rise—and equally dramatic fall—of communism; specific developments in Israel and America, in the Christian, Muslim, and Bahá'í Faiths, in physics, cosmology, palaeontology, and medicine—any of these might have turned out differently in such a way as to cast doubt upon Bahá'u'lláh's claim. Napoleon III, Sulṭán 'Abdu'l-'Azíz, or Náṣiri'd-Dín Sháh might have been spared an untimely end. Queen Victoria might, like most of her royal contemporaries, have fallen from power. Germany might have won (or avoided altogether) either of the great wars on which it embarked. Communism might never have gained worldwide importance, or, having gained such importance, it might have gone on to gain world domination as well. Bahá'u'lláh might have died in prison. His Faith, like every world religion before it, might have broken into sects and factions. Nuclear power and transmutation of elements might have proved impossible. Piltdown Man might have been established as a genuine "missing link" as more fossil specimens came to light. Classical physics might have successfully fought off the challenges posed by relativity and quantum mechanics.

None of these things came to pass. Instead, the Bahá'í prophecies, most of which sounded preposterous when they first were revealed, were in every instance fulfilled by seemingly improbable events that clicked into place with clockwork precision.

Coincidence? Hardly. This is an imposing array of facts, one that calls for a serious and considered explanation. One such explanation is that Bahá'u'lláh's claim is true: He was indeed a Manifestation of God with inspired knowledge. Whether this is the most reasonable of the available hypotheses can hardly be decided without first exploring the others. I will attempt such an exploration in a later chapter; for the moment, however, I would suggest only that the evidence presented so far is strong enough to greatly enhance the credibility of Bahá'u'lláh's claim.

We might naturally ask, at this point, whether the list of prophecies presented in the two preceding chapters is complete. Quite clearly, it is not. Bahá'í scriptures contain a great many other prophecies that I have not cited. Most of these seem to fall into several broad categories:

1. *Prophecies concerning lesser-known individuals*

The Báb, Bahá'u'lláh, and 'Abdu'l-Bahá corresponded with thousands of persons—some of them believers, some not—and in a number of instances made predictions about events in those persons' lives. In every case with which I am familiar, the predictions came true, and my impression is that any comprehensive review of such prophecies would acquire enormous size. I am not, however, in a position to undertake such a review and have chosen to include only prophecies of which the outcome may be verified by the average reader using a good library.

Those wishing to pursue this subject on their own will find ample material in Shoghi Effendi's *God Passes By*; in Adib Taherzadeh's four-volume survey, *The Revelation of Bahá'u'lláh*; and in many other historical works on the Bahá'í Faith. A particularly striking example of this type of prophecy is recounted in *Not Every Sea Hath Pearls,* the autobiography of Loulie Albee Mathews (not a relative of mine).

2. Prophecies of the Báb concerning Bahá'u'lláh

The Báb's writings contain many predictions, most of which were designed to prepare His followers to recognize the Promised One to Whom He referred as "Him Whom God shall make manifest." He indicated, for example, that the years 1852 and 1863 would be significant in the ministry of the one to come. (It was in the former year that Bahá'u'lláh awoke to His own prophetic mission and in the latter that He declared it to His associates.) These and countless similar prophecies were important to Bábís seeking to identify "Him Whom God shall make manifest." Most such prophecies, however, were expressed as hints or clues rather than as specific forecasts, and a detailed exposition of them seems out of place here. Bahá'u'lláh Himself discusses this subject thoroughly in His *Epistle to the Son of the Wolf*, as does Shoghi Effendi in *God Passes By*.

3. Anecdotal prophecies

In reported conversations with the Central Figures of the Bahá'í Faith, one finds a number of interesting prophecies. Many of these accounts come from credible witnesses and were widely circulated before their fulfillment. Others, however, are of debatable authenticity, and it is sometimes hard to separate wheat from chaff. In the foregoing compilation, I have relied only on prophecies from authenticated writings of the Bahá'í founders or from authorized transcripts of their formal talks. In a few cases, I have quoted from their conversational remarks, but only where such remarks accompany and shed light on prophecies from their writings or formal talks.

4. Symbolic prophecies

The Bahá'í scriptures contain a number of predictions expressed in poetic symbolism or otherwise deliberately cryptic language. Some of these, such as Bahá'u'lláh's Tablet of the

Holy Mariner, written in Baghdad in 1863 to prepare His followers for impending attacks on the Cause, were fairly well understood by their intended audience. Others apparently were meant to be understood, if at all, only after their fulfillment. I have generally refrained from quoting such prophecies, preferring to focus on those which, as Bahá'u'lláh states, have "in most explicit language foretold future events."[211] The only symbolic or metaphorical prophecies I have considered suitable for this book are those that were specifically interpreted, in advance of the events to which they referred, by 'Abdu'l-Bahá or Shoghi Effendi, the sole authorized interpreters of the Bahá'í teachings.

5. *Long-range prophecies*

Some Bahá'í prophecies refer to events and conditions of the distant future. Bahá'u'lláh predicts, for example, the gradual emergence over centuries of a Bahá'í Commonwealth, the flowering of which will produce a world culture so glorious it cannot today be even faintly imagined. He also states that after the lapse of a thousand or more years, another Manifestation of God will appear—One Who (like all those gone before) will at first face rejection and persecution but ultimately will prevail and raise civilization to new and still greater heights. Such prophecies are encouraging and valuable to Bahá'ís for a variety of reasons. They do not, however, constitute evidence for anyone seeking at this time to determine whether Bahá'u'lláh's revelation is authentic. One must decide, if at all, on the basis of facts available in one's own lifetime.

This leaves, of course, one major category containing some of the most significant prophecies from the entire range of Bahá'í scripture.

6. *Short-range prophecies that have not yet been completely fulfilled*

Bahá'u'lláh and 'Abdu'l-Bahá predict a number of developments for humanity's short-term future—developments that by their nature must occur, if at all, far in advance of the long-range prophecies mentioned above.

It is these short-range, yet-to-be-completely-fulfilled prophecies that I will review in this chapter. Since the primary purpose of this book is to compile evidence with a bearing on the truth or falsity of Bahá'u'lláh's revelation-claim, this chapter represents, in some respects, a digression. These are prophecies concerning which the facts are not all in; to that extent, they do not yet count either for or against Bahá'u'lláh. Nor am I suggesting that anyone wait to see the outcome of the prophecies before deciding on Bahá'u'lláh's genuineness. The issue seems to me so urgent, and the available evidence already so compelling, that I see no justification for such an attitude.

Still, it seems natural that an inquirer would want to know more, at this point, about Bahá'u'lláh's not-yet-fulfilled predictions for the near future. Such prophecies, whatever their outcome, will soon become evidence even if they are not today. Moreover, the situation is less cut-and-dried than the preceding paragraph may imply. Several of these predictions apparently refer not to isolated events but to ongoing processes taking place all around us. Thus, though not completely fulfilled, they seem already to be partially fulfilled. Insofar as this is true, they carry at least some weight as evidence.

Since I have indicated that the list of prophecies in chapters 4 and 5 is not complete, one further question comes naturally to mind: *Has a single prediction of the Báb, Bahá'u'lláh, or 'Abdu'l-Bahá ever been contradicted by later events?* My answer would have to be "No." In every case with which I am familiar (whether or not I have recorded it here), events have remained true to Bahá'u'lláh's promise: "All that hath been sent down hath and will come to pass, word for word, upon earth. No possibility is left for anyone either to turn aside or protest."[212]

Let us now examine the remaining prophecies.

Flags of Freedom

Bahá'u'lláh wrote: "After a time, all the governments on earth will change. Oppression will envelop the world. And following a universal convulsion, the sun of justice will rise from the horizon of the unseen realm."[213] Shortly after World War I, 'Abdu'l-Bahá described the "prevailing state of the world" as one of "irreligion and consequent anarchy," which He said would bring in its wake a "temporary reversion to coercive government."[214] The accent was on "temporary," for He wrote elsewhere that the world must eventually achieve "unity in freedom."[215] Stressing the connection between peace and freedom, He said: "To cast aside centralization which promotes despotism is the exigency of the time. This will be productive of international peace."[216]

Repressive government was nothing new, of course, but during the twentieth century it gained ground and momentum as never before. Colonialism, Stalinism, Nazism, fascism, and other "isms" engulfed much of the human race and terrorized the rest. Centrally planned economies and state-directed lives became the norm for thousands of millions of people. Radical new forms of government control far more ambitious and intrusive than any previously attempted came into being, and a new word—"totalitarianism"—had to be coined to describe them.

The baneful effects of tyranny have been felt everywhere—not just in those countries most closely identified with it. As militant ideologies, vying for world domination, carved humanity into armed camps, freedom inevitably suffered even in the so-called "free world." During the past century, generations in every land have had to live with the certainty that they could die at any moment in a nuclear holocaust; they have, in addition, borne the brunt of military conscription, onerous taxation, and frequent curtailment of civil liberties—all in the name of resisting outside oppression. Other indirect effects include the widespread hunger, disease, and misery that could easily be removed but for humanity's obsession with conflict.

(How free are the forty thousand children who, at present, die every day of preventable neglect and starvation?)

So vigorous was the spread of totalitarianism that the very survival of liberty often seemed doubtful. The Bahá'í view—that the future belongs not to oppression but to freedom—would once have been dismissed by many international observers as little more than a naive hope. Two developments, however, have radically altered this perception.

First came the achievement, in the second half of the twentieth century, of independence by most of the countries and peoples formerly under colonial domination. This titanic and as yet unfinished struggle has, of course, had mixed results, with external control sometimes giving way to home-grown tyranny. Nevertheless, these scores of independence movements have borne witness to the depth and fervor of humanity's longing for freedom and have set the stage for its further evolution.

Within the last few years there has occurred a second development, equally auspicious and dramatic: A seemingly irresistible pro-democracy movement has burst upon the world stage, as if from nowhere, and has scored victory after victory in every continent. So stunning have been its achievements that the presidents of the United States and the former Soviet Union have, on separate occasions, been moved to declare: "The day of the dictator is over."

This is, of course, not yet literally true: Dictatorships there still are, as well as many other forms of oppression and exploitation. The point, however, is that the tide of history seems clearly to have turned at last, making the worldwide triumph of freedom likely if not inevitable. There may yet be generations of struggle punctuated by countless setbacks before such a vision can become reality, but it no longer seems naive to believe in it. Small wonder that the Universal House of Justice has written: "The spirit of liberty which in recent decades has swept over the planet with such tempestuous force is a manifestation of the vibrancy of the Revelation brought by Bahá'u'lláh."[217]

As Bahá'ís see it, the chief remaining obstacle to worldwide political freedom is attachment to the outworn concept of absolute national sovereignty—the unrestricted freedom of nations to make war. Anarchy is the worst of all tyrannies, and a world of interdependent yet absolutely sovereign states is the deadliest of all anarchies. Humanity's coming liberation from this paralyzing condition is the subject of one of Bahá'u'lláh's most momentous prophecies—the Lesser Peace.

The Lesser Peace

As chapter 4 explains, Bahá'u'lláh indicates that world peace will come in two stages, described as the "Lesser Peace" and the "Most Great Peace." The first stage, the Lesser Peace, will arrive when the world's nations jointly erect a political mechanism adequate to prevent wars. Such a peace may, in the beginning, be little more than an uneasy truce among suspicious and belligerent parties. The second stage, the Most Great Peace, refers to the emergence of a truly global society rooted in spiritual brotherhood and world citizenship. Although Bahá'ís expect that the Most Great Peace may take centuries to achieve, they regard the Lesser Peace as much nearer.

Describing the Lesser Peace, Bahá'u'lláh writes:

> The time must come when the imperative necessity for the holding of a vast, an all-encompassing assemblage of men will be universally realized. The rulers and kings of the earth must needs attend it, and, participating in its deliberations, must consider such ways and means as will lay the foundations of the world's Great Peace amongst men. Such a peace demandeth that the Great Powers should resolve, for the sake of the tranquility of the peoples of the earth, to be fully reconciled among themselves. Should any king take up arms against another, all should unitedly arise and prevent him. If this be done, the nations of the world will no longer require any armaments, except for the purpose of preserving the security of their realms and of maintaining internal order within their territories.[218]

'Abdu'l-Bahá writes:

True civilization will unfurl its banner in the midmost heart of the world whenever a certain number of its distinguished and high-minded sovereigns . . . arise, with firm resolve and clear vision, to establish the Cause of Universal Peace. They must make the Cause of Peace the object of general consultation, and seek by every means in their power to establish a Union of the nations of the world. They must conclude a binding treaty and establish a covenant, the provisions of which shall be sound, inviolable and definite. They must proclaim it to all the world and obtain for it the sanction of all the human race. . . . In this all-embracing Pact the limits and frontiers of each and every nation should be clearly fixed, the principles underlying the relations of governments towards one another definitely laid down, and all international agreements and obligations ascertained. In like manner, the size of the armaments of every government should be strictly limited, for if the preparations for war and the military forces of any nation should be allowed to increase, they will arouse the suspicion of others. The fundamental principle underlying this solemn Pact should be so fixed that if any government later violate any one of its provisions, all the governments on earth should arise to reduce it to utter submission, nay the human race as a whole should resolve, with every power at its disposal, to destroy that government. Should this greatest of all remedies be applied to the sick body of the world, it will assuredly recover from its ills and will remain eternally safe and secure.[219]

While fully recognizing the difficulties to be overcome, 'Abdu'l-Bahá states categorically that this peace plan will be fully implemented: "Surely the day will come," He says, "when its beauteous light shall shed illumination upon the assemblage of man."[220]

In a Tablet, 'Abdu'l-Bahá identifies seven historical trends, or "candles," through which the unity of humankind will gradually appear:

Behold how its light is now dawning upon the world's darkened horizon. The first candle is unity in the political realm, the early glimmerings of which can now be discerned.

The second candle is unity of thought in world undertakings, the consummation of which will ere long be witnessed. The third candle is unity in freedom which will surely come to pass. The fourth candle is unity in religion which is the corner-stone of the foundation itself, and which, by the power of God, will be revealed in all its splendor. The fifth candle is the unity of nations—a unity which in this century will be securely established, causing all the peoples of the world to regard themselves as citizens of one common fatherland. The sixth candle is unity of races, making of all that dwell on earth peoples and kindreds of one race. The seventh candle is unity of language, i.e. the choice of a universal tongue in which all peoples will be instructed and converse. Each and every one of these will inevitably come to pass, inasmuch as the power of the Kingdom of God will aid and assist in their realization.[221]

This passage—one of the most remarkable and prophetic in the entire range of Bahá'í scripture—has become known to Bahá'ís as the "Seven Candles of Unity." Shoghi Effendi has stated that the seven "lights" or "candles" identified by 'Abdu'l-Bahá "will not necessarily appear in the order given."[222] Some of them (such as the unity of religions and races) seem to allude to the Most Great Peace of the distant future. Others, however, seem to refer to, or represent aspects of, the Lesser Peace described by Bahá'u'lláh.

Of particular interest is the fifth candle, which 'Abdu'l-Bahá says "is the unity of nations—a unity which in this century will be securely established, causing all the peoples of the world to regard themselves as citizens of one common fatherland." Elsewhere, commenting on a similar statement of 'Abdu'l-Bahá ("All will dwell in one common fatherland, which is the planet itself"), Shoghi Effendi writes: "This is the stage which the world is now approaching, the stage of world unity, which, as 'Abdu'l-Bahá assures us, will, in this century, be securely established."[223]

This fifth candle might easily be construed as referring to the future world government that, according to the prophecies, will provide the institutional structure for the Lesser Peace. One must note, however, that 'Abdu'l-Bahá's first candle—"unity in the political realm"—is an even more explicit reference to the Lesser Peace, a peace that the Universal House of Justice (using almost identical wording) defines as "the political unification of the world."[224] Apparently we must distinguish between the first candle of political unity (to which 'Abdu'l-Bahá assigns no definite time limit) and the fifth candle, unity of nations ("a unity which in this century will be securely established"). This suggests that the fifth candle may refer not necessarily to the political machinery of world government but to some broader form of unity such as technological and economic interdependence. If this was the intended meaning, the prophecy has already been largely fulfilled. As early as 1936, Shoghi Effendi wrote: "The interdependence of the peoples and nations of the earth, whatever the leaders of the divisive forces of the world may say or do, is already an accomplished fact. Its unity in the economic sphere is now understood and recognized."[225] The truth of this statement is, of course, immeasurably more obvious today than when the Guardian wrote it.

'Abdu'l-Bahá goes on to say that the unity of nations symbolized by the fifth candle will cause "all the peoples of the world to regard themselves as citizens of one common fatherland." The prophecy, then, envisages two phenomena: (1) some important level of unity (not necessarily political) destined in the twentieth century to bind together the nations of the earth, and (2) a widespread consciousness of world citizenship that will follow as a result of that unity. It is not clear to me from His wording whether 'Abdu'l-Bahá meant that both these phenomena or merely the first would appear "in this century"—that is, in the twentieth century. In any case, it seems conceivable that the upsurge in global thinking foreseen by 'Abdu'l-Bahá might precede the formal creation of a functioning world government. In my view, therefore, this prophecy stops short of stating that the political institutions of the Lesser Peace will arrive by the end of the year 2000.

A more explicit promise comes from a newspaper interview 'Abdu'l-Bahá granted in Canada during His North American tour. When asked, "Are there any signs that the permanent peace of the world will be established in anything like a reasonable period?" He reportedly answered: "It will be established in this century. It will be universal in the twentieth century. All nations will be forced into it." Asked whether economic pressure would be a telling factor in this momentous development, He was quoted as saying, "Yes: the nations will be forced to come to peace and to agree to the abolition of war. The awful burdens of taxation for war purposes will get beyond human endurance. . . ."[226]

This oral statement, representing the reporter's recollection and understanding of what 'Abdu'l-Bahá said through an interpreter, carries none of the authority of His formally authenticated writings and talks. Like the unconfirmed notes of visiting pilgrims, such statements—however interesting or illuminating they may be—form no part of recognized Bahá'í scripture and are not binding upon members of the Bahá'í Faith.*

Shoghi Effendi stated that another process—the erection of administrative buildings for the major institutions of the Bahá'í World Center—would "synchronize" with the emergence of the Lesser Peace.[227] This ambitious construction project was completed shortly before the end of the twentieth century. As the first edition of this book suggested, however, synchronization need not imply that the two processes will

---

* In the 1993 and 1999 editions of this work, the above paragraph concluded: "Still, without becoming dogmatic, one is free to trust such a report if it appears credible. This one is widely regarded as such, and its resemblance to the 'Seven Candles' Tablet is unmistakable." This newspaper account helped foster a widespread Bahá'í impression that world government would materialize during the twentieth century.

I am therefore glad those same editions emphasized, as this one does, the unconfirmed nature of the interview notes. Internal evidence from his article long ago suggested to me that the reporter had perhaps misunderstood and sensationalized 'Abdu'l-Baha's remarks. Such things can too easily happen even under ideal circumstances, and are all but inevitable when communicating through an interpreter, as was the case here.

terminate simultaneously: It can mean simply that they move together towards fruition. These uncertainties notwithstanding, the Universal House of Justice cites numerous signs that "the Lesser Peace cannot be too far distant. . . ."[228]

As to the precise timing of these events, Shoghi Effendi's secretary wrote on his behalf: "World government will come, but we do not know the date."[229] "All we know is that the Lesser and the Most Great Peace *will* come—their exact dates we do not know."[230]

What is to be the role of the Bahá'í Faith in this process? A letter written on behalf of the Universal House of Justice makes the following points:

> As to the Lesser Peace, Shoghi Effendi has explained that this will initially be a political unity arrived at by decision of the governments of various nations; it will not be established by direct action of the Bahá'í community. This does not mean, however, that the Bahá'ís are standing aside and waiting for the Lesser Peace to come before they do something about the peace of mankind. Indeed, by promoting the principles of the Faith, which are indispensable to the maintenance of peace, and by fashioning the instruments of the Bahá'í Administrative Order, which we are told by the beloved Guardian is the pattern for future society, the Bahá'ís are constantly engaged in laying the groundwork for a permanent peace, the Most Great Peace being their ultimate goal.[231]

Humanity's Ordeal

Few things worth having come easily—least of all world peace. Bahá'u'lláh makes it clear that the road to peace will be rocky and painful. We have already quoted His words to the effect that the "sun of justice" will rise only after a "universal convulsion" and that "imperative necessity" will drive the world's leaders to establish peace. Bahá'í scriptures frequently suggest that a key factor in the emergence of world order will be a great calamity or catastrophe destined to shake mankind out of its apathy in this regard.

Many of these references to a calamity are simply hints or allusions. Like most concepts from scripture, that of calamity has multiple meanings—some figurative, others literal. For Bahá'ís, the greatest calamity is the spiritual one that occurs when the world's peoples and leaders hear of Bahá'u'lláh yet refuse to investigate or even consider His claim to be God's Messenger for this age. A particularly tragic aspect of this calamity is the suffocating materialism that pervades every aspect of modern life, creating untold misery and destruction on both spiritual and physical levels.

Some passages from Bahá'í scripture seem to refer to calamity in the spiritual sense; others may refer generally to the entire period of turmoil separating the declaration of Bahá'u'lláh from the Most Great Peace. Some, however, seem (without going into detail) to point to a specific future event. Bahá'u'lláh writes, for example:

> The world is in travail and its agitation waxeth day by day. Its face is turned towards waywardness and unbelief. Such shall be its plight that to disclose it now would not be meet and seemly. Its perversity will long continue. And when the appointed hour is come, there shall suddenly appear that which shall cause the limbs of mankind to quake. Then and only then will the Divine Standard be unfurled and the Nightingale of Paradise warble its melody.[232]

Though Bahá'u'lláh does not reveal the nature of the dire event which at "the appointed hour" will "suddenly appear," He seems clearly to regard it as something more specific than the general "travail" and "agitation" leading up to it. Shoghi Effendi draws a similar distinction between the "retributive calamity" predicted by Bahá'u'lláh and sixteen signs that "must either herald or accompany" it:

> Against the background of these afflictive disturbances—the turmoil and tribulations of a travailing age—we may well ponder the portentous prophecies uttered well-nigh four-score years ago, by the Author of our Faith, as well as the dire predictions made by Him Who is the unerring Interpreter

of His teachings, all foreshadowing a universal commotion, of a scope and intensity unparalleled in the annals of mankind.

The violent derangement of the world's equilibrium; the trembling that will seize the limbs of mankind; the radical transformation of human society; the rolling up of the present-day Order; the fundamental changes affecting the structure of government; the weakening of the pillars of religion; the rise of dictatorships; the spread of tyranny; the fall of monarchies; the decline of ecclesiastical institutions; the increase of anarchy and chaos; the extension and consolidation of the Movement of the Left; the fanning into flame of the smoldering fire of racial strife; the development of infernal engines of war; the burning of cities; the contamination of the atmosphere of the earth—these stand out as the signs and portents that must either herald or accompany the retributive calamity which . . . must, sooner or later, afflict a society which, for the most part, and for over a century, has turned a deaf ear to the Voice of God's Messenger in this day —a calamity which must purge the human race of the dross of its age-long corruptions, and weld its component parts into a firmly-knit world-embracing Fellowship. . . .[233]

It might appear that World War II, with its fifty-five million deaths, represented a calamity of sufficient magnitude to fulfill Bahá'u'lláh's predictions. Yet the Guardian's statement above was written in April 1957, long after the war. Even more explicit is a 1954 statement in which Shoghi Effendi, citing Bahá'u'lláh's forecast of the baneful effects of materialism, described World War II as simply a "foretaste" of things to come:

Indeed a foretaste of the devastation which this consuming fire [materialism] will wreak upon the world, and with which it will lay waste the cities of the nations participating in this tragic world-engulfing contest, has been afforded by the last World War, marking the second stage in the global havoc which humanity, forgetful of its God and heedless of the clear warnings uttered by His appointed Messenger for this day, must, alas, inevitably experience.[234]

The foregoing statement indicates that the catastrophe will involve, or be somehow connected with, a "tragic world-engulfing contest" between nations. The prophecies do not, however, state what form that catastrophe will take—military, economic, environmental, or something completely unforeseen and unexpected. In a 1949 letter, Shoghi Effendi's secretary wrote on his behalf:

> We have no indication of exactly what nature the apocalyptic upheaval will be: It might be another war . . . but as students of our Bahá'í writings it is clear that the longer the "Divine Physician" (i.e., Bahá'u'lláh) is withheld from healing the ills of the world, the more severe will be the crises, and the more terrible the sufferings of the patient.[235]

Whatever happens, Bahá'u'lláh makes it clear that the calamity will neither annihilate the human race, nor prevent it from attaining its high destiny of world peace and unity. He indicates, on the contrary, that its consequences, however tragic they may be in the short run, will ultimately prove beneficial. "My calamity," He writes, "is My providence; outwardly it is fire and vengeance, but inwardly it is light and mercy."[236] Shoghi Effendi writes:

> The flames which His Divine justice have kindled cleanse an unregenerate humanity, and fuse its discordant, its warring elements as no other agency can cleanse or fuse them. It is not only a retributory and destructive fire, but a disciplinary and creative process, whose aim is the salvation, through unification, of the entire planet. Mysteriously, slowly, and resistlessly God accomplishes His design, though the sight that meets our eyes in this day be the spectacle of a world hopelessly entangled in its own meshes, utterly careless of the Voice which, for a century, has been calling it to God. . . .[237]

Bahá'u'lláh likens the current state of the world to that of pregnancy. Applying this analogy, we could interpret labor pains as the recurrent crises agitating humanity, birth as the "apocalyptic upheaval," and the soon-to-be-born infant as the

Lesser Peace, the federation of the world. Carrying further the image of an earth in labor, Bahá'u'lláh writes: "The day is approaching when it will have yielded its noblest fruits, when from it will have sprung forth the loftiest trees, the most enchanting blossoms, the most heavenly blessings."[238] Shoghi Effendi explains:

> God's purpose is none other than to usher in, in ways He alone can bring about, and the full significance of which He alone can fathom, the Great, the Golden Age of a long-divided, a long-afflicted humanity. Its present state, indeed even its immediate future, is dark, distressingly dark. Its distant future, however, is radiant, gloriously radiant—so radiant that no eye can visualize it.[239]

Given this perspective, Bahá'ís view the cataclysmic events of the present era with hope and optimism. Even though they expect world conditions to worsen before improving, their eyes are focused on a bright future. They seek to follow the golden mean, neither overreacting to the uncertain dangers ahead nor ignoring them altogether. The following letter, written on Shoghi Effendi's behalf to the Bahá'ís of the United States, describes a balanced and constructive response to the situation:

> He does not feel that the Bahá'ís should waste time dwelling on the dark side of things. Any intelligent person can understand from the experiences of the last world war, and keeping abreast of what modern science has developed in the way of weapons for any future war, that big cities all over the world are going to be in tremendous danger. . . .
>
> Entirely aside from this, he has urged the Bahá'ís, for the sake of serving the Faith, to go out from these centers of intense materialism, where life nowadays is so hurried and grinding and, dispersing to towns and villages, carry the Message far and wide throughout the cities of the American Union. He strongly believes . . . that the Bahá'ís in the end will be happier for having made this move, and that, in case of an outbreak of war, it stands to reason they will be safer, just the way any other person living in the country, or away from the big industrial areas, is safer.

... He sees no cause for alarm, but he certainly believes that the Bahá'ís should weigh these thoughts, and take action for the sake of spreading the Faith of Bahá'u'lláh, and for their own ultimate happiness as well. Indeed the two things go together.[240]

The Destiny of America

The writings of the Bahá'í Faith state that America will play a leading role in establishing both the world's political unity (the Lesser Peace) and its subsequent spiritual unity (the Most Great Peace).

Bahá'u'lláh, in the Kitáb-i-Aqdas, addresses the "Rulers of America and the Presidents of the Republics therein," saying: "Bind ye the broken with the hands of justice, and crush the oppressor who flourisheth with the rod of the commandments of your Lord, the Ordainer, the All-Wise."[241] 'Abdu'l-Bahá writes: "The continent of America is, in the eyes of the one true God, the land wherein the splendors of His light shall be revealed, where the mysteries of His Faith shall be unveiled, where the righteous will abide and the free assemble."[242] "The American people," He said during His visit to the United States,

> are indeed worthy of being the first to build the tabernacle of the great peace and proclaim the oneness of mankind. . . . May they rise from their present material attainments to such a height that heavenly illumination may stream from this center to all the peoples of the world. . . . This American nation is equipped and empowered to accomplish that which will adorn the pages of history, to become the envy of the world and be blest in both the East and the West for the triumph of its people. . . . The American continent gives signs and evidences of very great advancement. Its future is even more promising, for its influence and illumination are far-reaching. It will lead all nations spiritually.[243]

'Abdu'l-Bahá realized that America could never fulfill such hopes without first overcoming a number of grave weaknesses.

We have already seen, for example, that He regarded racial prejudice as a threat to America's very survival. He held a similar view of the dangers inherent in materialism and moral decline. Commenting on these warnings and promises, Shoghi Effendi writes of America:

> Tribulations, on a scale unprecedented in its history, and calculated to purge its institutions, to purify the hearts of its people, to fuse its constituent elements, and to weld it into one entity with its sister nations in both hemispheres, are inevitable.[244]

> The woes and tribulations which threaten it are partly avoidable, but mostly inevitable and God-sent, for by reason of them a government and people clinging tenaciously to the obsolescent doctrine of absolute sovereignty and upholding a political system, manifestly at variance with the needs of a world already contracted into a neighborhood and crying out for unity, will find itself purged of its anachronistic conceptions, and prepared to play a preponderating role, as foretold by 'Abdu'l-Bahá, in the hoisting of the standard of the Lesser Peace, in the unification of mankind, and in the establishment of a world federal government on this planet. These same fiery tribulations will not only firmly weld the American nation to its sister nations in both hemispheres, but will through their cleansing effect, purge it thoroughly of the accumulated dross which ingrained racial prejudice, rampant materialism, widespread ungodliness and moral laxity have combined, in the course of successive generations, to produce, and which have prevented her thus far from assuming the role of world spiritual leadership forecast by 'Abdu'l-Bahá's unerring pen—a role which she is bound to fulfill through travail and sorrow.[245]

The Future of the Faith

Bahá'u'lláh and 'Abdu'l-Bahá have predicted several important developments affecting the future of the Bahá'í Faith itself. Among these, two seem especially noteworthy:

1. *The appearance of a ruler in Persia who will extend protection to the Bahá'ís of that country*

The Faith has been bitterly persecuted in Bahá'u'lláh's native land since its inception. Hundreds of Bahá'ís were executed following Persia's Islamic revolution of 1979, and hundreds of thousands more are, at this time, denied work, education, legal marriage, pensions, freedom of assembly, and other basic rights.

In the Kitáb-i-Aqdas, Bahá'u'lláh addresses the capital of Persia, saying that God "shall, if it be His Will, bless thy throne with one who will rule with justice, who will gather together the flock of God which the wolves have scattered. Such a ruler will, with joy and gladness, turn his face towards, and extend his favors unto, the people of Bahá."[246] Shoghi Effendi states in a summary of Bahá'í prophecies: "The sovereign who, as foreshadowed in Bahá'u'lláh's Most Holy Book, must adorn the throne of His native land, and cast the shadow of royal protection over His long-persecuted followers, is as yet undiscovered."[247]

2. *The future growth of the Bahá'í Faith and the opposition it will face as a result of that growth*

Bahá'í scripture forecasts a remarkable increase in the membership of the Faith, swelling from a trickle to a steady stream, and finally to large-scale enrollments in many countries. No one who has tracked the history of the movement can fail to see the beginning of this process in India, Africa, South America, the Caribbean, and other lands. Bahá'ís, however, see these victories as only the first signs of the mass acceptance promised in their scriptures.

These writings also indicate that the Faith's expansion and consolidation will eventually bring strong opposition "in the West, in India and in the Far East."[248] According to Shoghi Effendi, the prophecies of 'Abdu'l-Bahá "foreshadow the turmoil which [the Faith's] emancipation from the fetters of religious orthodoxy will cast in the American, the European, the Asiatic and African continents."[249]

It should be stated that Bahá'ís do not court opposition or seek controversy. Wherever they live, they are law-abiding citizens, loyal to their respective governments; they strictly avoid political entanglements; and they foster cordial relations with all religions and progressive social movements. Neither in appearance nor in reality are they a threat to the well-being of others. The Faith's claims, however, are imposing, its laws and principles challenging, and the social changes it seeks to bring about deep and far-reaching. One must expect these to excite misgivings and, at times, resistance from various quarters.

Bahá'ís are confident that opposition will not harm the long-term prospects of their Cause. Rather, they feel that such opposition will invite greater public scrutiny and discussion of the Faith, lead to a clearer understanding of its claims and purposes, and eventually dispel the apprehension that prompted resistance in the first place.

Some Closing Thoughts

As stated near the outset of this chapter, it is in some respects a digression from the main topic of this book, which is evidence bearing on the truth of Bahá'u'lláh's claim. These are prophecies on which the jury is still out. To that extent they do not yet constitute evidence for or against that claim, though they must sooner or later do so.

These predictions may, to someone learning of them for the first time, sound frankly incredible. It is, however, a characteristic of most great historical and scientific developments that they seem incredible or even impossible until after the fact; only in hindsight do they appear as steps in a logical progression. The dozens of explicit Bahá'í prophecies that have already been fulfilled seemed every bit as startling, when first uttered, as the handful that remain.

It is also clear that while none of these remaining prophecies has been completely fulfilled, several are already partially so; and new events are moving daily in the direction they indicate. The ending of the Cold War and the astounding progress now being made towards "unity in freedom" have swept away age-old barriers to world peace and world unification—barriers that only recently appeared insurmountable. It is one thing, however, to demolish barriers to peace and quite another actually to move towards it. Unless and until the Great Powers initiate dialogue aiming towards world federation, the "anarchy inherent in state sovereignty" will, in Shoghi Effendi's words, continue to move "towards a climax."[250]

The plain fact is that 'Abdu'l-Bahá's confident assertion, uttered more than ninety awesomely turbulent years ago, today rings truer than ever:

> . . . all that was recorded in the Tablets to the Kings is being fulfilled: if from the year A.D. 1870 we compare the events that have occurred, we will find everything that has happened has appeared as predicted; only a few remain which will afterward become manifested.[251]

ADDENDUM

Most of chapter 6 was written in 1989. It first saw print in 1993 with the first edition of *The Challenge of Baha'u'llah*. When we updated the book for the 1999 edition, the publisher supported my request to leave this sixth chapter untouched. Why? Because this chapter, more than any other, deals explicitly with future developments and trends in process. We therefore felt readers were entitled to see for themselves how well its predictions stood the test of time. Personally, I also wanted to steer clear of anything that might tempt anyone to wonder whether prophecies were being revised along the way, better to conform to unexpected events.

Today, a good fifteen years after the chapter was first written, this book is again being updated. But despite significant revisions to several other chapters, I again am resisting any temptation to rewrite chapter 6: It remains essentially unchanged.

The word "essentially" reflects the following minor concessions: (1) Here and there, the alert reader will note that a sentence or paragraph changes from present or future tense to past tense. These edits are necessary because I sometimes referred in the original edition to "this century," meaning the twentieth century. (2) Syntax and punctuation now conform to the new publisher's house style. (3) Two sentences under the "Lesser Peace" section are moved—unaltered—into a footnote for additional comment. Otherwise, this chapter remains exactly as it first appeared: Nothing is added, nothing taken away.

This decision surprises even me. During the past fifteen years, the world has been stirred to its depths by a vortex of changes. Many of these have been fantastic and far-reaching. I therefore expected to find that this chapter, had I written it today, would have been quite different. On rereading, however, I found hardly anything that would have changed had I composed it this very week. Naturally, there would have been references to the Internet and the World Wide Web. Space would have gone to the 11 September 2001 attack on the World Trade Center, the ensuing antiterrorist campaign, the Iraq conflict, and other developments. Dramatic though they are, however, such developments only reinforce the trends and expectations the chapter already emphasizes. None of them would have entailed any substantive revision.

My editors therefore once again supported my request to leave this chapter as it originally appeared in 1993.

Chapter 7

THE OBJECT OF ALL KNOWLEDGE

We have decreed, O people, that the highest and last end of all learning be the recognition of Him Who is the Object of all knowledge; and yet, behold how ye have allowed your learning to shut you out, as by a veil, from Him Who is the Dayspring of this Light. . . .

—*Bahá'u'lláh*

Knowledge is a light which God casteth into the heart of whomsoever He willeth.

—*Muhammad*

The historical predictions and scientific disclosures we have been considering can help us decide whether Bahá'u'lláh displayed knowledge not readily available to Him through normal human channels. However, there also are other avenues by which we can test the nature and extent of His knowledge. These, like the ones we have already explored, have a distinct bearing on the broader question of His identity and the validity of His claim to be the bearer of a divine message.

The term "Manifestation of God," as defined by Bahá'u'lláh, obviously means much more than an inspired predictor of future events. It signifies, among other things, a world educator guided by God to deliver spiritual and social principles for a new civilization and endowed by Him with "a divine power to put them into effect."[252] As 'Abdu'l-Bahá frequently remarked, the proof of an educator lies not in miraculous displays but in his power to educate. The teachings of a Divine Manifestation must both anticipate the needs of the age to come and help shape that age. This requires knowledge of the future, but it requires a vast amount of other knowledge as well.

136

Bahá'u'lláh stipulates, moreover, that the knowledge of a Manifestation is *innate*. Being a divine gift, it is inborn, intuitive—not acquired through study or reflection. To show that someone's knowledge was the product of ordinary human learning would therefore be to show that that person was not, in the Bahá'í sense, a Manifestation of God. This would be true no matter how brilliant or well-read the individual in question happened to be.

These considerations open several promising lines of inquiry. How extensive was Bahá'u'lláh's knowledge? Did He undergo schooling or engage in research? Were His insights radically beyond the established learning of His day? Did He display skills or abilities that no amount of training could confer? Most important, was His knowledge really comprehensive enough to fit Him for the mission He undertook—the launching of a new and higher civilization?

The answers to such questions ought to shed considerable light on the authenticity of Bahá'u'lláh's inspiration. Should the answers prove strongly consistent with His claim, they would greatly strengthen the probability that it is true. These matters are of course fraught with value judgments that reasonable people may well make differently. Nevertheless, the facts of Bahá'u'lláh's life are sufficiently well documented that any serious inquirer can proceed with considerable confidence. For anyone seeking to assess the validity of the Bahá'í revelation, these questions bear directly on our central issue: *Who was Bahá'u'lláh?*

Bahá'u'lláh's Background

Bahá'u'lláh's native Persia was a land of rich culture and startling contrasts. It was the remnant of an ancient civilization that, at its height, had dominated most of the civilized world. In Old Testament days, Zoroastrian Persia had ruled an empire stretching from "the inner confines of India and China to the farthermost reaches of Yemen and Ethiopia."[253] During her long and glamorous history, Persia produced kings such as Cyrus and Darius; poets such as Ḥáfiẓ, Rúmí, Saʿdí and ʿUmar Khayyám; and artisans who dazzled the world with unrivaled carpets, steel blades, pottery and other handiwork. "This fairest of lands," writes ʿAbduʾl-Bahá, "was once a lamp, streaming with the rays of Divine knowledge, of science and art, of nobility and high achievement, of wisdom and valor."[254]

By the eighteenth and nineteenth centuries, however, Persia had sunk into an appalling state of backwardness and decay. It had become, in the words of Sir Valentine Chirol, "a country gangrened with corruption and atrophied with indifferentism."[255] Persia's people—rich and poor, learned and illiterate—were drowning in superstition and fanaticism. The country was a feudal autocracy whose rulers wielded iron control over a docile and apathetic populace. Its Muslim priesthood, vested with enormous political power, maintained sway over both rulers and populace by regularly whipping both into an emotional frenzy. Women were regarded as little more than livestock, foreigners and religious minorities as accursed heathen, and liberal ideas generally as satanic. Criminals were tortured to death in carnival-like public celebrations, the word "criminal" being loosely construed to mean anyone who happened to displease the local priest or governor. Bribery was the indispensable lubricant of every transaction, public or private.

This was the environment of Bahá'u'lláh's formative years—the only one He knew prior to assuming His prophetic ministry. The suffocating effects of this benighted social atmosphere pervaded every department of life, including education. Most Persians were entirely uneducated, and even the upper classes (which included the nobility, government officials and well-to-do merchants) seldom aspired to anything beyond functional literacy. Male children of privileged families customarily received a few years of home tutoring in reading and writing, with emphasis on the Koran, Persian religious poetry, and ornate penmanship. Despite its artistic flavor, such training was rudimentary, far greater importance being attached to marksmanship, swordplay, horseback riding and other physical skills. With rare exceptions, formal schooling was reserved for the professional clergy, whose members were accepted without question as the divinely intended custodians of knowledge. These men, fiercely protective of their elite status, regarded both the nobility and the peasantry as inferior beings unfit for higher learning.

Bahá'u'lláh, being the child of a prominent government official, received the same sketchy tutoring as others of His high rank. By the standards of His own society, He was literate but not learned. At no time did He attend school or devote Himself to scholarly pursuits. This very lack of academic grounding soon excited comment as He acquired a reputation for unusual knowledge and insight. As a young man, He repeatedly astounded the divines by unraveling mysteries that had defied their collective ingenuity. Both before and after He became known as the head of the Bahá'í movement, His erudition won the respect of outstanding scholars and men of letters throughout the Middle East, including many who did not accept Him as divinely inspired. Experts in diverse fields sought and received His help in solving problems peculiar to their own specialties, and even His enemies were wont to call Him "the renowned Bahá'u'lláh." His voluminous letters, addressed to persons from a wide assortment of ethnic and religious communities, show intimate familiarity with the diverse scriptural, historical, and literary traditions of those individuals.

That an unschooled individual should gain such preeminence among the foremost scholars and savants of His time is surely without precedent. An extraordinary example is cited in *God Passes By*, Shoghi Effendi's history of the Bahá'í Faith. Shortly after His banishment to Iraq, Bahá'u'lláh, for various reasons, withdrew for two years into the wilderness of Kurdistan. This was almost a decade before the formal declaration of His mission, and the region's intelligentsia at that time knew nothing of His identity. For a while He lived in a cave on a mountain called Sar-Galú. Soon, however, He happened to meet the head of an outstanding theological seminary* in nearby Sulaymáníyyih. This man, taking a liking to Bahá'u'lláh, persuaded Him to move to that town and accept a room owned by the seminary. His appearance there brought Bahá'u'lláh into contact with three leading lights of Sunní Islam—men who, despite their own stature, quickly became devoted admirers and freely acknowledged Him as their superior. These were Shaykh 'Uthmán, leader of the Naqshbandíyyih Order, whose adherents included the sulṭán himself and his court; Shaykh 'Abdu'r-Raḥmán, leader of the Qádiríyyih Order, who commanded the unswerving allegiance of at least a hundred thousand devout followers; and Shaykh Ismá'íl, head of the seminary and leader of the Khálidíyyih Order—a man so venerated that his supporters considered him coequal with the illustrious Khálid, famed founder of the order. Shoghi Effendi describes the sequence of events:

> When Bahá'u'lláh arrived in Sulaymáníyyih none at first, owing to the strict silence and reserve He maintained, suspected Him of being possessed of any learning or wisdom. It was only accidentally, through seeing a specimen of His exquisite penmanship shown to them by one of the students who waited upon Him, that the curiosity of the learned instructors and students of that seminary was aroused, and they were impelled to approach Him and test the degree of His knowledge and the extent of His familiarity with the arts and sciences current amongst them. That seat of learning had been renowned for its vast endowments, its numerous takyihs [religious establishments], and its association with Ṣaláḥí'd-Dín-i-Ayyúbí and his descendants; from it some of the most illustrious exponents of Sunní Islám had gone forth to teach its precepts, and now a delegation, headed by Shaykh Ismá'íl himself, and consisting of its most eminent doctors and most distinguished students, called upon Bahá'u'lláh, and, finding Him willing to reply to any questions they might wish to address Him, they requested Him to elucidate for them, in the course of several interviews, the abstruse passages contained in the Futúḥát-i-Makkíyyih, the

---

* The seminary was called Takyiy-i-Mawláná Khálid.

celebrated work of the famous Shaykh Muḥyi'd-Dín-i-'Arabí. "God is My witness," was Bahá'u'lláh's instant reply to the learned delegation, "that I have never seen the book you refer to. I regard, however, through the power of God . . . whatever you wish me to do as easy of accomplishment." Directing one of them to read aloud to Him, every day, a page of that book, He was able to resolve their perplexities in so amazing a fashion that they were lost in admiration. Not contenting Himself with a mere clarification of the obscure passages of the text, He would interpret for them the mind of its author, and expound his doctrine, and unfold his purpose. At times He would even go so far as to question the soundness of certain views propounded in that book, and would Himself vouchsafe a correct presentation of the issues that had been misunderstood, and would support it with proofs and evidences that were wholly convincing to His listeners.[256]

Shoghi Effendi adds that

an increasing number of the 'ulamás, the scholars, the shaykhs, the doctors, the holy men and princes who had congregated in the seminaries of Sulaymáníyih and Karkúk, were now following [Bahá'u'lláh's] daily activities. Through His numerous discourses and epistles He disclosed new vistas to their eyes, resolved the perplexities that agitated their minds, unfolded the inner meaning of many hitherto obscure passages in the writings of the various commentators, poets and theologians, of which they had remained unaware, and reconciled the seemingly contradictory assertions which abounded in these dissertations, poems and treatises. Such was the esteem and respect entertained for Him that some held Him as One of the "Men of the Unseen," others accounted Him an adept in alchemy and the science of divination, still others designated Him "a pivot of the universe," whilst a not inconsiderable number among His admirers went so far as to believe that His station was no less than that of a prophet. Kurds, Arabs, and Persians, learned and illiterate, both high and low, young and old, who had come to know Him, regarded Him with equal reverence, and not a few among them with genuine and profound affection. . . . Small wonder that Bahá'u'lláh Himself should have, in the Lawḥ-i-Maryam, pronounced the period of His retirement [to Sulaymáníyyih] as "the mightiest testimony" to, and "the most perfect and conclusive evidence" of, the truth of His Revelation.[257]

Such was the impression Bahá'u'lláh made upon His most illustrious contemporaries. We cannot, of course, afford to rely blindly on their judgment any more than we would rely blindly on those who denounced Him as a subversive madman. Fortunately, most of Bahá'u'lláh's original writings have been preserved; a comprehensive and representative selection of these has been translated into English and many other languages, and more translations are appearing all the time. Bahá'u'lláh did not restrict these writings to such stereotypically "religious" topics as metaphysics and character development. He revealed divine principles governing issues in law, international relations, arms control, political administration, education, group dynamics, economics, health, psychology, medicine and science, to name just a few. These writings, along with the large and growing body of scholarly literature they have evoked, make it fairly easy for any thoughtful reader to assess Bahá'u'lláh's contributions objectively. Many distinguished people, familiar with these contributions in their respective fields yet themselves not Bahá'ís, have praised His work in terms scarcely less glowing than those of His nineteenth-century admirers.

Vast erudition is not necessarily a token of divine inspiration. We do not regard men such as Aristotle, Leonardo da Vinci, Isaac Newton, or Albert Einstein as bearers of revealed truth. The reason is that we can, by studying their lives, trace their gradual acquisition of knowledge through years of schooling and research. Westerners often approach the study of Bahá'u'lláh with the preconception that He can be explained in the same way—that His was a brilliant and creative mind blossoming under the benign influence of a cosmopolitan environment, advanced education, and contact with other similarly gifted individuals. His brilliance and creativity are not, of course, in doubt; but every other element of this explanation is false. Bahá'u'lláh grew to adulthood in an atmosphere of extreme prejudice, fanaticism, superstition, and ignorance. The limited education He received offered nothing to counteract the pernicious influence of His early conditioning or to explain the phenomenal knowledge and vision He displayed. We may—indeed we must—say He rose above the limitations of His environment. We cannot explain Him as its product.

Recognizing this fact, we may suspect that Bahá'u'lláh was simply a self-taught prodigy. Living in the modern West, we are accustomed to believing that any sufficiently motivated person can acquire an education by voracious reading. However, matters were not so simple in nineteenth-century Persia. Bahá'u'lláh was, from His earliest youth, a well-known, highly visible figure at a time when it was unthinkable for a man of his station to pursue higher learning. Public libraries were unknown. Books—often hand-copied—were rare and exorbitantly expensive. Scholarly reference libraries were confined to Muslim theological universities, where they were haunted by the clergy—men who would have bristled at the thought of a "lesser mortal" invading their sacred turf. Bahá'u'lláh might have found a way to gain access to a university library, or He might (by spending a large chunk of the family fortune) have built up a useful private collection. But He could not have carried out either project, much less devoted years of His life to personal research, without attracting widespread attention. So brazen an affront to the rigid customs of Persian society would have raised eyebrows and aroused indignation throughout much of the country.

The fact that Bahá'u'lláh did none of these things is one of the strongest points of agreement between His supporters and His avowed enemies. When He advanced His claim to be a Manifestation of God, His adversaries—missing the point altogether—countered by stressing His entire lack of higher education. Many found it impossible to believe that God might choose as His instrument of revelation someone who had never earned a degree in theology. Bahá'u'lláh acknowledged their protests:

Lay not aside the fear of God, O ye the learned of the world, and judge fairly the cause of this unlettered One. . . .

Certain ones among both commoners and nobles have objected that this wronged One is neither a member of the ecclesiastical order nor a descendant of the Prophet. Say: O ye that claim to be just! Reflect a little while, and ye shall recognize how infinitely exalted is His present state above the station ye claim He should possess. The Will of the Almighty hath decreed that out of a house wholly devoid of all that the divines, the doctors, the sages and scholars commonly possess His Cause shall proceed and be made manifest.[258]

His Tablet to the <u>sh</u>áh states:

. . . the breezes of the All-Glorious were wafted over Me, and taught me the knowledge of all that hath been. . . . The learning current amongst men I studied not; their schools I entered not. Ask of the city wherein I dwelt, that thou mayest be well assured that I am not of them who speak falsely.[259]

Still, a fact is one thing, its interpretation quite another. There is no serious doubt that Bahá'u'lláh was "unlettered" (as He and His detractors insisted). A skeptic may naturally wonder, however, whether His supposedly innate knowledge has been exaggerated. We can always construct elaborate scenarios purporting to show how Bahá'u'lláh might have acquired the necessary training in secrecy. However unwarranted or farfetched such ideas may be, many people understandably will find them more plausible than the idea of divine revelation. It would therefore be helpful if we could identify specific features of Bahá'u'lláh's knowledge that cannot easily be dismissed as overblown or explained away as the result of clandestine study.

As it happens, there are several such features. One of them we have already explored in detail—namely, the occurrence in Bahá'u'lláh's writings of many daring but accurate predictions. However, there are at least three other factors that, given His situation, weigh heavily against any effort to equate His knowledge with ordinary human learning. These are

(1) the farsightedness of Bahá'u'lláh's social principles, (2) His phenomenal mastery of Arabic, and (3) the speed and spontaneity with which He composed His writings. Let us examine each of these factors more closely.

Farsightedness

The characteristic I call "farsightedness" refers to the way Bahá'u'lláh's teachings have consistently proved to be ahead of their time. A century after His passing—a century during which the world has changed more than in all previous recorded history—His writings remain astoundingly modern in tone, outlook, and substance; in fact, this modernity becomes more striking each year. The change, of course, has been not in His writings but rather in the world itself as it has developed along lines that render His teachings ever more suitable to its needs. Bahá'u'lláh did not write only about the world in which He lived. He also wrote, explicitly and with exceptional insight, about the world in which we live today—a global village entering the twenty-first century. In so doing He gave humanity its *first comprehensive inventory* of the principles now generally held to be on the cutting edge of social advancement. His proposals have set the agenda for all the great upheavals and reform struggles that have raged ever since.

The result of this evolutionary process has been described by George Townshend in the following words:

> The humanitarian and spiritual principles enunciated decades ago in the darkest East by Bahá'u'lláh and molded by Him into a coherent scheme are one after the other being taken by a world unconscious of their source as the marks of progressive civilization.[260]

Commenting on the same phenomenon, Townshend again writes:

> Slowly the veil lifts from the future. Along whatever road thoughtful men look out they see before them some guiding

truth, some leading principle, which Bahá'u'lláh gave long ago and which men rejected.[261]

This gradual and largely unconscious adoption of Bahá'í ideals as symbols of enlightened modernism has become the single most pervasive trend of our time. Examples abound; an especially revealing one occurred in April 1963, the month when Bahá'ís celebrated the centenary of Bahá'u'lláh's formal declaration of His mission.

In that very month, Pope John XXIII issued his last pastoral letter, the encyclical *Pacem in Terris* (Peace on Earth). This brilliant document—a summary of the prerequisites for peace and progress in the decades ahead—evoked worldwide praise from non-Catholics and Catholics alike. Pope John did not claim originality for any of his points. He presented them simply as a fusion and synthesis of the best in contemporary thought, weaving them into a single package in order to bring them to the forefront of public discussion. The principles were: (1) creation of a world community; (2) independent investigation of truth; (3) universal education; (4) equality of men and women; (5) abolition of prejudice; (6) recognition of the oneness of God; (7) the reconciliation of science and religion; (8) world disarmament; (9) a spiritual approach to economics; and (10) loyalty to government. Also included was a warning on the dangers of atomic energy.[262]

Every one of these points is a recurring theme of Bahá'u'lláh's writings.* With the exception of His own warning on atomic energy (circa 1890), they all are major planks of the peace program He drafted in the late 1860s and early 1870s, and which He in that same period called to the attention of world leaders including Pope Pius IX. Bahá'u'lláh, unlike

---

* There is no "official" list of Bahá'í principles. Bahá'u'lláh's writings seldom contain descriptive headings; they cover thousands of topics and defy easy categorization. To indicate the spirit of His teachings, however, Bahá'í writers generally list eight to twelve thematic ideas, rewording or rearranging them slightly to suit the context. Two important Bahá'í principles are missing from *Pacem in Terris*—the essential unity of all religions and the adoption of a universal auxiliary language. Otherwise, its main points correspond closely to the familiar principles listed and described in hundreds of Bahá'í publications since the Faith's beginning.

Pope John, gave detailed guidance on translating these matters from theory into practice. By the time the Pope announced the principles, they already had become familiar to enlightened men and women everywhere. Bahá'u'lláh, however, announced them at a time when they were largely unknown both to leaders of thought and to the public, their feasibility had not been seriously explored in any part of the world, and their interconnectedness as peace prerequisites was quite unheard of.

A Bahá'í might naturally interpret Bahá'u'lláh's advanced outlook as simply one more aspect of His ability to see the future—an ability attested by the review of prophecies in previous chapters. However, I have chosen not to discuss it under that heading because it seems to me to involve much more than mere predictive power. We can easily imagine a psychic who is able to predict the future with pinpoint accuracy (right down to, say, stock market fluctuations) but unable to produce anything of lasting spiritual or social value. Bahá'u'lláh clearly was much more than this. It is His analysis of policy questions, as distinct from mere predictions or statements of fact, that most powerfully demonstrates His grasp of modern realities.

However we interpret His modernity, it clearly betokens a knowledge far ahead of anything He might have learned or deduced from any course of study available in His lifetime. We cannot realistically say that Bahá'u'lláh "merely" displayed an unusual gift for extrapolating future trends from existing conditions. Modern sociologists consider it humanly impossible—even with the aid of up-to-the-minute research libraries, electronic databanks, computer simulations, and the like—to project social trends more than a few years into the future. Every attempt at scientific forecasting of social changes has been a dismal failure. Even if we suppose Bahá'u'lláh might somehow have succeeded where today's science fails, such a feat would have required an extraordinary amount of raw data. The requisite information for such far-reaching deductions certainly was not to be found in nineteenth-century

Middle Eastern literature. Whether it was available in the West is doubtful but entirely moot: Bahá'u'lláh had no access to Western literature and no contact, save for one brief visit in the closing days of His life, with any Western scholar.

We must also remember that the nineteenth century produced many outstanding intellectuals and visionaries who studied in the best universities, worked in the best libraries, and shared ideas and insights with one another. Not one of these thinkers in the East or the West even came close to matching Bahá'u'lláh's vision. He alone, with none of their advantages, produced the writings that have best stood the test of time—the only writings that each year become more relevant to world events, rather than less, and the only ones conspicuously free of the narrow outlook, naive misconceptions, and outright superstition that plagued the thought of His day. Surely these considerations challenge us to weigh seriously Bahá'u'lláh's own explanation: "This thing is not from Me, but from One Who is Almighty and All-Knowing."[263]

Bahá'u'lláh's Use of Arabic

Bahá'u'lláh's insight into the problems and conditions of a future age undoubtedly is impressive. As evidence of inspired knowledge, however, it is admittedly circumstantial. If nothing else, we can always chalk it up to a series of fantastically lucky guesses. Can we point to some specific, highly technical body of knowledge that Bahá'u'lláh demonstrably mastered without study—a subject that normally cannot be acquired without years of training?

Such a subject is not hard to find. It is the Arabic written language. 'Abdu'l-Bahá, discussing proofs of Bahá'u'lláh's inspiration, cites His virtuosity with classical Arabic as a clear example of innate knowledge:

> Bahá'u'lláh had never studied Arabic; He had not had a tutor or teacher, nor had He entered a school. Nevertheless, the eloquence and elegance of His blessed expositions in Arabic, as well as His Arabic writings, caused astonishment

and stupefaction to the most accomplished Arabic scholars, and all recognized and declared that He was incomparable and unequaled.[264]

This point deserves careful consideration. One of the first things a student of the Bahá'í Faith learns is that Bahá'u'lláh wrote both in Persian and in Arabic. This fact, in itself, hardly seems surprising: Millions of people are bilingual, with or without formal training. For an uninformed Westerner, there is a natural tendency to assume that Persian and Arabic probably are similar languages, widely used by Bahá'u'lláh's countrymen, from whom He might have acquired both by simple exposure. Such an assumption, however, turns out to be flawed in two key respects.

First, Persian and Arabic do not especially resemble one another. They have similar alphabets, to be sure (Persian has four extra letters), and there has been some mutual influence. This derives in part from the fact that they are spoken in adjacent countries. A more fundamental reason is that Islam, the prevailing religion of Persia, reveres as its holy book the Koran, which was originally revealed in Arabic. But the differences are profound, and they far outweigh any cosmetic similarities. The two do not even belong to the same family of languages: Arabic is Semitic while Persian is Indo-European.

Second, Arabic is not widely used or spoken in Persia; nor was it so used or spoken in Bahá'u'lláh's lifetime. Neither the nobility nor the peasantry, as a rule, knew anything of the language. The one class for which knowledge of Arabic was considered important was the Islamic clergy, who used it in their study of the Koran. These Muslim divines labored for years to master the subtleties of Arabic grammar and vocabulary, as well as its complex literary conventions. Most of them regarded no treatise as worthy of attention unless it was written in Arabic, and they tended to pepper their sermons and discourses with complex Arabic expressions that few if any members of their congregations could fathom.

It is certainly possible to acquire a working knowledge of conversational Arabic through association with persons who speak it. This is how all children first learn their native tongues. There is, however, a peculiarity of Arabic that takes on extreme importance in this connection. "In Arabic," explains Phillip K. Hitti, "distinction should be made between the written, or classical form, and the spoken, or colloquial."[265] Ordinary spoken Arabic takes the form of various local dialects or vernaculars, which are used in everyday commerce but rarely written. None of these has much in common with any of the others. In contrast, written Arabic (also known as "standard" or "formal" Arabic) is the same throughout the Arabic-speaking world. It is therefore used for literary and technical communication as well as for diplomatic correspondence. It is, however, markedly different from any of the standard dialects in its vocabulary, its grammar, its syntax, and its stylistic requirements.* Simply put, written and conversational Arabic differ enough to constitute, for all practical purposes, different languages.

This radical distinction between the written and spoken word has consequences that might seem odd to an English-speaking individual. Much Arabic fiction, for instance, gives the impression of being written in two languages, the classical for narrative and a local vernacular for dialogue. Other fiction uses the classical form throughout, producing dialogue with little resemblance to actual speech anywhere, and a few works use the vernacular only. We are accustomed to the idea that anyone who speaks excellent English and who knows script well enough to transcribe that English word for word can write excellent English as well. Indeed, the best advice an English teacher can give a student is "Speak correctly, and write the way you speak." But this would be terrible advice for a student of Arabic! One might learn to converse in fluent or even eloquent Arabic and learn in addition to copy one's speech onto paper verbatim. Yet doing so would not enable anyone to write Arabic that is correct or even necessarily

---

* Though rarely used in face-to-face communication, the spoken form of classical Arabic is employed on certain formal occasions and, today at least, is used increasingly on Arabic radio. (Radio was of course nonexistent in Bahá'u'lláh's lifetime.)

comprehensible. One would remain, in every way that matters, quite illiterate.

Learning to write adequately—not brilliantly, just adequately—in Arabic requires years of disciplined instruction. A. F. L. Beeston, author of *The Arabic Language Today*, states flatly that the classical Arabic used for writing and formal speech "must be learned in school."[266] The details of the language are subtle, intricate, and arbitrary. They are acquired through painstaking drill and memorization. A structured training program administered by a competent instructor is generally deemed indispensable. With this sort of grounding, one may become passably literate.

Even more difficult, by a whole order of magnitude, is the specialized literary Arabic used in Muslim religious writing. "In this latter case," says *Collier's Encyclopedia*, "the knowledge of Arabic is restricted to the learned."[267] This form presents technical challenges so imposing as to daunt any but the most accomplished experts. Native Arabic-speaking scholars, steeped from childhood in the richness and beauty of the language, intimately familiar with its culture and traditions, can and do spend lifetimes augmenting their knowledge of this seemingly infinite subject.

Bahá'u'lláh, as stated above, had no training in Arabic and no experience that might have equipped Him to deal with its complex literary formalities. However, from the earliest beginnings of His forty-year prophetic ministry, He wrote interchangeably in Persian and Arabic, proving Himself equally adept in both languages. His Arabic compositions—some in prose, others in poetry—are unrivaled whether from the standpoint of literary beauty or technical proficiency. Though He often broke with convention, preferring to originate His own distinctive styles, His command of established patterns was complete. Time and again He demonstrated His ability to work in any classical or traditional form, adhering strictly to its most rigorous requirements.

Among the many experts who marveled at His mastery of Arabic were the learned doctors of the theological seminary in Sulaymáníyyih, who, as described above, interrogated Him during His sojourn in Kurdistan. Having received satisfying answers to their preliminary questions, they resolved to put Bahá'u'lláh's Arabic wizardry to a supreme test. Quoting again from Shoghi Effendi's account:

> Amazed by the profundity of His insight and the compass of His understanding, they were impelled to seek from Him what they considered to be a conclusive and final evidence of the unique power and knowledge which He now appeared in their eyes to possess. "No one among the mystics, the wise, and the learned," they claimed, while requesting this further favor from Him, "has hitherto proved himself capable of writing a poem in a rhyme and meter identical with that of the longer of the two odes, entitled Qaṣídiy-i-Tá'íyyih composed by Ibn-i-Fárid [a famous Egyptian poet]. We beg you to write for us a poem in that same meter and rhyme." This request was complied with, and no less than two thousand verses, in exactly the manner they had specified, were dictated by Him, out of which He selected one hundred and twenty-seven, which He permitted them to keep, deeming the subject matter of the rest premature and unsuitable to the needs of the times. It is these same one hundred and twenty-seven verses that constitute the Qaṣídiy-i-Varqá'íyyih, so familiar to, and widely circulated amongst, His Arabic speaking followers.
>
> Such was their reaction to this marvelous demonstration of the sagacity and genius of Bahá'u'lláh that they unanimously acknowledged every single verse of that poem to be endowed with a force, beauty and power far surpassing anything contained in either the major or minor odes composed by that celebrated poet.[268]

Many of Bahá'u'lláh's writings, both Persian and Arabic, are available in English translation. Through these (particularly the superb renderings of Shoghi Effendi) one may obtain a glimpse of the towering eloquence and beauty of His composition and the diversity of styles at His command. Regrettably, it is a glimpse and nothing more: According to all competent testimony, the originals are in every respect incomparably superior to the translations. Shoghi Effendi describes one of his own finest translations as "one more attempt . . . in language however inadequate" to "assist others in their efforts to approach what must always be regarded as the unattainable goal—a befitting rendering of Bahá'u'lláh's matchless utterance."[269] Some of the more intricate Arabic compositions of Bahá'u'lláh—especially His poetry—are said to be virtually impossible to translate. The Qaṣídiy-i-Varqá'íyyih mentioned above is one of these. One may paraphrase the meaning, but it is no simple task to capture, in an alien tongue, the subtle rhythms and nuances which bring that meaning vividly to life. Those of us who cannot read Arabic must therefore rely for information upon those who can, just as students of the Bible, unless they understand Greek or Hebrew, must obtain much of their knowledge from scholars able to study the original manuscripts.

Literary Arabic traditionally incorporates subtle wordplay, often involving the deliberate breaking of grammatical rules to achieve a desired effect. The Koran, which Arabs regard as the ultimate stylistic model, employs this technique throughout with superb finesse. This is harder than it may sound: Anyone who attempts it without knowing precisely what he is doing will butcher the language, producing text that is clumsy or even incomprehensible. In some of His works, Bahá'u'lláh upholds textbook standards with scrupulous consistency, while in others He manipulates or disregards them at will—always enhancing the eloquence of His message by so doing. His own footnotes to the Qaṣídiy-i-Varqá'íyyih call attention to a couple of apparent deviations from standard grammar but argue convincingly that His usage is, in the context, entirely proper.

Despite the clearly conscious nature of these decisions and the scholarly precedents behind them, Bahá'u'lláh's liberties with language sometimes occasioned criticism from Arabic purists. These same purists, ironically, censured 'Abdu'l-Bahá (Who learned Arabic from Bahá'u'lláh) for the opposite practice—that of adhering strictly to grammatical rules.*

---

* Why He chose to do this, we can only speculate: My guess is that it was His way of subordinating His writing to that of His father.

Facing this impossible double standard, 'Abdu'l-Bahá ex-
claimed, "What can We do? If We make mistakes, they criticize
us on those grounds. If We make no mistakes, they criticize
us on those grounds!"[270]

Bahá'u'lláh's choice of Arabic for many of His most important works* was appropriate on several counts. First, Arabic
traditionally is regarded in Islamic countries (including Persia)
as the "language of revelation" since it is used in the Koran.
Second, the Koran itself—a book of almost magical beauty,
and one that laid the foundation for a mighty civilization—is
revered in Islam as a literary miracle because Muḥammad, its
author, was illiterate. Bahá'u'lláh of course was not illiterate
in Arabic; but by human standards He should have been. By
matching Muḥammad's achievement, He produced the one
sign that, above all others, had for centuries been hailed by
His countrymen as the most incontrovertible proof of prophetic authenticity. Finally, Persia's Islamic clergy (most of
whose members inevitably opposed Him) had taken Arabic
as their own primary badge of learning, a badge they strug-
gled endlessly to polish. When Bahá'u'lláh, meeting them in
their own chosen arena, effortlessly dwarfed their highest
attainments, He not only caused consternation within their
ranks but exposed the hollowness of their opposition.

A Torrent of Eloquence

A third token of the superhuman origin and nature of Bahá'-
u'lláh's knowledge is the seemingly impossible speed and
spontaneity with which He composed His writings. Further
enumerating the "signs" of His father's prophetic authenticity,
'Abdu'l-Bahá writes:

> Another of His signs is the marvel of His discourse, the
> eloquence of His utterance, the rapidity with which His

---

* Bahá'u'lláh's Persian writing was as exquisite and technically competent
as His Arabic. This fact, however, is less surprising because Persian was His
native language and one in which (unlike Arabic) He received some childhood tutoring.

Writings were revealed. . . . By thy very life! This thing is plain as day to whoever will regard it with the eye of justice.[271]

This phenomenon—documented both by eyewitness accounts and by empirical evidence—is one that no amount of education could adequately explain.

Any human mind, however great its capacity, is finite and fallible unless aided by some higher power. It follows that writing is a trial-and-error procedure for any normal author. Some writers, to be sure, are extremely prolific; a few of these are able to work long hours at high speed and produce relatively good work much of the time. But even for this select minority, serious writing involves certain necessities. These include preliminary thought and research, occasional hesitation and backtracking, and a certain amount of polishing and revision. Any composition a writer dashes off without these essential steps will be, at best, a "rough draft." Such work—however fine it may be overall—will show wide variations in quality, more or less obvious lapses in consistency and organization, and a general lack of attention to detail. The entire history of secular literature demonstrates that no ordinary human author, composing extemporaneously, can create perfectly finished work at all times and under all conditions.

So much for human writing. But what of revelation—a form of composition which, if it exists at all, must by definition emanate from an infinite, all-powerful, all-knowing, and perfect Intelligence? Presumably such a Being, transcending time and space and combining all-encompassing knowledge with boundless creativity, could know in advance precisely what He wished to convey through His human intermediary and how to formulate that message most befittingly to produce any desired effect.

The manner in which Bahá'u'lláh's writings were composed is therefore highly significant. Most of His "writings" are not, strictly speaking, writings at all: They were dictated by Him to one or more secretaries, who would later recopy them. Bahá'u'lláh would then verify the accuracy of the transcripts and affix His seal or signature. During dictation the words would cascade from His lips in a steady stream so rapidly as to tax the abilities of the most gifted stenographer. He seldom had any opportunity for prior reflection or rehearsal, since the bulk of His work consists of replies to letters He had not seen or heard until moments before He began to speak. During dictation He did not grope for words, lose His train of thought, or, having spoken, retract one phrase in order to substitute another.

After the secretary's notes were neatly recopied, Bahá'u'lláh, in checking the final version, would sometimes add margin notes or correct a word or two that had been transcribed incorrectly. In so doing, however, He did not revise or polish His own actual utterances.* When the workload was heavy and time short, He would sometimes dispense with the step of checking the transcript Himself. Instead, He would dictate the Tablet a second time from memory while the secretary followed along, proofreading the transcript from Bahá'u'lláh's utterances.[272]

Until the end of His life, Bahá'u'lláh poured out His writings in sessions that often lasted for hours at a time. Within two days and nights, for example, He composed the Kitáb-i-Íqán, or Book of Certitude, one of His major works: Its English translation exceeds 250 pages. Most of these writings He produced under conditions of bitter adversity, often when He was weak from hunger, illness, or exhaustion, stricken with grief, harassed by enemies, or mortally endangered by their schemes. He Himself describes His words as "a copious

---

* Bahá'u'lláh sometimes would adapt His own previous works to a new context by means of minor editing. In publishing, for example, a general-audience version of a Tablet revealed earlier for an individual, He might change tense or gender, omit personal references, clarify allusions that would have been obvious to His original recipient, and so forth. Thus we sometimes have two authentic yet subtly different versions of the same Tablet (the Book of Certitude being a case in point). Their triviality aside, however, such variations serve generally obvious purposes having nothing to do with the merit of the work in question. In this respect they differ fundamentally from the corrective rewriting in which most authors (myself included) compulsively engage.

rain,"[273] commenting: "Such are the outpourings ... from the clouds of Divine Bounty that within the space of an hour the equivalent of a thousand verses hath been revealed."[274]

A believer named Siyyid Asadu'lláh-i-Qumí, who was present during some of these sessions, left the following account:

> I recall that as Mírzá Áqá Ján [Bahá'u'lláh's primary secretary] was recording the words of Bahá'u'lláh at the time of revelation, the shrill sound of his pen could be heard from a distance of about twenty paces. . . .
>
> Mírzá Áqá Ján had a large ink-pot the size of a small bowl. He also had available about ten to twelve pens and large sheets of paper in stacks. In those days all letters which arrived for Bahá'u'lláh were received by Mírzá Áqá Ján. He would bring these into the presence of Bahá'u'lláh and, having obtained permission, would read them. Afterwards [Bahá'u'lláh] would direct him to take up his pen and record the Tablet which was revealed in reply. . . .
>
> Such was the speed with which he used to write the revealed Word that the ink of the first word was scarcely yet dry when the whole page was finished. It seemed as if someone had dipped a lock of hair in the ink and applied it over the whole page. None of the words was written clearly and they were illegible to all except Mírzá Áqá Ján. There were occasions when even he could not decipher the words and had to seek the help of Bahá'u'lláh. When revelation had ceased, then . . . Mírzá Áqá Ján would rewrite the Tablet in his best hand and dispatch it to its destination. . . .[275]

Nabíl-i-A'zam, a Bahá'í historian who accompanied Bahá'u'lláh throughout much of His exile and imprisonment, and who chronicled both his own firsthand observations and the eyewitness accounts of others, adds the following details:

> A number of secretaries were busy day and night and yet they were unable to cope with the task. Among them was Mírzá Báqir-i-Shírází. . . . He alone transcribed no less than two thousand verses every day. He labored during six or seven months. Every month the equivalent of several volumes would be transcribed by him and sent to Persia. About twenty volumes, in his fine penmanship, he left behind as a remembrance. . . .[276]

Many other observers have left similar accounts. However, we need not rely entirely on their testimony to verify this phenomenon. After Bahá'u'lláh's Tablets were dispatched, the original notes of Mírzá Áqá Ján and other secretaries were generally distributed to resident Bahá'ís and visiting pilgrims as souvenirs. The early believers treasured these keepsakes and called them "revelation writing." Countless specimens of this stenography have since been collected at the Bahá'í World Center. To appreciate the value of these historical documents, simply suppose the disciples of Christ had taken notes as He spoke and had preserved them for study by future generations of scholars. Handwritten dictation, scribbled frantically without pause by a secretary working under high pressure, looks much the same in any language. The "revelation writing" therefore bears eloquent testimony to the circumstances of its origin. By comparing its almost illegible scrawl with careful Arabic or Persian penmanship, anyone—even knowing nothing of the languages—can visualize the speed and continuity with which Bahá'u'lláh's secretaries worked.*

The torrential flow of Bahá'u'lláh's utterance could more easily be explained away if the resulting writings were occasionally of lackluster quality. Such is not the case, however. The caliber of His work is not only strikingly uniform but uniformly superlative. This of course does not mean His writings are all alike; one of the very things that makes them excellent is the astounding diversity they incorporate. "At one time," says Bahá'u'lláh, "We spoke in the language of the lawgiver; at another in that of the truth seeker and the mystic. . . ."[277] However, all His compositions are from beginning to end highly polished, meticulously organized, lucidly presented, and vibrant with spiritual power and beauty.

There are various standards by which to judge quality in writing; some of these—such as eloquence or beauty—will vary

---

* For photostatic copies of "revelation writing," see page 110 of Adib Taherzadeh's *The Revelation of Bahá'u'lláh*, vol. 1. Contrast them, for example, with the neatly transcribed Arabic Tablet reproduced as the frontispiece of the same book.

considerably according to individual taste. Other yardsticks are not so flexible. If, for instance, an author quotes from the works of others, or even from his own works, we are entitled to ask how accurately he has done so. Bahá'u'lláh would sometimes quote liberally from scriptures of past religions, or from works by sages, mystics, historians, and the like. Many of these excerpts are from obscure or little-known works to which He seemingly had no access at the time; He could not, in any event, have stopped to look them up without interrupting His pacing and His dictation. Both the original notes and eyewitness reports indicate that He always dictated these passages afresh: He did not simply instruct the secretary to look up the necessary text and insert it. Sometimes verification of His sources required hours or even months of research by scholars. Bahá'u'lláh's citations are always scrupulously precise. So rigorous is His use of such secondary material that we would never know (if the historical record were less clear) that we are reading extemporaneous composition.

Closing Comments

This chapter explored further the issue of whether Bahá'u'lláh displayed knowledge not readily available to Him through normal human channels. It attempted to do so in ways that look beyond the various historical and scientific prophecies detailed in previous chapters. To restate the main points:

Bahá'u'lláh spent His crucial formative years in an atmosphere of profound superstition and prejudice, receiving only the most perfunctory education. Despite these disadvantages, His knowledge aroused the wonder and admiration of many eminent scholars. Three especially striking features of that knowledge testify to its intuitive and seemingly superhuman character: (1) His farsightedness—Bahá'u'lláh in His writings analyzed and foreshadowed all the sweeping social changes of the twentieth century, displaying a thorough grasp of future global policy issues that had not yet even begun to engage the attention of His contemporaries. (2) His mastery of Arabic literary writing—He demonstrated, apparently without study or training, a flawless command of this highly technical subject, which normally takes many years of drill and discipline to acquire. (3) His creative speed and spontaneity—He consistently produced highly polished, superbly organized, deeply thoughtful writing embellished with exact quotes from a wide variety of sources at phenomenal speed in completely extemporaneous fashion.

This chapter has said nothing, until now, about the Báb or 'Abdu'l-Bahá. Because Bahá'u'lláh Himself teaches that both these men also were divinely illumined (the Báb directly, as a Manifestation of God, and 'Abdu'l-Bahá indirectly, as the Perfect Exemplar and appointed Interpreter of the Faith), it is fair to ask whether They showed similar signs of innate knowledge. Any thoughtful student of Bahá'í history will discover such signs in abundance. Since a detailed discussion of these issues would extend far beyond the useful length of this book, the reader is referred to the bibliography for more information. Briefly, however, I will say that while the outward circumstances differ, they paint the same picture in each case: All three Central Figures of the Bahá'í Faith manifested an apparently intuitive grasp of skills and subjects entirely foreign to Their backgrounds, and all three displayed the same torrential spontaneity in composing perfectly polished text. ('Abdu'l-Bahá, when pressed for time, would dictate to as many as five secretaries at once, moving rapidly from one to another, speaking of different subjects and even using different languages, without ever losing the thread of His thought.[278])

Do these observations prove Bahá'u'lláh was a Messenger from God? Certainly not—not in any everyday sense of the word "prove." In religion, as in science, there is never any fact or body of facts, however large, that cannot be explained in more than one way. So long as we can explain our findings in more than one way, we can never "prove" absolutely which explanation is correct. All we can do is try to weigh the evidence as fairly as possible and exercise our best judgment. I have tried in this chapter to sharpen the focus, to present facts which, added to the successful historical and scientific predictions described in previous chapters, simplify such a decision.

However, the facts are not all in. All information we have discussed so far has pertained, directly or otherwise, to the question of Bahá'u'lláh's knowledge. Important as this may be, knowledge is not the only, or even the most important, characteristic we should expect to find in a Divine Manifestation. The next chapter will discuss some of these other characteristics and will suggest ways to test for them that could shed light on our central question: *Who was Bahá'u'lláh?*

Chapter 8

THE SUN: ITS OWN PROOF

He Who is everlastingly hidden from the eyes of men can
never be known except through His Manifestation, and His
Manifestation can adduce no greater proof of the truth of
His Mission than the proof of His own Person.
                                               —*Bahá'u'lláh*

. . . the Sun of Righteousness [shall] arise, with healing in
His wings.
                                               —*Malachi 4:2*

We have been exploring the claim of Bahá'u'lláh by repeatedly
asking two questions. First, what phenomena may reasonably
be expected to occur if His claim is true? Second, do those
phenomena actually occur?

To sum up the main points so far: Anyone claiming to be
a Manifestation of God (as the term is defined by Bahá'u'lláh)
must be, among other things, "omniscient at will." Such a
person should be able correctly to describe events of the
future. Bahá'u'lláh did this. Such a person should understand
scientific facts not yet discovered in His time. Bahá'u'lláh did
this. Such a person should possess skills not acquired in any
school and display a deep understanding of spiritual and
social problems beyond the experience of His learned contemporaries. Bahá'u'lláh did these things.

But a Manifestation of God, if such a Being exists at all,
cannot be merely a fountain of knowledge. An individual
might conceivably be a walking encyclopedia, able to divulge
all manner of fascinating and useful information, and still lack
many other admirable qualities such as compassion, fairness,
humor, courage, or many others. No such person could be

considered a Manifestation of God in the Bahá'í sense. The periodic Manifestations, according to Bahá'u'lláh, fully reflect the infinite perfections of the Creator Himself: They are "endowed with all the attributes of God, such as sovereignty, dominion, and the like. . . ."[279] Whatever They do or say is what God would do or say were He to appear in human form. Beyond this, They are Spiritual Suns, ablaze with divine energy powerful enough to transform the world and redirect its history for hundreds or even thousands of years. They "manifest" God as a flawless mirror manifests or reflects the sun. Christ Himself—the "Word made Flesh"—said no less: "If ye had known Me, ye should have known My Father also."[280]

It follows that any true Manifestation of God must be extraordinary in ways that go far beyond intellectual attainment. As the exponent and representative of God on earth, He is not literally God, but His presence is in a very real sense the presence of God. What would such a presence be like? How would it feel to enter the company of a Divine Manifestation, to converse and interact with Him and thus obtain a glimpse of His true nature?

Perhaps the first thing we must say about such questions is that we can never truly know the answers—not, at least, without first having had the experience. Since we ordinarily have no direct contact with infinite perfection, we cannot logically hope to imagine such contact in any realistic way. This very futility, however, allows us to say one thing with considerable assurance: To be in the presence of a Manifestation must be a rare experience indeed, unforgettable and indescribable. Presumably it would be unlike any other experience on earth. We may reasonably expect that the personality of a Manifestation of God should make an overpowering impression and should have a lasting impact on persons who encounter Him—even on those of high rank and capacity.

Since Bahá'u'lláh left this earth in 1892, we can no longer physically enter His presence and thus judge firsthand how well He satisfied these expectations. The best we can do is study the reactions of those who met Him and try to see Him through their eyes. This does not mean we should substitute their judgment for our own, nor does it bind us to accept their explanations of what they experienced. (Different witnesses, in any case, explained their experiences in different and sometimes contradictory ways.) Just the same, such a study is clearly relevant for anyone wishing to evaluate Bahá'u'lláh's claim in systematic fashion. We can say, at the very least, that if someone claims to be a Manifestation of God, but ordinarily makes no unusual impression on those who meet him and demonstrates no extraordinary qualities of character, that person's claim must be considered suspect. If the opposite is true, then, by the same token, that impression and those qualities must to some extent strengthen his claim.

THE PROOF OF HIS PERSON

As previous chapters have indicated, the life of Bahá'u'lláh is extensively documented. His photograph, surrounded by a wide array of personal effects, is reverently displayed in the Archives Building at the Bahá'í World Center in Haifa. Thousands of people met Him—believers and skeptics, rich and poor, high government officials, noted scholars, and ordinary people from all walks of life. These individuals left unnumbered public records, diplomatic papers, diaries, memoirs, interviews, oral histories, and anecdotes reflecting His movements and activities on an almost daily basis. What can we learn from such documentation?

His Magnetic Presence

From this array of primary source material, one fact leaps out again and again, at every turn and in every possible way. That fact is Bahá'u'lláh's spellbinding personal magnetism. "An atmosphere of majesty," says 'Abdu'l-Bahá, "haloed Him as the sun at midday."[281] The almost irresistible charm of His personality thrilled His friends and confused His enemies; the latter warned inquirers to avoid Him lest they become mesmerized by His "sorcery." Complete strangers, knowing nothing of His station or identity, would often bow spontaneously on the occasion of a surprise meeting. High-ranking skeptics and cynics, accustomed to dealing on an equal footing with notables of every description, would become awestruck and speechless in His presence. His loyal followers, having known Him, could not bear to be separated from Him; many abandoned lives of comfort and affluence in order to share His exile and imprisonment. His hard-boiled jailers and custodians routinely became devoted admirers, placing their resources at His disposal and offering to help Him escape— offers He would kindly but firmly refuse.

"If you had come to this blessed place ['Akká] in the days of the manifestation of the evident Light," says 'Abdu'l-Bahá,

> if you had attained to the court of His presence, and had witnessed His luminous beauty, you would have understood that His teachings and perfection were not in need of further evidence.
>
> Only through the honor of entering His presence, many souls became confirmed believers; they had no need of other proofs. Even those people who rejected and hated Him bitterly, when they had met Him, would testify to the grandeur of Bahá'u'lláh, saying: "This is a magnificent man, but what a pity that He makes such a claim! Otherwise, all that He says is acceptable."[282]

Ḥájí Mírzá Haydar-'Alí, a Bahá'í residing in 'Akká who witnessed many such encounters, comments as follows:

> Although [Bahá'u'lláh] showed much compassion and loving-kindness, and approached anyone who came to His presence with tender care and humbleness, and often used to make humorous remarks to put them at ease, yet in spite of these, no one, whether faithful or disbelieving, learned or unlettered, wise or foolish, was able to utter ten words in His presence in the usual everyday manner. Indeed, many would find themselves to be tremulous with an impediment in their speech.

Some people asked permission to attain His presence for the sole purpose of conducting arguments and engaging in controversies. As a favor on His part, and in order to fulfill the testimony and to declare conclusively the proofs, He gave these permission to enter the court of His majesty and glory. As they entered the room, heard His voice welcoming them in, and gazed at His countenance beaming with the light of grandeur, they could not help but prostrate themselves at His door. They would then enter and sit down. When He showed them where to sit, they would find themselves unable to utter a word or put forward their questions. When they left they would bow to Him involuntarily. Some would be transformed through the influence of meeting Him and would leave with the utmost sincerity and devotion, some would depart as admirers, while others would leave His presence, ignorant and heedless, attributing their experience to pure sorcery. . . . To be brief, the bounties which were vouchsafed to a person as a result of attaining His presence were indescribable and unknowable. The proof of the sun is the sun itself.[283]

One of the most overworked and debased words in the English language is "charisma"—a word currently applied to any performer with crowd appeal and to every politician or preacher with an engaging personality. To any thoughtful student of Bahá'u'lláh's life, it will be obvious that His uncanny effect on others was of an entirely different and higher order. Much of what passes today for charisma is actually the work of "image consultants" who teach their clients how to manipulate news media, stage publicity stunts, "dress for success," and surround themselves with symbols of leadership and authority. Bahá'u'lláh did none of these things. He lived frugally, wore simple clothing, conducted Himself in a modest and unassuming manner, and (despite His audacious claim) avoided the limelight. Such was His radiance of spirit, however, that those who felt its warmth often remarked they felt transported to paradise.

Few if any firsthand descriptions of Bahá'u'lláh dwell on details of His physical appearance. Instead, they speak of such things as His kingly dignity, His flashing eyes and penetrating gaze, and His melodious voice that always carried a sense of calm authority. Time and again such reports mention the ineffable sense of serenity and exhilaration one felt in His presence. Perhaps the best-known pen portrait of Bahá'u'lláh is the following account by Edward Granville Browne, the distinguished Cambridge Orientalist who met Him at 'Akká in 1890:

> Though I dimly suspected whither I was going and whom I was to behold (for no distinct intimation had been given to me), a second or two elapsed ere, with a throb of wonder and awe, I became definitely conscious that the room was not untenanted. In the corner where the divan met the wall sat a wondrous and venerable figure, crowned with a felt head-dress of the kind called *taj* by dervishes (but of unusual height and make), round the base of which was wound a small white turban. The face of him on whom I gazed I can never forget, though I cannot describe it. Those piercing eyes seemed to read one's very soul; power and authority sat on that ample brow; while the deep lines on the forehead and face implied an age which the jet-black hair and beard flowing down in indistinguishable luxuriance almost to the waist seemed to belie. No need to ask in whose presence I stood, as I bowed myself before one who is the object of a devotion and love which kings might envy and emperors sigh for in vain![284]

Many specific incidents could be culled from Bahá'u'lláh's life story to illustrate His awe-inspiring majesty and the various reactions it evoked. One extreme instance occurred when the Persian consul-general in Baghdad hired a Turkish ruffian named Riḍá to assassinate Bahá'u'lláh. Armed with a pistol, Riḍá tried twice to carry out his mission—once by approaching the Bahá'í leader in a public bath and again by lying in ambush for Him as He walked the city's streets. Both times, when actually confronting his prey, the assassin lost his nerve. On the second occasion he became so frightened and bewildered that he dropped his weapon; whereupon an amused Bahá'u'lláh instructed that the pistol be handed back to him and arranged for an escort to help the dazed man find his way home![285] (Riḍá himself, in later years, circulated this story.)

The electrifying impact of Bahá'u'lláh's presence is clear not only from the testimony of His followers, but also—in an ironic and backhanded way—from that of Muslim and Christian clergymen seeking to discredit Him. Realizing that this phenomenon required an explanation, His detractors labored to supply one that would not enhance the credibility of His prophetic claim. One oft-repeated theory was that visitors were carefully conditioned in advance to see Bahá'u'lláh as a godlike being. Each pilgrim was told (so the story went) that what he would experience depended on his own spiritual capacity: If he was a material being he would see Bahá'u'lláh only as a man, but if he was sufficiently spiritual, he would see God. Only after the visitor had been aroused to a frenzy of anticipation (the story continued) would he be allowed, for a few moments, to enter the Holy Presence and gaze adoringly at the face of his Lord. The almost magical effect of such visits was thus attributed to psychological manipulation.

This superficially plausible explanation might well convince someone who had only minimal knowledge about Bahá'u'lláh; it cannot, however, stand up to serious examination. Its fictitious character is clearly exposed by the testimony of many credible and independent eyewitnesses. E. G. Browne, for example, whose soul-stirring encounter with Bahá'u'lláh is quoted above, was aware of this cynical theory but regarded it as nonsense. He himself, as he states, only "dimly suspected" that he was being taken to see Bahá'u'lláh, "for no distinct intimation had been given"[286] to him. Browne, though skeptical of Bahá'u'lláh's claims, was hardly an enemy, but reactions similar to his were commonplace even among those who initially were far less receptive. As Ḥájí Mírzá Haydar-'Alí comments:

> When a believer describes what he has experienced in the presence of Bahá'u'lláh, his impressions may be interpreted as being formed through his attitude of self-effacement and a feeling of utter nothingness in relation to Him. But to what

can it be attributed when one enters into His presence as an antagonist and leaves as a believer, or comes in as an enemy but goes out as a friend, or comes to raise controversial arguments, but departs without saying anything and, due to willful blindness, attributing this to magic?[287]

The fact is, Bahá'u'lláh's Muslim opponents were painfully aware of His power to bewitch even those who were hostile or indifferent. Aside from warning inquirers to avoid His presence and avoiding it themselves, they introduced a further explanation for these reactions by nonbelievers. Their idea was, quite simply, that Bahá'u'lláh and His followers administered hypnotic drugs to their contacts. Elaborate refinements were added as the story spread: The drug—purportedly an "extract of dates"—was said to be slipped into the delicious Persian tea customarily served to guests at Bahá'u'lláh's home. For those too wise to accept the spiked tea, there supposedly was a further stratagem: The drug would be compressed into a tiny pill and, at an opportune moment, surreptitiously tossed into the visitor's open mouth. The hypno-drug theory, ludicrous though it was, was widely aired and believed in Persia for a number of decades.

This chapter has so far discussed only Bahá'u'lláh, arguing that His stupendous personal magnetism was consistent with His claim fully to reveal and manifest the infinite perfections of God. He demonstrated precisely those signs we should expect to see in Him if that claim is true. This raises a further question: What of the Báb, Whose own claim to be a Manifestation is endorsed by Bahá'u'lláh Himself? If Bahá'u'lláh was genuine, then the Báb was genuine, and we should expect to observe in Him the same remarkable signs.

On this question the facts of history are, once again, too clear to invite serious debate. The Báb's presence, like that of Bahá'u'lláh, was by all accounts riveting; it affected even indifferent or apathetic onlookers like a thunderbolt. Having experienced it, many former opponents preferred to die rather than part from Him or deny their belief. His enemies, like bats fleeing from light, steered clear of Him and warned others to do the same lest they fall under His spell.

Reverend T. K. Cheyne, a well-known Oxford Bible scholar, wrote of the Báb:

> His combination of mildness and power is so rare that we have to place him in a line with super-normal men. . . . We learn that, at great points in His career, after he had been in an ecstasy, such radiance of might and majesty streamed from his countenance that none could bear to look upon the effulgence of his glory and beauty. Nor was it an uncommon occurrence for unbelievers involuntarily to bow down in lowly obeisance on beholding His Holiness. . . .[288]

Comte de Gobineau, one of the first European historians to investigate the story of the Báb in depth, writes that He was "of extreme simplicity of manner, of a fascinating gentleness, those gifts were further heightened by his great youth and his marvelous charm. . . . He could not open his lips (we are assured by those who knew him) without stirring the hearts to their very depths."[289] Furthermore, Gobineau writes, "Those who came near him felt in spite of themselves the fascinating influence of his personality, of his manner and of his speech. His guards were not free from that weakness."[290] Concerning the Báb's effect on unbelievers, Gobineau says: ". . . even the orthodox Muhammadans who were present [at encounters with Him] have retained an indelible memory of them and never recall them without a sort of terror. They agreed unanimously that [His] eloquence . . . was of an incomparable kind, such that, without having been an eyewitness, one could not possibly imagine."[291]

Of the Bahá'í Faith's three Central Figures, 'Abdu'l-Bahá is in many ways the most paradoxical. He is not regarded by Bahá'ís as a Manifestation of God, and He never for a moment pretended to be cut from the same cloth as the Báb and Bahá'u'lláh. Still, if Bahá'u'lláh was a reflection of God, 'Abdu'l-Bahá was in some sense a reflection and extension of Bahá'u'lláh, Who called Him "the Gulf that hath branched out of this Ocean that hath encompassed all created things."[292] From texts already cited, it should be clear that just as Bahá'u'lláh's spiritual majesty towered above that of His son, so must that of His son (if the Faith's claims be true) have towered above that of humanity in general.

'Abdu'l-Bahá was, to Western eyes, the most accessible of the Faith's major figures. His travels throughout America, as well as His visits to Canada, the United Kingdom, France, Germany, Austria, and Hungary, brought Him into direct contact with the Western press and public, as well as with numerous dignitaries and leaders of thought. It is fair to say that wherever He went, He was mobbed by enthusiastic admirers, most of whom had never before heard of Him. Judging from the crowds that thronged His public talks and from the sensational press coverage that followed His every move, one would have thought He was a world-class celebrity—not the obscure head of an even more obscure Eastern religion. The volumes of prose written by those who remembered Him reflect a clear consensus as to His remarkable qualities. One could hardly summarize that consensus more aptly than by quoting these words of Mrs. Phoebe Hearst (mother of William Randolph Hearst): "Tho He does not seek to impress one at all, strength, power, purity, love and holiness are radiated from His majestic, yet humble, personality, and the spiritual atmosphere which surrounds Him and most powerfully affects all those who are blest by being near Him, is indescribable."[293] Another recurring comment was that merely to sit beside Him in an automobile, even when He was physically exhausted from His hectic speaking schedule, was to feel oneself being charged with spiritual energy.

'Abdu'l-Bahá always insisted that He was but a drop compared to Bahá'u'lláh's ocean. However, those who knew only the son often found it difficult to conceive that His father (or anyone else) could have surpassed His transcendent majesty or His irresistible power of attraction. 'Abdu'l-Bahá asked the Bahá'ís to contemplate, in light of His own astounding impact on Westerners, what might have been achieved by the One who was immeasurably greater:

How foolish are the people of the East to have incarcerated for well-nigh fifty years the like of this glorious personage! But for His chains and prison, Bahá'u'lláh by this time would have gained absolute ascendancy over the minds and thoughts of the peoples of Europe. . . . Consider and reflect upon the result of My few days in London and the profound effect it has had here and in the surrounding regions. Ponder then in your heart, what the coming of Bahá'u'lláh would have achieved! Had He appeared in Europe, its people would have seized their opportunity, and His Cause, by virtue of the freedom of thought, would by this time have encompassed the earth. But, alas! This Cause, though it first appeared in Persia, yet eventually it shall be seen how the peoples of Europe have wrested it from its hands! Take note of this and remember it in future. Ultimately you shall see how it has come to pass. And yet behold! how the Bahá'ís are still persecuted by the people of Persia![294]

As stated above, we can no longer physically meet such remarkable beings as Bahá'u'lláh, the Báb and 'Abdu'l-Bahá; thus we cannot experience for ourselves the dynamic influence Their presence is said to have exerted. We are free to explain in any way we like the subjective reactions of others. But we cannot deny, as a matter of historical fact, what those reactions were; nor can we doubt that such reactions were typical not only of believers but of unbelievers—people of capacity whose impressions can in no way be ascribed to simpleminded credulity. We may well ask ourselves: What manner of being can consistently produce so unforgettable an impact upon human consciousness, and how can we explain the successive appearance of three such extraordinary beings, closely linked as Central Figures of one world faith?

Certainly the answers to these questions are not so self-evident as to force acceptance of Bahá'u'lláh's claim. Still, the observations that prompt such questions clearly have some bearing upon, and relevance to, the probable truth or falsity of that claim. The nature of that bearing and relevance is of course for each inquirer to judge, impartially and independently.

His Luminous Character

Another way to test the claim of any purported Divine Messenger is to examine the claimant's character. What can we learn about the moral and ethical stature of the candidate? Like the other issues we have been considering, unusual nobility of character falls short of "proving" in any absolute sense that its possessor is a Manifestation of God. Lack of such nobility, however, would most assuredly prove someone was not. Therein lies the question's importance. The Manifestations must be more than "good people": They are, by definition, beings who fully personify all the divine attributes. Since one of those attributes, presumably, is moral perfection, it stands to reason that any genuine Manifestation must exemplify an exalted standard of conduct that few people would be able to uphold.

We must exercise care in approaching this issue. One thorny obstacle is deciding how to define character. Throughout history, followers of every faith have applied their own standards to the founders of other faiths and judged those founders defective. Jews criticized Jesus for breaking the Sabbath. Christians condemned Muḥammad for taking several wives and for defending His religion by force of arms. Muslims expressed moral outrage when Bahá'u'lláh established equality of women with men. Examples could be multiplied without end.

Bahá'ís reply that it is not man but God Who, through His Manifestation, reveals the social norms and moral values that are to prevail until the coming of a new Manifestation. Right and wrong are whatever He says they are, until His Dispensation ends: The Manifestation "doeth whatsoever He willeth, and ordaineth whatsoever He pleaseth"[295]; moreover, "He shall not be asked of His doings."[296] Being guided by God, each Manifestation is free to keep the law of His predecessor, modify it, or discard it altogether as He deems appropriate. This in no way implies that divine revelation is arbitrary: 'Abdu'l-Bahá says, "The Laws of God are not imposition of will, or of power, or pleasure, but the resolutions of truth, reason and justice."[297] The point is that God sees the entire puzzle while we see only pieces; therefore only He can correctly weigh the infinite variables and decide, based on the circumstances of history and man's spiritual readiness, what will best promote human development in a given period.

It may seem, at first glance, that this concept denies by implication the very possibility of evaluating the character of anyone claiming to be a Divine Manifestation. If He and He alone defines the standard by which He is to be judged, all previous criteria being ruled out of order, will He not appear to be a saint whether His claim is true or false? The answer is, "Not necessarily." In theory, this may seem to be a problem; but in practice it resolves itself quite neatly for two reasons.

First, the teachings of religion fall into two quite different categories: social laws and spiritual principles. Social laws cover marriage and divorce, dietary practices, devotional observances, the lending of money, treatment of criminals, governmental policies, and thousands of other practical concerns. These laws are subject to change in every revelation. For instance, the dietary restrictions and penal code of Moses, perfectly tailored to the nomadic heritage of the Children of Israel, were no longer appropriate by the time of Jesus; Christianity therefore modified them. Fundamental spiritual principles, however, are quite another matter. While different faiths employ different terminologies to express them, these principles are the same in every religious dispensation: They rest on truths that are eternal and immutable. The Golden Rule, for example, is central to the holy scriptures of every religion. The same may be said of exhortations to love, kindness, justice, mercy, patience, courtesy, cleanliness, honesty, self-discipline, and the like. Attributes such as these clearly derive their importance from the inward, eternal aspect of religious morality and not from the outward, temporary social aspect. These unnumbered virtues are of course the same in the teachings of Bahá'u'lláh as in the teachings of Abraham, Christ, or Buddha.

Second, Bahá'u'lláh Himself stipulates that a Manifestation of God is the first to put His own teachings into practice: "...whatsoever thou dost behold in His deeds, the same wilt thou find in His sayings, and whatsoever thou dost read in His sayings, that wilt thou recognize in His deeds."[298] For a Manifestation of God or anyone else to behave in this way is no small accomplishment, particularly when the standard He inculcates is uncommonly lofty and challenging. History is filled with examples of wise men and philosophers who preached one thing while practicing another. No one whose deeds and words are in manifest conflict can plausibly claim to be a Manifestation of God, as Bahá'ís understand the term.

These considerations suggest two ways in which we can study the personal characters of Bahá'u'lláh, the Báb, and 'Abdu'l-Bahá. First, disregarding for the moment whether we agree with Their social principles, we can ask how fully They exemplified those eternal qualities of spirit upheld as essential in all religions. Second, we can ask how consistent Their behavior was with Their own teachings, remembering that only the rarest individuals act as nobly as they speak. These two questions, of course, overlap considerably; for many purposes they are simply different ways of looking at a single yardstick.

Studying Bahá'u'lláh's life from this perspective, we see clearly that the deep devotion He inspired was due to more than the force of His personality or the sublimity of His teachings. It followed, just as surely, from His exemplary personal life and rectitude of conduct. The common thread tying together all the diverse events of His life was this: He was forced to choose, on an almost daily basis, between His own welfare and that of others. In literally every instance, He sacrificed Himself for the betterment of humanity.

Scores of incidents and anecdotes illustrate this theme; we have space here to touch only the barest highlights. It is well known that sometime before the declaration of the Báb, Bahá'u'lláh had turned down the lucrative government post previously occupied by His late father, Mírzá Buzurg. Instead,

He devoted His considerable fortune entirely to charitable and humanitarian work. He and His wife Navváb, who shared His priorities, were known to the masses as the "Father of the Poor" and the "Mother of Consolation." Public officials and the clergy (not yet faced with the challenge of accepting or rejecting Him as the Promised One) also held him in high esteem but warned Him that His continued generosity towards the poor would soon impoverish Him.

The point became moot when Bahá'u'lláh espoused the cause of the Báb, for so bold and public a stance seemed tantamount to suicide. His reputation, however, protected Him until state-sponsored persecution boiled over in the massacres that followed the Báb's martyrdom. Even then, He could have chosen safety, for the anti-Bábí hysteria erupted during a time when He was away from home, visiting the brother of the prime minister. Friends in the country offered to hide Him until the storm abated. Spurning their offer, Bahá'u'lláh headed for the capital to confront the foes of the Faith, turning Himself in along the way to a military detail sent to arrest Him. He was conducted "on foot and in chains, with bared head and bare feet"[299] under the pitiless August sun, from the hill villages north of Tehran to the city's great dungeon. Along the way He was pelted with stones and filth by the crowds. At one point an old woman, wishing to play her part in punishing the vile heretic (as authorities now were depicting Him), ran alongside, begging the soldiers to pause long enough-for her to cast her stone. Bahá'u'lláh gave a revealing glimpse of His nature by telling the soldiers, "Suffer not this woman to be disappointed. Deny her not what she regards as a meritorious act in the sight of God."[300] To cheer her blind and hardened heart, He then submitted patiently to the added injury.

While Bahá'u'lláh was personally forgiving, His forbearance and compassion sprang not from weakness but from deep strength. We are reminded of the way in which "gentle Jesus, meek and mild" used a bullwhip to clear the temple of money-changers who had made of His Father's house a den of thieves. Bahá'u'lláh was lionlike in His defense of the Faith, routing His enemies in debate and brilliantly exposing their hypocrisy. Although He endured persecution when He had to do so to prosecute His mission, He never sought it out: Throughout His life, in fact, He strenuously protested the campaign of terror the authorities waged against Him and His followers. (In one instance, an outraged Bahá'u'lláh risked torture and death by rebuking the Sulṭán of Turkey for the latter's cruelty to Bahá'í women and children.)

When Bahá'u'lláh entered the dungeon of Tehran—the unutterably foul "Black Pit"—He was in His mid-thirties and in the prime of health. He left it four months later an emaciated shadow, scarred for life. He had been forced, along with a number of other Bábís, to wear chains so heavy that they cut through to His collarbone; to eat food poisoned, at one point, by His enemies; to breathe air polluted with the stench of human waste and festering wounds; and to stay in a position that made sleep virtually impossible. Each day one of the Bábís would be taken out and executed, reminding the others that their turn might come next. Bahá'u'lláh and His fellow-prisoners fueled their courage by chanting songs of praise and glorification to God—songs that could be heard even in the palace of the sháh, some distance away.

In that dungeon in 1852, the conviction came to Bahá'u'-lláh that He and He alone was the Promised One Whose imminent appearance the Báb had proclaimed. "One night in a dream," He wrote many years later,

> these exalted words were heard on every side: "Verily, We shall render Thee victorious by Thyself and by Thy pen. Grieve Thou not for that which hath befallen Thee, neither be Thou afraid, for Thou art in safety. Ere long will God raise up the treasures of the earth—men who will aid Thee through Thyself and through Thy Name, wherewith God hath revived the hearts of such as have recognized Him."[301]

Bahá'u'lláh did not, until 1863, announce His claim to be the Redeemer foretold by the Báb. However, He referred to it often in barely veiled allusions contained in the odes, essays, and letters that began to flow from His pen immediately after His release from prison. At the same time, coinciding with His initial banishment to Baghdad, He arose to regenerate the devastated Bábí community. He succeeded, by precept and example, in transforming its members into the "treasures of the earth" who, as promised in His dream, would bring victory to the Cause of God.

Throughout the long years of exile, persecution, and imprisonment that followed, Bahá'u'lláh faced danger and hardship with superhuman fortitude. Wherever He went He earned a reputation as a great humanitarian, a man of deep compassion, truthfulness, and integrity. Even those who refused to accept His claims and doctrines frequently expressed admiration for His personal life; the words "saintly" and "Christ-like" appear frequently in their descriptions of Him. In the following admonition addressed to one of His sons, He clearly set forth the standard of which He was a walking embodiment:

> Be generous in prosperity, and thankful in adversity. Be worthy of the trust of thy neighbor, and look upon him with a bright and friendly face. Be a treasure to the poor, an admonisher to the rich, an answerer of the cry of the needy, a preserver of the sanctity of thy pledge. Be fair in thy judgment, and guarded in thy speech. Be unjust to no man, and show all meekness to all men. Be as a lamp unto them that walk in darkness, a joy to the sorrowful, a sea for the thirsty, a haven for the distressed, an upholder and defender of the victim of oppression. Let integrity and uprightness distinguish all thine acts. Be a home for the stranger, a balm to the suffering, a tower of strength for the fugitive. Be eyes to the blind, and a guiding light unto the feet of the erring. Be an ornament to the countenance of truth, a crown to the brow of fidelity, a pillar of the temple of righteousness, a breath of life to the body of mankind, an ensign of the hosts of justice, a luminary above the horizon of virtue, a dew to the soil of the human heart, an ark on the ocean of knowledge, a sun in the heaven of bounty, a gem on the diadem of wisdom, a shining light in the firmament of thy generation, a fruit upon the tree of humility.[302]

The seamless consistency between Bahá'u'lláh's words and actions revealed itself in countless ways. He taught His followers, for example, to obey the laws and decrees of duly constituted governments, except in certain extremely grave matters of conscience. For example, a Bahá'í may not, even to save his own life, renounce his faith.* Bahá'u'lláh Himself upheld this principle even at immense personal cost. One such occasion was when, in Adrianople, on the eve of His imprisonment in the fortress of 'Akká, a number of foreign diplomats begged Him to flee and offered Him asylum in their own countries. Spurning their advice, He submitted to the imperial edict, knowing all too well that 'Akká was worse, in many respects, than the notorious "Black Pit" of Tehran. Long afterward, when the governor of 'Akká (who by this time had entrusted his own son to Bahá'u'lláh's family for education and moral guidance) urged Him to leave the prison and offered to take full responsibility, He still refused, pointing out that such action would be contrary to the sulṭán's decree. Though Bahá'u'lláh deeply loved the beauty of the countryside and His confinement deprived Him of seeing so much as a blade of grass, He voluntarily remained a prisoner for years after the original sentence had become a dead letter. He was finally persuaded to leave only in the sunset of His life, after it had become obvious that neither the sulṭán (a new one, by this time) nor anyone else in authority objected to His doing so.

Bahá'u'lláh spent His last years in the country mansion of Bahjí in 'Akká, surrounded by the scenic beauty He cherished. By this time the Bahá'í Faith had grown considerably and the body of the believers had placed substantial funds at His disposal. Even so, He maintained a lifestyle of extreme austerity, spending the money not on Himself but in promoting the Faith and helping the poor of 'Akká. So generous were Bahá'u'lláh and His family that they themselves often went without

---

* Shoghi Effendi's secretary, in a letter written on his behalf, states the Bahá'í position as follows: "We must obey in all cases except where a spiritual principle is involved, such as denying our Faith. For these spiritual principles we must be willing to die." (*Bahá'í News*, No. 241, March 1951, p. 14.); *Lights of Guidance*, 1453, p. 445.

things that in other households would have been considered necessities. Thus He ended His career with the same solicitude for the needy that had marked its inception.

As mentioned previously, there were Muslim and Christian ecclesiastics who represented Bahá'u'lláh as a selfish charlatan. It would be grossly unfair, however, to imply that all clergy have shown hostility to the Bahá'í Faith and its founder. Theological differences aside, many have paid tribute to the purity and heroism of Bahá'u'lláh's life. One such was the Reverend T. K. Cheyne (mentioned earlier) who researched Bahá'u'lláh thoroughly and expressed his findings in *The Reconciliation of Races and Religions:*

> There was living quite lately a human being of such consummate excellence that many think it is both permissible and inevitable even to identify him mystically with the invisible Godhead. . . . If there has been any prophet in recent times, it is to Bahá'u'lláh that we must go. Character is the final judge. Bahá'u'lláh was a man of the highest class—that of prophets.[303]

A non-Bahá'í scholar, Alfred W. Martin, delivered an excellent summation in *Comparative Religion and the Religion of the Future*. He writes that since its inception the Bahá'í Faith

> has been identified with Bahá'u'lláh, who paid the price of prolonged exile, imprisonment, bodily suffering, and mental anguish for the faith He cherished—a man of imposing personality as revealed in His writings, characterized by intense moral earnestness and profound spirituality, gifted with the selfsame power so conspicuous in the character of Jesus, the power to appreciate people ideally, that is, to see them at the level of their best and to make even the lowest types think well of themselves because of potentialities within them to which He pointed, but of which they were wholly unaware; a prophet whose greatest contribution was not any specific doctrine He proclaimed, but an informing spiritual power breathed into the world through the example of His life and thereby quickening souls into new spiritual activity.[304]

What of the Báb and 'Abdu'l-Bahá? Space precludes any attempt to provide here even a sketchy outline of their lives, about which many fact-packed volumes have been written. What I will do, however, is quote the judgment of respected observers who were familiar with those lives and who cannot be accused of partiality, the more so because they were not Bahá'ís.

As to the Báb's moral character, independent historians have expressed remarkable agreement. "Who can fail to be attracted by the gentle spirit of [the Báb]?" writes E. G. Browne,

> His sorrowful and persecuted life; his purity of conduct, and youth; his courage and uncomplaining patience under misfortune . . . but most of all his tragic death, all serve to enlist our sympathies on behalf of the young Prophet of Shíráz. The irresistible charm which won him such devotion during his life still lives on. . . .[305]

Sir Francis Younghusband, in his book *The Gleam*, writes:

> The story of the Báb . . . was the story of spiritual heroism unsurpassed. . . . The Báb's passionate sincerity could not be doubted, for he had given his life for his faith. And that there must be something in his message that appealed to men and satisfied their souls was witnessed to by the fact that thousands gave their lives in his cause and millions now follow him. If a young man could, in only six years of ministry, by the sincerity of his purpose and the attraction of his personality, so inspire rich and poor, cultured and illiterate . . . his life must be one of those events in the last hundred years which is really worth study.[306]

A. L. M. Nicolas, the prominent French historian who meticulously researched the episode of the Báb, writes:

> His life is one of the most magnificent examples of courage which it has been the privilege of mankind to behold. . . . He sacrificed himself for humanity, for it he gave his body and his soul, for it he endured privations, insults, torture and martyrdom. He sealed, with his very lifeblood,

the covenant of universal brotherhood. Like Jesus he paid with his life for the proclamation of a reign of concord, equity and brotherly love. More than anyone he knew what dreadful dangers he was heaping upon himself . . . but all these considerations could not weaken his resolve. Fear had no hold upon his soul and, perfectly calm, never looking back, in full possession of his powers, he walked into the furnace.[307]

'Abdu'l-Bahá, Who was more accessible to Western observers than either the Báb or Bahá'u'lláh, was the object of many similar testimonies. Rather than quote several short impressions, I have decided to reprint one moderately long one by Myron H. Phelps, a prominent New York attorney who was not a Bahá'í but who visited 'Akká in December 1902. Phelps recorded his experiences and observations in a book about 'Abdu'l-Bahá entitled *Abbás Effendi, His Life and Teachings*. One passage describes a typical gathering of the Palestinian poor— "a crowd of human beings with patched and tattered garments." Phelps continues:

It is a noteworthy gathering. Many of these men are blind; many more are pale, emaciated, or aged. . . . Most of the women are closely veiled, but enough are uncovered to cause us well to believe that, if the veils were lifted, more pain and misery would be seen. Some of them carry babes with pinched and sallow faces. There are perhaps a hundred in this gathering, and besides, many children. They are of all the races one meets in these streets—Syrians, Arabs, Ethiopians, and many others.

These people are ranged against the walls or seated on the ground, apparently in an attitude of expectation;—for what do they wait? Let us wait with them.

We have not long to wait. A door opens and a man comes out. He is of middle stature, strongly built. He wears flowing light-colored robes. On his head is a light buff fez with a white cloth wound about it. He is perhaps sixty years of age. His long grey hair rests on his shoulders. His forehead is broad, full, and high, his nose slightly aquiline, his moustaches and beard, the latter full though not heavy, nearly white. His eyes are grey and blue, large, and both soft and penetrating. His bearing is simple, but there is grace, dignity, and even majesty about his movements. He passes through the crowd, and as he goes utters words of salutation. We do not understand them, but we see the benignity and the kindliness of his countenance. He stations himself at a narrow angle of the street and motions to the people to come towards him. They crowd up a little too insistently. He pushes them gently back and lets them pass him one by one. As they come they hold their hands extended. In each open palm he places some small coins.* He knows them all. He caresses them with his hand on the face, on the shoulders, on the head. Some he stops and questions. An aged negro who hobbles up, he greets with some kindly inquiry; the old man's broad face breaks into a sunny smile, his white teeth glistening against his ebony skin as he replies. He stops a woman with a babe and fondly strokes the child. As they pass, some kiss his hand. To all he says, "Marhabbah, marhabbah" —"Well done, well done!"

So they all pass him. The children have been crowding around him with extended hands, but to them he has not given. However, at the end, as he turns to go, he throws a handful of coppers over his shoulder, for which they scramble.

During this time this friend of the poor has not been unattended. Several men wearing red fezes, and with earnest and kindly faces, followed him from the house, stood near him and aided in regulating the crowd, and now, with reverent manner and at a respectful distance, follow him away. When they address him they call him "Master."

This scene you may see almost any day of the year in the streets of 'Akká. There are other scenes like it, which come only at the beginning of the winter season. In the cold weather which is approaching, the poor will suffer, for, as in all cities, they are thinly clad. Some day at this season, if you are advised of the place and time, you may see the poor of 'Akká gathered at one of the shops where clothes are sold, receiving cloaks from the Master. Upon many, especially the

---

* Describing a similar occasion, Corinne True points out that 'Abdu'l-Bahá's charity was reserved for the truly needy: ". . . once in a while we would see Him send someone away empty-handed and He would reprimand him for his laziness." (Quoted in Honnold, *Vignettes from the Life of 'Abdu'l-Bahá*, no. 53, p. 80.)

most infirm or crippled, he himself places the garment, adjusts it with his own hands, and strokes it approvingly, as if to say, "There! Now you will do well." There are five or six hundred poor in 'Akká, to all of whom he gives a warm garment each year.

On feast days he visits the poor at their homes. He chats with them, inquires into their health and comfort, mentions by name those who are absent, and leaves gifts for all.

Nor is it the beggars only that he remembers. Those respectable poor who cannot beg, but must suffer in silence— those whose daily labor will not support their families—to these he sends bread secretly. His left hand knoweth not what his right hand doeth.

All the people know him and love him—the rich and the poor, the young and the old—even the babe leaping in its mother's arms. If he hears of any one sick in the city— [Muslim] or Christian, or of any other sect, it matters not— he is each day at their bedside, or sends a trusty messenger. If a physician is needed, and the patient poor, he brings or sends one, and also the necessary medicine. If he finds a leaking roof or a broken window menacing health, he summons a workman, and waits himself to see the breach repaired. If any one is in trouble—if a son or a brother is thrown into prison, or he is threatened at law, or falls into any difficulty too heavy for him—it is to the Master that he straightway makes appeal for counsel or for aid. Indeed, for counsel all come to him, rich as well as poor. He is the kind father of all the people. . . .

For more than thirty-four years this man has been a prisoner at 'Akká. But his jailors have become his friends. The Governor of the city, the Commander of the Army Corps, respect and honor him as though he were their brother. No man's opinion or recommendation has greater weight with them. He is the beloved of all the city, high and low. And how could it be otherwise? For to this man it is the law, as it was to Jesus of Nazareth, to do good to those who injure him. Have we yet heard of any one in lands which boast the name of Christ who lived that life?

Hear how he treats his enemies. One instance of many I have heard will suffice.

When the Master came to 'Akká there lived there a certain man from Afghanistan, an austere and rigid [Muslim]. To him the Master was a heretic. He felt and nourished a great enmity towards the Master, and roused up others against him. When opportunity offered in gatherings of the people, as in the Mosque, he denounced him with bitter words.

"This man," he said to all, "is an imposter. Why do you speak to him? Why do you have dealings with him?" And when he passed the Master on the street he was careful to hold his robe before his face that his sight might not be defiled.

Thus did the Afghan. The Master, however, did thus: The Afghan was poor and lived in a mosque; he was frequently in need of food and clothing. The Master sent him both. These he accepted, but without thanks. He fell sick. The Master took him a physician, food, medicine, money. These, also, he accepted; but as he held out one hand that the physician might take his pulse, with the other he held his cloak before his face that he might not look upon the Master. *For twenty-four years* the Master continued his kindnesses and the Afghan persisted in his enmity. Then at last one day the Afghan came to the Master's door, and fell down, penitent and weeping, at his feet.

"Forgive me, sir!" he cried. "For twenty-four years I have done evil to you, for twenty-four years you have done good to me. Now I know that I have been in the wrong."

The Master bade him rise, and they became friends.

The Master is as simple as his soul is great. He claims nothing for himself—neither comfort, nor honor, nor repose. Three or four hours of sleep suffice him; all the remainder of his time and all his strength are given to the succour of those who suffer, in spirit or in body. "I am," he says, "the servant of God."

Such is 'Abbás Effendi, the Master of 'Akká.[308]

We must remember that apart from His ceaseless charitable labors, 'Abdu'l-Bahá devoted hours of each day to writing letters, holding meetings, giving talks, directing the far-flung affairs of the Faith, constructing—often with His own hands—the Shrine of the Báb, and developing a detailed plan of expansion destined to carry the Bahá'í Faith into the twenty-first century and beyond. When World War I broke out, it was He Who launched medical and agricultural relief projects in

Palestine, preventing mass starvation—a service for which He later received a title He never used: Sir 'Abdu'l-Bahá 'Abbás, Knight of the British Empire. As the war drew to a close, Haifa remained in the hands of Turks who vowed to crucify 'Abdu'l-Bahá and all His family on Mount Carmel. When General Allenby's British forces swept into the region, the general went first for counsel to the Master, then cabled his astonished superiors in London: "Have today taken Palestine. Notify the world that 'Abdu'l-Bahá is safe."[309]

'Abdu'l-Bahá was a man Who would—and often did, literally—give one the shirt off His back. Many a time He took aside some needy passerby or street urchin, bestowing upon that astonished person some garment He had on: robe, cloak, coat, occasionally even trousers. As He lay dying in 1921, His daughter sought to change His nightshirt, only to discover He was wearing the only one He had—the others He had all given away. His funeral brought together, in a vivid and united experience of grief, what almost certainly was the largest-ever public gathering of Haifa's many religious, ethnic, and cultural communities.

To present someone's character through selected highlights and personal impressions is unsatisfactory at best. It risks being unfair, both to the reader and to the person thus presented. The vignettes I have offered are intended primarily to whet curiosity and spur independent research. Any inquirer will find at his or her disposal a great deal of well-documented biographical material on the lives of the Central Figures of the Bahá'í Faith.

A world-renowned expert on character once said: "Ye shall know them by their fruits. Do men gather grapes of thorns, or figs of thistles?"[310] My conviction that the Báb, Bahá'u'lláh, and 'Abdu'l-Bahá lived lives of towering, almost unheard-of goodness and nobility might not by itself cause me to conclude that They were channels of divine authority. Without such conviction as a catalyst, however, I would remain unmoved by any purely logical clues or indications such as prophecies, scientific revelations, innate knowledge, spellbinding personal magnetism, and the like. One whose heart is touched by the beauty of these men's lives, and who not only understands but feels Their never-failing harmony of word and action—only such a person, I would wager, will be inclined to take seriously any other evidence of inspiration, however compelling or tantalizing it might appear.

THE DIVINE WORD

This chapter has focused, until now, on Bahá'u'lláh's teaching that the Manifestation of God is His own proof. We have explored two potentially useful ways of understanding this statement: first, that the Manifestation should make a uniquely powerful impression on those who encounter Him, and second, that He must distinguish Himself by peerless character and iron consistency. Bahá'u'lláh admirably fulfilled both expectations.

In His writings, however, Bahá'u'lláh carries this idea a step further. He states that just as the Manifestation is His own proof to those who know Him, so is His revealed word—the Word of God—its own proof to those who read and reflect upon it. This intriguing concept warrants close attention. Of all the evidence Bahá'u'lláh offers, His own written word is the one to which we have the most immediate access. It is something we can experience directly without need to rely on data compiled by historians, biographers, scientists, literary scholars, and the like. What, then, does He mean when He says the revealed word is its own proof?

His meaning, as I have come to understand it, is this: The words that descend upon the Messenger of God through divine revelation are distinguished from human writing by certain characteristics—characteristics that we as human beings can discern but can never reproduce or emulate. The proof of the divine word is our inability to create anything like it. "No breeze," He says, "can compare with the breezes of Divine Revelation, whilst the Word which is uttered by God shineth and flasheth as the sun amidst the books of men.

Happy the man that hath discovered it, and recognized it. . . ."[311] He states:

> He, the divine King, hath proclaimed the undisputed supremacy of the verses of His book over all things that testify to His truth. For compared with all other proofs and tokens, the divinely-revealed verses shine as the sun, whilst all others are as stars. To the peoples of the world they are the abiding testimony, the incontrovertible proof, the shining light of the ideal King. Their excellence is unrivaled, their virtue nothing can surpass. They are the treasury of the divine pearls and the depository of the divine mysteries. . . . Through them floweth the river of divine knowledge, and gloweth the fire of His ancient and consummate wisdom.[312]

What are the specific qualities of revealed writing that no human author can replicate? Bahá'u'lláh identifies two characteristics that set apart the Word of God from the words of men: (1) its creative power to stimulate spiritual growth—a power different both in degree and in kind from anything else in existence; and (2) its limitless depth of meaning.

The Creative Power

The Word of God, according to Bahá'u'lláh, is the outward form of an inward reality—the mysterious spiritual energy released into the world when God speaks through His Manifestation. This celestial force, channeled through the Manifestation and expressed through His speech, shares with the Manifestation Himself the distinction of reflecting perfectly all the attributes of God such as knowledge, love, justice, dominion, and an infinity of others.

We have previously discussed what Bahá'u'lláh says about the indirect influence of revelation—the spiritual energy diffused throughout the world when God reveals Himself. It is not, however, with such an indirect effect that we are here concerned. We are interested rather in the creative power by which, Bahá'u'lláh says, the Word acts directly upon those who turn towards it and open themselves to its influence:

Intone, O My servant, the verses of God that have been received by thee, as intoned by them who have drawn nigh unto Him, that the sweetness of thy melody may kindle thine own soul, and attract the hearts of all men. Whoso reciteth, in the privacy of his chamber, the verses revealed by God, the scattering angels of the Almighty shall scatter abroad the fragrance of the words uttered by his mouth, and shall cause the heart of every righteous man to throb. Though he may, at first, remain unaware of its effect, yet the virtue of the grace vouchsafed unto him must needs sooner or later exercise its influence upon his soul. Thus have the mysteries of the Revelation of God been decreed by virtue of the Will of Him Who is the Source of power and wisdom.[313]

Such claims are not, of course, confined to the revelation of Bahá'u'lláh. In the Old Testament, God says:

For as the rain cometh down, and the snow from heaven, and returneth not thither, but watereth the earth, and maketh it bring forth and bud, that it may give seed to the sower, and bread to the eater: So shall my word be that goeth forth out of my mouth: it shall not return unto me void, but it shall accomplish that which I please, and it shall prosper in the thing whereto I sent it.[314]

Jesus put it simply: "The words that I speak unto you, they are spirit, and they are life."[315] Bahá'u'lláh likens the divine word to "bread from heaven," "life-giving water," and sunlight that causes the seed of the human heart to germinate and grow. Of its influence on individual growth He says:

Through the Teachings of this Day Star of Truth every man will advance and develop until he attaineth the station at which he can manifest all the potential forces with which his inmost true self hath been endowed.[316]

Now let us consider the second distinguishing attribute of the Divine Word:

The Hidden Mysteries

According to Bahá'u'lláh, the Word of God is the storehouse not only of infinite creative power but of infinite meaning:

"Know assuredly . . . that its meaning can never be exhausted."[317] Each of the revealed utterances, He teaches, can
be understood on countless levels, and within each level there
are unnumbered implications—some veiled, others obvious.

In His own commentaries on other scripture, Bahá'u'lláh
often returns to this theme. Regarding a Gospel passage, He
writes: "This servant will now share with thee a dewdrop out
of the fathomless ocean of the truths treasured in these holy
words."[318] He then spends many pages unfolding the author's
purpose and intent. Of a similar verse from the Koran He
says: "Were We to expound its inner meanings and unfold its
hidden mysteries, eternity would never suffice to exhaust their
import, nor would the universe be capable of hearing
them!"[319] Finally, concerning His own words He makes this
astounding assertion:

> My holy, My divinely ordained Revelation may be likened
> unto an ocean in whose depths are concealed innumerable
> pearls of great price, of surpassing luster. It is the duty of
> every seeker to bestir himself and strive to attain the shores
> of this ocean, so that he may, in proportion to the eagerness
> of his search and the efforts he hath exerted, partake of such
> benefits as have been pre-ordained in God's irrevocable and
> hidden Tablets.[320]

Nor is any seeker restricted to the "shores of this ocean,"
for Bahá'u'lláh writes elsewhere: "Immerse yourselves in the
ocean of My words, that ye may unravel its secrets, and discover all the pearls of wisdom that lie hid in its depths."[321]

Diving into the Divine Ocean

When we dive for pearls in a literal ocean, we gain more than
pearls: We experience the force and beauty of the ocean itself.
So it is when we dive for "pearls of wisdom" in the symbolic
ocean of revelation—"the Ocean Whose waters refresh, by
virtue of the Will of God, the souls of men."[322] By searching
out the deeper meanings and hidden implications of Bahá'u'-
lláh's writings, we experience directly their vitalizing power.

We can never do this merely by skimming the surface—a point Bahá'u'lláh makes succinctly in the following prayer:

> Number me not with them who read Thy words and fail to find Thy hidden gift which, as decreed by Thee, is contained therein, and which quickeneth the souls of Thy creatures and the hearts of Thy servants.[323]

What does this mean, in practical terms, to an inquirer who seeks to determine whether the words of Bahá'u'lláh are divine or human in origin? Simply this: Plunge into a personal study of His writings! Do not rely on the opinions, interpretations, or commentaries of others: Go directly to the source. Read Bahá'u'lláh with an open mind and an open heart; delve below the surface to determine whether His words really do contain "hidden pearls" of meaning and implication. If they seem to do so, then explore and reflect upon those deeper meanings. This in no way implies that one must start out by believing Bahá'u'lláh is Who He claims to be; the goal, after all, is to find out. Nor does it mean that an uncommitted reader must necessarily agree with everything that Bahá'u'lláh says. If, at some point, one comes to believe in Bahá'u'lláh's divine authority, then logically one must also believe in His teachings—but an investigator is under no such obligation. The point is not to agree but to understand and, in seeking that understanding, to put oneself in a position to experience spiritual transformation.

The late Dr. Daniel C. Jordan, a Bahá'í who was a psychologist and educator, analyzes this process of transformation in a groundbreaking paper entitled "Becoming Your True Self". He makes one particularly crucial point:

> Personal transformation is a fundamental reason that people are attracted to the Faith, develop conviction as to its truth, and finally become Bahá'ís. The reason is simple. People who come in contact with the Faith and feel themselves being transformed by it have an experience that is self-validating. No one can take that experience away from them and no intellectual argument can make it appear insignificant or unreal. Feeling oneself becoming the best of what

one can potentially be constitutes the highest joy. It promotes a sense of self-worth, obviates the need for expressing hostility, and guarantees a compassionate social conscience— all prerequisites of world unity and peace.[324]

Immersing ourselves in the "ocean" of Bahá'u'lláh's writings is easy but not necessarily effortless. Bahá'u'lláh, as quoted earlier, states that the benefits one derives will be "in proportion to the eagerness of his search and the efforts he hath exerted." For Bahá'ís, the study of their sacred texts is a lifetime endeavor; it requires, among other things, willingness to entertain new ideas and to relinquish cherished prejudices and misconceptions as their understanding grows. Shoghi Effendi writes: "The more we read the Writings, the more truths we can find in them, the more we will see that our previous notions were erroneous."[325]

How one proceeds will necessarily depend on one's interests and spiritual orientation. One who believes in God, for example, and who feels inclined to turn towards Him in prayer, may try using Bahá'u'lláh's written prayers in his or her personal devotions. There are several translated volumes of such prayers, covering every imaginable need and topic— prayers for insight, for spiritual development, for aid and assistance, for praise and thanksgiving, for special occasions, for friends and family, and for innumerable other purposes. (Bahá'ís can and do pray in their own words, but they believe the prayers of Bahá'u'lláh, being divinely revealed, have a special potency that no human speech can match.) An agnostic or atheist will probably take a different approach (since one may well feel hypocritical speaking to a being in whom one does not believe). Such an approach might consist simply of meditating on Bahá'u'lláh's writings. Bahá'u'lláh Himself states that "One hour's reflection is preferable to seventy years of pious worship."[326]

One may choose a specific theme—life after death, world peace, the nature of God, or any other subject in which one takes an interest—and explore what Bahá'u'lláh says about it, pulling together His statements from various places in various books. Often, in this way, one will gain some sudden insight by realizing that a seemingly unrelated statement actually has a direct bearing on the matter. Or one may take a specific book by Bahá'u'lláh and study it from beginning to end— perhaps His Book of Certitude, in which He explores the symbolic meaning of age-old prophecy; or His Hidden Words, which sets forth the essentials of good character and spiritual development; or His Seven Valleys, in which He defines true mysticism; or His Epistle to the Son of the Wolf, in which He reminisces about His own life and presents a mini-anthology of His earlier writings. There are many others, including compilations of His most important letters and essays. The approach is less important than the effort, for Bahá'u'lláh promises divine assistance to anyone who sincerely tries to uncover the truth: "Whoso maketh efforts for Us," He says, quoting the Koran, "in Our ways shall We assuredly guide him."[327]

If Bahá'u'lláh is really the Voice of God, then by undertaking such an experiment open-mindedly and with reasonable patience, we should soon enough sense the superhuman power and potency with which He claims His words are charged: "Though he may, at first, remain unaware of its effect, yet the virtue of the grace vouchsafed unto him must sooner or later exercise its influence upon his soul." By putting this promise to the test, we gain the most direct and important evidence imaginable in our quest.

The Bahá'í Community

While personal exposure and introspection are the best ways to test the creative power of any purported revelation, they are not the only ways. We must expect any phenomenon so remarkable to have social consequences that we can investigate empirically. "Such," says Bahá'u'lláh, "is the binding force of the Word of God, which uniteth the hearts of them that have renounced all else but Him. . . ."[328]

This statement may surprise some people. There is an opinion, fashionable in some circles, that religion is the world's primary cause of war, disunity, and intolerance; that all human progress is achieved not because of, but in spite of, religion; and that society really would be better off without it. Whenever religion does cease to bring about love and unity, Bahá'ís would agree that its absence is preferable, for they believe the primary purpose of religion is the promotion of love and unity. Does it do this—or are the cynics correct in arguing that it does the opposite?

A Bahá'í would reply that religion serves its unifying purpose so long as its adherents remain true to the vision and spirit of the Manifestation of God Who revealed it. True religion is more than stately buildings; it is more than formal creeds and ceremonies; it is more than choirs, or stained glass, or any of the other outward trappings we may associate with it. These things are neither wrong nor harmful in themselves, but they are not what religion is about. "The essence of religion," says Bahá'u'lláh, "is to testify unto that which the Lord hath revealed, and follow that which He hath ordained in His mighty Book."[329] If we disregard religious institutions and look instead at the historical effects of the world's holy books, what do we see?

We see, with unmistakable clarity, that those books collectively have provided the most powerful unifying, civilizing force in human history. Every world faith has begun in darkest obscurity with the teachings of some lone individual—a Christ, a Buddha, a Muḥammad—Who claimed to be the mouthpiece of an invisible Supreme Intelligence. In each case the teachings of the founder were compiled into a book that became the rallying point for the religious community. Each religion grew slowly, usually over a period of centuries, and always against violent resistance, to establish itself as a major force in society. Each one, in doing so, brought under its umbrella hundreds of formerly hostile tribes, nationalities, cults, and cultures, infusing into its members a higher loyalty and a spirit of brotherhood under one God. This unifying impulse, on each such occasion, has brought into being a new civilization more advanced than any that previously had appeared.

This recurring cycle is more than a mere fact of history. It is the central, most significant fact of history. Unfortunately, every cycle has a down side as well as an up side. The down side is that humankind eventually loses touch with the pure teachings of the religion's founder. Prophetic enthusiasm gives way to custom and complacency. Then crusades and inquisitions are launched in the name of Christ, Who commanded His followers to turn the other cheek[330] and "Put up again thy sword into his place."[331] Then holy wars are waged in the name of Muḥammad, Who used force only in self-defense, and Who said: "Let there be no compulsion in religion."[332] Then it becomes easy for intellectuals, seeing religion in its decay, to condemn it as a source of hatred and fanaticism.

This is why, Bahá'ís believe, religion must be periodically renewed. This renewal cannot be accomplished by ecumenical movements that reach into the past in an effort to recapture the pristine purity of their faith. It can only be renewed by God, speaking through a new Messenger, adapting His laws to the new age, and providing new teachings in accordance with humanity's readiness.

Whatever our feelings about religion, we can hardly deny that the most influential books in history have been the world's great religious scriptures—the Bhagavad-Gita, the Upanishads, the Zend-Avesta, the Bible, the Koran. These, to an incomparably greater extent than the works of any secular writer or philosopher, have shaped the course of civilization; they have also uplifted thousands of millions of individual lives. As the Bahá'í writer Marzieh Gail once expressed it, "How many homes have ever had an Old Family Aristotle?" Viewing the matter in this way, we see why Bahá'u'lláh would say "The Word of God is the king of words and its pervasive influence is incalculable. It hath ever dominated and will continue to dominate the realm of being."[333]

I have suggested that if Bahá'u'lláh's words are genuine revelation, the creative force they embody can be expected to have observable social consequences. The implications of this point should now be a bit clearer. If Bahá'u'lláh is Who He claims to be, then the emerging worldwide Bahá'í community is actually the embryo of a new civilization, just as the early Jewish, Christian, or Muslim communities, at comparable stages of development, were embryonic civilizations. In that case it should display a dynamic cohesiveness, an evolutionary vigor contrasting starkly with the social disintegration prevalent in today's world. Such a phenomenon might not be obvious to a casual observer: Arnold Toynbee remarks in *A Study of History* that the Christian Faith, in the Hellenizing world of the second century, loomed no larger than the Bahá'í Faith does in the Westernizing world of today.[334] Still, the signs of such a development, if they exist, should be visible to anyone who consciously looks for them.

Those signs abound. The relative newness and smallness of the Bahá'í Faith serve to render all the more amazing two of its most striking characteristics: its human diversity and its geographical spread.

As to its diversity, the various races, tribes, nationalities, and religious and ethnic backgrounds represented within the Bahá'í community number in the thousands, while the community's continuing expansion leaves all official statistics obsolete long before they can be published. Every attempted membership breakdown runs to many pages of fine print; when we scan those pages, we usually find every human subgroup we have ever heard of, plus countless others we have not.

Marcus Bach, former professor of comparative religion at the University of Iowa, verified this diversity in his travels:

> Wherever I have gone to research the faith called Bahá'í, I have been astonished at what I have found. . . . I am continually intrigued by the Bahá'í people . . . representing the basic cultural and ethnic groups around the world and embracing obscure and little-known localities in far-flung lands where even Christianity has barely gone. . . . I have met

them in the most unexpected places, in a war-torn village in southeast Asia, in African cities, in industrial Mexico, in the executive branches of big industry in Iran, in schools and colleges on foreign campuses, in American cities and villages, wherever people dream of the age-old concept of the brotherhood of man and the fatherhood of God . . . the Bahá'ís are there.[335]

As Bach suggests, the Bahá'í commitment to diversity goes far beyond membership statistics: It transforms the personal lives of its adherents. Long before the civil rights movement in the American South or the dismantling of apartheid in South Africa, Bahá'í communities in those places were actively practicing racial integration and intermarriage. The Bahá'í Faith has brought together Brahmins and untouchables in caste-conscious India, Protestants and Catholics in strife-torn northern Ireland, Jews and Arabs in the Middle East. Robert Semple, a member of the Management Committee of the Presbyterian Church, is among many to make such comments as these:

> . . . nor can one wonder at the rapid growth in Christian Countries of the new Bahá'í World Faith, which is also gaining many adherents among the people of Asia and Africa; for that Faith has as its motive power a burning belief in the Fatherhood of God, the brotherhood of men, of all creeds and races, and, here is the point, like the early Christian Church, it practices what it preaches.[336]

Closely linked to this diversity is the astonishing geographical distribution of the international Bahá'í community. The *Encyclopaedia Britannica,* in its 1988 Yearbook and subsequent annual editions, published a table of comparative statistics for each of the important world religions. While the Bahá'í Faith was among the smallest of these numerically, *Britannica* ranked it as second only to Christianity in the number of countries where it has a "significant following."

In addition to human diversity and geographical spread, the worldwide Bahá'í community displays several other features that testify to the creative power of Bahá'u'lláh's revealed words. Among these is the indivisible unity of the Administrative Order through which Bahá'ís, wherever they reside, conduct and coordinate their activities. To the best of my knowledge, no other widespread, highly diversified religious movement has ever survived for more than a century without dividing into sects and factions.

Organizational unity, however, is simply a vessel for the far more important sense of spiritual fellowship that animates believers. Consider the effect of the Bahá'í belief in progressive revelation. Followers of any and all faiths—Jewish, Buddhist, Muslim, Christian, Hindu, or Zoroastrian—who rally around Bahá'u'lláh do so without sacrificing their spiritual roots. Bahá'ís of Christian background, for example, revere Jesus and the Bible no less than persons who consider themselves Christian in an exclusive sense. To accept Bahá'u'lláh as the spiritual reappearance of Christ is not to deny Christ; it is to follow Him in His Second Coming. Likewise, Bahá'ís of Buddhist origin need not abandon Buddha; those of Muslim background do not desert Muḥammad; and so forth. By accepting Bahá'u'lláh as the Promised One of *all* religions, devotees of diverse faiths find common ground while strengthening and clarifying their traditional beliefs. The result is a vibrant bond of brotherhood that no eclectic or ecumenical movement can duplicate.

A further sign of the community's cohesive vitality is its shared sense of history. Bahá'í historian Douglas Martin expresses the Faith's pride in a legacy that includes, among other things, twenty thousand early martyrs: "Apart from its lively interest in the spiritual giants of earlier Revelations it has its own archetypal heroes and saints (for whom its children are named) whose lives provide moral example and whose spiritual achievements have already begun to evoke the first halting response of Bahá'í artists, writers, and musicians. Today, all around the world, an entire generation of Japanese, Italian, Bolivian, Ugandan, Canadian and Persian children are being educated in this common tradition." Together they are learning, for instance, the story of the mother of Aṣẖraf, a young Persian Bahá'í. The mother was seated in a room with Ashraf's teenage wife when the two women heard an approaching mob chanting anti-Bahá'í hate slogans. Before either could react, someone in the crowd hurled into the room the severed head of Ashraf; whereupon the young bride fainted. The mother, however, calmly washed the blood from her son's head, then threw it back to the crowd with words now cherished by Bahá'ís everywhere: "What we have given to God we do not take back!"

Still another remarkable feature of Bahá'í community life is its effectiveness as a catalyst for harmonious social change. Bahá'í groups and individuals, working at the grassroots level in thousands of localities throughout the planet, are translating Bahá'u'lláh's universal ideals into practical programs of social and economic development. Their achievements have won, and are increasingly winning, not only the admiration but the active support of public and private agencies with which they coordinate their humanitarian efforts.

Combined with its astonishing diversity and its geographical spread, these characteristics—administrative and spiritual unity, a shared sense of history, and a demonstrated commitment to social change—invest the Bahá'í community with a pulsating evolutionary vigor that one must experience to understand. Having experienced it, we are free to explain it in any way we like; what we cannot do is ignore it or deny its reality.

The springboard for this discussion was Bahá'u'lláh's teaching that the revealed Word of God is its own proof by virtue of its inimitable qualities—one of these being the power to bring into being a new civilization. This audacious statement has led us to ask what facts, if any, support the Faith's vision of itself as the nucleus and prototype of a burgeoning world order. Is it reasonable, given conditions within the emerging Bahá'í community, to interpret its existence and momentum as deriving from the same spiritual impulse that produced the great religions and civilizations of the past?

There is, of course, no mathematically rigorous way to answer such a question; sociology is anything but an exact science. But however we interpret these signs, they testify to the awe-inspiring influence that Bahá'u'lláh's words have already exerted, and continue to exert, in the lives of an ever-swelling portion of humanity. Shoghi Effendi sums up the situation:

> The Faith of Bahá'u'lláh has assimilated, by virtue of its creative, its regulative and ennobling energies, the varied races, nationalities, creeds and classes that have sought its shadow, and have pledged unswerving fealty to its cause. It has changed the hearts of its adherents, burned away their prejudices, stilled their passions, exalted their conceptions, ennobled their motives, coordinated their efforts, and transformed their outlook. While preserving their patriotism and safeguarding their lesser loyalties, it has made them lovers of mankind. . . . While maintaining intact their belief in the Divine origin of their respective religions, it has enabled them to visualize the underlying purpose of these religions, to discover their merits, to recognize their sequence, their interdependence, their wholeness and unity. . . .
>
> . . . this world-enfolding System, this many-hued and firmly-knit Fraternity, infus[es] into every man and woman it has won to its cause a faith, a hope, and a vigor that a wayward generation has long lost, and is powerless to recover. They who preside over the immediate destinies of this troubled world, they who are responsible for its chaotic state, its fears, its doubts, its miseries will do well, in their bewilderment, to fix their gaze and ponder in their hearts upon the evidences of this saving grace of the Almighty that lies within their reach—a grace that can ease their burden, resolve their perplexities, and illuminate their path.[337]

Chapter 9

THE BOOK OF GOD IS OPEN

Extraordinary claims require extraordinary evidence.
—*Carl Sagan*

O ye that judge with fairness! If this Cause is to be denied
then what other cause in this world can be vindicated or
deemed worthy of acceptance?
—*Bahá'u'lláh*

No one, as the introduction to this book emphasizes, ever
followed a religion purely on the basis of rational evidence.
Nor should anyone ever do so. If one's heart does not respond
to the Prophet's message with a certainty that goes beyond
words and logic, if it does not ring true in the very core of
one's being, then it is neither wise nor rational to believe.

Just the same, we have at least two compelling reasons to
acquaint ourselves with the logical basis for religious faith.
First, as 'Abdu'l-Bahá explains, "arguments are a guide to the
path and by this the heart will be turned unto the Sun of
Truth. And when the heart is turned unto the Sun, then the
eye will be opened and will recognize the Sun through the Sun
itself."[338] Second, even after one gains assurance, reason can
support and clarify one's intuitive conviction. 'Abdu'l-Bahá
encouraged the believers to "exercise reason, analyze and
logically examine the facts presented so that confidence will
be inspired and faith attained";[339] He advised them to "acquire certainty of knowledge" concerning God and His Manifestations "through proofs and evidences and not through
susceptibilities."[340]

It is therefore necessary to investigate religion just as we would investigate any other aspect of reality. Shoghi Effendi states that the Bahá'í Faith is "scientific in its method"[341] (referring, I assume, to its method of investigating truth, since that is the entire purpose of the scientific method, and since independent investigation of truth is the "first principle" of the Faith).

The scientific method may sound daunting to a nonscientist, but it need not be. It is nothing more than organized common sense. Harking back to chapter 3, we may define scientific method as the *testing* of a proposed *explanation* (or "hypothesis") by means of *data* derived from *experience*. In gathering such data and testing such explanations, one can and should apply every legitimate human faculty—observation, reason, intuition, and validated authority. The process must be potentially *public*; that is, based on data that can be verified, and procedures that can be successfully repeated, by any qualified investigator.

Any set of facts—however large—can be explained in more than one way. This means one can never really "prove" any useful scientific hypothesis. What scientists do, therefore, is to sneak up on an idea from behind: They try by every means at their disposal to disprove it. Each time a hypothesis survives a test that might have disproved it (or at least called it into question), the likelihood grows that it is true, and one's confidence in it increases. When an explanation consistently passes a large number of tests from many different directions, ties together a wide range of observations that previously seemed unrelated, correctly predicts new and unexpected findings, and accounts for a maximum of data with a minimum of complexity, we may rationally embrace that explanation as true (subject always to further testing).

This description is light-years away from popular stereotypes of scientific method, which mistakenly assume that science is concerned only with "laboratory facts" leading to "absolute proof." Any good scientist would scoff at such a notion. In science, as in law, one may hope to prove a hypothesis "beyond a reasonable doubt," but one can never eliminate every vestige of theoretical uncertainty. Once we become accustomed to this idea, there is nothing necessarily unsettling about it. It can be refreshing and even comforting: On the one hand, it allows us to act on our convictions with a high degree of confidence; on the other, it reminds us, ever so gently, that we must always remain open to new ideas and evidence.

There exists a pervasive feeling among Western intellectuals—believers and skeptics alike—that religion is "beyond" science and scientific method. Followers of traditional faiths frequently maintain that religious knowledge is of a higher order than scientific knowledge and that submitting those beliefs to the methods of science would demean or degrade them. Skeptics uphold the distinction for a quite different reason: They feel the basic tenets of religion are either patently superstitious, or else so vague, so unclear in their implications, that no conceivable test could prove them false. This would mean, from a scientific standpoint, that such tenets also could never be proved true. Any statement so general that no possible observation could contradict it, so nebulous that no real-life experience could call it into question, is a statement we can never confirm or validate by scientific means. The best we can do is suspend judgment. Modern doubters would banish all spiritual or mystical thinking to this limbo.

The claim of Bahá'u'lláh presents a ringing challenge to both camps. He identifies Himself as the bearer of a modern-day revelation from God—as One Whose appearance is, moreover, the fulfillment of the promises and prophecies of all other religions. He states His case, however, in terms so specific, so rich with concrete and testable implications, that it is fully open to evaluation by the methods of modern science. He says, for example, that the successive "Manifestations of God" (founders of religion and civilization, of Whom He claims to be the latest) have certain invariable attributes: They are infallible; They are omniscient at will; They see the future; They understand even the hidden secrets of physical reality; They possess innate knowledge not learned or learnable in any school. Their powers and perfections make Them stand out like the sun from ordinary men; Their characters are flawless models of resolve and consistency, even under bitterest adversity; and Their words resonate with creative power—power sufficient to transform individuals and change the course of history. Born in the appalling darkness of nineteenth-century Persia, deprived of anything resembling even a modern elementary school education, Bahá'u'lláh wrote hundreds of works tackling head-on the most intractable problems of today's world—a world not one of His learned contemporaries even dimly visualized. He left, moreover, the legacy of His life, itself an open book of which unnumbered details are preserved and documented.

Today's people of learning can tell us astounding things: the internal structure of the smallest atom, the composition of the farthest star, the appearance of animals that lived eons before the first human being. They deduce these facts from the most insubstantial wisps of evidence: a phantom trail in a cloud chamber, a glimmer of light that traveled towards earth for thousands of millions of years, a handful of fossilized bone splinters. With Bahá'u'lláh, however, the evidence is not wispy; it is mountainous. Cannot the same scientific method used by these intrepid explorers of reality—a method capable of unlocking such marvelous secrets—tell us whether Bahá'u'lláh was Who and What He claimed to be?

This book argues that anyone who really wishes to do so can find out whether Bahá'u'lláh was telling the truth about His identity. It further argues that in a world pregnant with promise on the one hand and dissolving in chaos on the other, we cannot afford to skirt the issue: We need to know whether He really was a Messenger from God. The stakes are extraordinarily high. Moreover, this is an issue that confronts each individual human being. The so-called "leaders of thought," into whose hands humanity seems to entrust its collective conscience, have for well over a century refused to acknowledge or even consider the claim of Bahá'u'lláh—much less examine the supporting evidence He offers.

Against this background, I have presented some of that evidence as I see it:

The writings of Bahá'u'lláh (along with those of the Báb and 'Abdu'l-Bahá, which bear the stamp of His authority) are liberally sprinkled with prophecies. These prophecies are detailed and specific; they name names and give locations; most refer to an identifiable time frame of limited duration. They cover, according to Bahá'u'lláh Himself, "most of the things which have come to pass on this earth" in such wise that "No possibility is left for anyone either to turn aside or protest."[342] Most of them ran counter to the conventional wisdom of the time. All were published well in advance of the events to which they refer, giving skeptics every opportunity to show that Bahá'u'lláh was capable of making mistakes. Yet not one prophecy proved to be in error. The great majority of these have been spectacularly fulfilled, sometimes at the last possible moment and against seemingly insuperable odds. The fulfillment of the few remaining others seems to be materializing before our eyes.

Prophecies of a historical nature taken from the Bahá'í scriptures include: the unexpected defeat and downfall of Napoleon III, emperor of France; the defeat of Germany in two bloody wars, resulting in the "lamentations of Berlin"; the conspicuous success and stability of Queen Victoria's reign; the dismissal of 'Álí Páshá, prime minister of Turkey; the subsequent overthrow and assassination of his chief, Sultán 'Abdu'l-'Azíz; the dismantling of the Ottoman Empire and the extinction of the "outward splendor" of its capital, Constantinople; the fate of Persia's Náṣiri'd-Dín Sháh as an "object lesson for the world"; the restrictions imposed upon the Persian monarchy by that country's Constitutional Revolution; the precipitous decline in the fortunes and prestige of monarchy throughout the world; the steady erosion of political and social power wielded by ecclesiastical institutions; the extinction of the caliphate, which held a position in Sunní Islam similar to that of the papacy in Roman Catholicism; the spread of communism—the "Movement of the Left"—and its rise to world power; the subsequent collapse of that same movement as a direct result of its obsession with forced economic equality; the rise of Israel as a Jewish homeland; the persecution of Jews on the European continent, which materialized in the Nazi holocaust; America's violent racial struggles, which, as foretold, threatened the country's survival by polarizing it during the tensest moments of the Cold War; Bahá'u'lláh's own release from the prison of 'Akká and the pitching of His tent on Mount Carmel; the seizure and desecration in Baghdad of Bahá'u'lláh's house—a Bahá'í shrine—by Muslim fanatics; and the complete collapse of every attempt to create sects and factions within the Bahá'í Faith.

Bahá'í prophecies that anticipated scientific discoveries include: the explosive acceleration of scientific and technological progress; the discovery of atomic weaponry as a force capable of poisoning the entire atmosphere of the earth; the transmutation of elements, a long-sought technology now known to be responsible for nuclear power and which, as foreseen by Bahá'u'lláh, has therefore brought humanity to the brink of catastrophe; the discovery that complex chemical elements evolve in nature from simpler ones; the recognition that planets are a universal consequence of normal star formation; space travel "with the rapidity of rising lightning," reaching out not only to other planets but "from the globe of the earth to the globe of the sun"; the realization that certain forms of cancer are communicable; the failure of all efforts to identify a "missing link" or common ancestor between man and ape; the collapse in physics of the theory of a mechanical ether and its replacement by an intellectual abstraction ("spacetime"); and the breakdown of mechanical models as a basis for understanding the physical world.

Other prophecies of Bahá'u'lláh and 'Abdu'l-Bahá seem intimately related to events taking place in the world today. These foretold, among other things, that a worldwide tide of oppression would be followed by a renaissance of liberty, leading ultimately to "unity in freedom"; that a "new world order" would emerge in which all nations, driven by "imperative necessity," would collectively resist aggression by any recalcitrant member; that these and other trends would lead ultimately to "the unity of nations—a unity which in this century will be firmly established, causing all the peoples of the world to regard themselves as citizens of one common fatherland"; the cataclysmic "rolling up" of the "present-day Order" as a prelude to world peace; the preponderating role to be played by America in the forging of that peace; the emergence of the Bahá'í Faith from obscurity and, as a temporary consequence, its repression in various parts of the world.

Bahá'u'lláh's seeming ability to peer into the future was not the only sign of His otherworldly knowledge. He spent His entire life in an atmosphere dominated by nineteenth-century Islamic fundamentalism, first in Persia, then as a prisoner of the Turks. He received only the most perfunctory tutoring, never went to school, never studied Western literature, indeed never experienced any outward influence that might plausibly have broadened His horizons or countered any of the deleterious effects of His early conditioning. Yet there is the startling modernity of His writing—a modernity that becomes more, rather than less, conspicuous every year as His social prescriptions appear increasingly relevant to world events, and which has evoked praise and appreciation from a host of independent observers. It was Bahá'u'lláh Who gave to the world its first comprehensive inventory of the spiritual and humanitarian principles that today constitute the essence of leading-edge thought. It was Bahá'u'lláh Who, long before such a concept had occurred to even His most advanced contemporaries, first described the world in detail as a global village and perceptively analyzed the problems it would face. He wrote with high eloquence and technical virtuosity not only in His native Persian, but also in Arabic—a language He never had any opportunity to study, yet which, according to scholars, cannot be mastered without years of arduous formal training. He composed His writings in both languages without premeditation, hesitation, or revision, dictating for hours at a time with such speed as to tax the most skilled stenographers. These spontaneous outpourings consistently display the very qualities one would expect of revelation: highly polished style, lucid organization, and exceptional literary force. At the same time, they exclude the lapses and inconsistencies typical of human extemporaneous rambling.

Bahá'u'lláh's personality and character were what one would logically expect of a Divine Manifestation. His personality was by all accounts so radiant, so majestic and magnetic as to lift Him high above the rank and file of humanity. Even hardened skeptics and high-ranking officials, upon meeting Him, would bow spontaneously; would-be debaters would find themselves speechless and humble in His presence. His enemies in the clergy warned curiosity-seekers to avoid Him lest they fall under His spell; they circulated absurd theories to account for His soul-stirring impact on credible witnesses. Bahá'u'lláh's character was as outstanding and unusual as His force of personality. His lifelong conduct was marked by courage, a passion for justice, self-sacrificing love for humanity, and airtight symmetry of word and deed.

Beyond such considerations as these, Bahá'u'lláh offers a subjective but highly intriguing proof of His divine mission: He claims—and millions of His followers believe—that His very words throb with spiritual power such as no human author can duplicate. He invites seekers to immerse themselves in the ocean of His words and, by seeking out the "hidden pearls" of meaning those words contain, to experience for themselves the creative and transforming influence of this power. This personal experiment enables any inquirer to evaluate, through the promptings of his or her own heart, whether Bahá'u'lláh's writings are of divine or merely human origin. One can further test such a power by observing its apparent effects in the emergence of the Bahá'í worldwide community.

These are some of the findings that, in my experience, seem to emerge from a systematic probing of Bahá'u'lláh's claim. No one needs to take my word for any of these statements. The evidence is open to any seeker who chooses to examine it. Let us suppose, therefore, that others repeat this investigation and verify these findings. In that case, how are we to explain them?

To me, the simplest, most elegant explanation is also the most obvious: Bahá'u'lláh's claim is true. He spoke and acted not of His own accord, but at the bidding of an all-encompassing Higher Power. This hypothesis neatly correlates and predicts everything we can discover about Bahá'u'lláh through empirical study. It is a scientific hypothesis in the strictest sense of the word; that is, any number of simple observations could conceivably remove it from serious consideration. Yet those observations, when performed, consistently have the opposite effect: Rather than rule it out, they fall into place in such a way as to strengthen our faith in the hypothesis.

Moreover, this explanation is, for me, the one that feels right. I try it on for size and find that somehow, in some way I cannot quite explain, it fits. It fits everything I can learn about Bahá'u'lláh, about myself, about other people, about life, religion, civilization, and whatnot. This intuitive "ring of truth" is not a strictly scientific consideration, although every true scientist uses it in evaluating scientific conclusions. It is a personal sense of rightness one cannot easily convey to others.

Does this mean one can "prove" Bahá'u'lláh was Who He claimed to be? That depends. When I investigate the evidence for myself, I find it both satisfying and compelling. I therefore choose to act on it, confident that my decision to do so is rational and correct. Still, we may recognize that there are other ways to explain the facts about Bahá'u'lláh; other observers may prefer one of these alternative explanations.

A professor of the Moody Bible Institute, asked to comment on the Bahá'í Faith, replied: "There is no question about it. It is the work of the Devil." There we have an undeniably straightforward explanation which, with one bold stroke, covers all the facts—the successful prophecies, the scientific insights, the innate abilities, the uncanny attraction of Bahá'u'-lláh's presence, and all the rest. I have not the first clue as to how one might disprove this hypothesis. My personal reason for rejecting it has to do with the words of Jesus Christ (Whose divine authority every Bahá'í accepts without reservation): "Ye shall know them by their fruits. Do men gather grapes of thorns, or figs of thistles?"[343] Different readers interpret this touchstone in different ways; it may well have more than one correct interpretation. But whenever I try to apply it in any reasonable manner, it strengthens my confidence in the divine origin of Bahá'u'lláh's revelation. The overwhelmingly positive results, or "fruits," of His life and teachings speak for themselves.

We might attempt to explain Bahá'u'lláh as a time traveler from the distant future or as a space alien with telepathic powers. The former hypothesis would account for His scientific and prophetic knowledge; the latter might explain His extraordinary subjective impact on those who met Him. We could say He was a saintly superpsychic who—simply to perpetrate an elaborate hoax—willingly endured agonizing persecution and humiliation, a kind of living crucifixion lasting forty years. However amusing such ideas may seem, they remind us that there is no mathematically rigorous way to exclude even the most fanciful alternatives.

Any hypothesis intended to account for the qualities, accomplishments and motives of Bahá'u'lláh must also explain the appearance of similar signs in the Báb and 'Abdu'l-Bahá. The rapid and successive appearance of three figures with such unheard-of abilities is itself a phenomenon almost as remarkable as any single achievement by any one of them.

One may play endlessly with speculative theories designed to account for the facts surrounding the rise and establishment of the Bahá'í revelation. Most such theories, it seems to me, ignore at least some of the facts and still bog down in complexity. I know only one hypothesis that (1) explains all the facts in a simple, straightforward manner, (2) yields a variety of testable implications, and (3) survives every attempt to discredit it through observation and experience. That hypothesis is the one proposed earlier: Bahá'u'lláh really was a Manifestation of God.

Let Bahá'u'lláh state the case in His own words:

> Consider this wronged One. Though the clearest proofs attest the truth of His Cause; though the prophecies He, in an unmistakable language, hath made have been fulfilled; though, in spite of His not being accounted among the learned, His being unschooled and inexperienced in the disputations current among the divines, He hath rained upon men the showers of His manifold and Divinely-inspired knowledge; yet, behold how this generation hath rejected His authority, and rebelled against Him.... God grant that, with a penetrating vision and radiant heart, thou mayest observe the things that have come to pass and are now happening, and, pondering them in thine heart, mayest recognize that which most men have, in this Day, failed to perceive.[344]

* * *

This book has set forth, to the best of my ability and understanding, the rational basis for my personal belief in Bahá'u'lláh. In writing it I have discussed a variety of subjects and presented a number of related arguments. Certain things, however, I have refrained from doing:

(1) I did not begin by attempting to demonstrate the existence of God through logical arguments. This does not mean I am writing only for those who already believe in God, nor does it mean I expect the reader necessarily to accept His existence as self-evident. It simply means I believe the strongest proof of God's reality is His periodic intervention in history through the founders of world religions—Moses, Christ, Buddha, Muḥammad, and all the others. Above all, it is the recurrence of His self-revelation in the person of Bahá'u'lláh, in this promised day of all ages. If we discover a broadcast coming over a radio, we need not precede our discussion of that discovery by proving logically the existence of a distant broadcaster. The voice of the broadcaster is proof enough. In a similar vein, Bahá'u'lláh says that "the gift of Divine Revela-

tion . . . is God's supreme testimony, the clearest evidence of His truth."[345]

(2) While discussing the fulfillment of prophecies contained in Bahá'í scripture, I have neglected a large category of related evidence: the fulfillment by Bahá'u'lláh Himself of prophecies from the Bible and other ancient scriptures. My reason for omitting this important topic is simply that it is treated fully in many other sources. Those wishing to pursue the matter are referred to such books as *Thief in the Night* by William Sears and *I Shall Come Again* by Hushidar Motlagh.

(3) I have not mentioned physical miracles. Every religion has its tales of supernatural healings and other wonderful acts purportedly performed by its founder; the Bahá'í Faith is no exception. Bahá'ís do not deny the reality of such happenings, for they believe God's Manifestations embody all His attributes —including divine omnipotence. Still, Bahá'ís are forbidden to offer such events as proofs of their religion's validity. Most "miracle" stories, even if true, are undocumented and anecdotal. Some refer to events that took place only in an inward or metaphorical sense. Even those that may have occurred literally are significant, as evidence, only to those who actually see them. Accordingly, I have omitted any and all reports of inexplicable physical phenomena. Certain abilities cited as evidence by Bahá'u'lláh Himself, such as prophecy and rapid revelation-writing, may in some sense be regarded as miraculous; but that sense clearly is a non-physical one.

(4) I have not presumed to suggest what any reader should do about the conclusions offered here. Any person who, after investigation, accepts the claim of Bahá'u'lláh must of course decide how to integrate that insight into his or her life. Religious conviction has obvious and urgent implications for action. But such decisions are logically distinct from questions of truth or falsity. The more determined one is to follow the facts wherever they lead, without regard to personal considerations, the more reliably one will be able to determine Bahá'u'lláh's real identity.

That said, it remains my earnest conviction that incalculable benefits await anyone willing to investigate dispassionately the claim of Bahá'u'lláh and to follow through on the results of that investigation. If society collectively is not yet ready to reap those benefits, it will be ready in the none-too-distant future. Meanwhile, we as individuals can enjoy those benefits today. We can also hasten that future for the society in which we live. There is nothing to stop us.

"The Book of God is wide open," writes Bahá'u'lláh,

> and His Word is summoning mankind unto Him. No more than a mere handful, however, hath been found willing to cleave to His Cause, or to become the instruments for its promotion. These few have been endued with the Divine Elixir that can, alone, transmute into purest gold the dross of the world, and have been empowered to administer the infallible remedy for all the ills that afflict the children of men.[346]

> Take heed that ye do not vacillate in your determination to embrace the truth of this Cause—a Cause through which the potentialities of the might of God have been revealed, and His sovereignty established. With faces beaming with joy, hasten ye unto Him. . . . Through it the poor have been enriched, the learned enlightened, and the seekers enabled to ascend unto the presence of God. Beware, lest ye make it a cause of dissension amongst you. Be ye as firmly settled as the immovable mountain in the Cause of your Lord, the Mighty, the Loving.[347]

NOTES

INTRODUCTION

1. 'Abdu'l-Bahá, in *Bahá'í World Faith*, pp. 383–4.
2. 'Abdu'l-Bahá, *Promulgation*, p. 327.

Chapter 1: *A TURNING POINT IN HISTORY*

3. Matthew 6:10.
4. Isaiah 2:4.
5. John 10:16.
6. Isaiah 11:9.
7. Bahá'u'lláh, *Gleanings*, III, p. 5.
8. Shoghi Effendi, *Promised Day*, ¶302.
9. See 'Abdu'l-Bahá, *Bahá'í World Faith*, p. 383.
10. Bahá'u'lláh, *Summons*, Súriy-i-Haykal, ¶192.
11. Bahá'u'lláh, *Gleanings*, XVIII, p. 45.
12. Ibid., VII, p. 11.
13. Ibid., L, p. 103.

Chapter 2: *DIVINE SPRINGTIME*

14. Ibid., CXVII, p. 250.
15. Bahá'u'lláh, *Hidden Words*, Arabic, no. 1.
16. Bahá'u'lláh, *Tablets*, p. 157.
17. Bahá'u'lláh, *Gleanings*, XXXIV, pp. 78–9.
18. 'Abdu'l-Bahá, *Paris Talks*, no. 44:14, 44:26.
19. 'Abdu'l-Bahá, *Promulgation*, p. 250.
20. 'Abdu'l-Bahá, *Some Answered Questions*, p. 154.
21. Ibid., p. 163.
22. 'Abdu'l-Bahá, quoted in Shoghi Effendi, *World Order*, p. 39.
23. Bahá'u'lláh, quoted in Shoghi Effendi, *Promised Day*, ¶39.
24. Shoghi Effendi, *God Passes By*, p. 222.
25. See Bahá'u'lláh, *Kitáb-i-Aqdas*, ¶121, ¶174, p. 141, n1.
26. See statistical table compiled by David B. Barrett, *1989 Britannica Book of the Year*, p. 299.
27. Shoghi Effendi, *God Passes By*, p. 139.
28. Shoghi Effendi's secretary on his behalf, 21 April 1939, quoted in *Lights of Guidance*, no. 1574, p. 478.
29. Bahá'u'lláh, quoted in Shoghi Effendi, *World Order*, p. 113.

30. Bahá'u'lláh, *Gleanings*, XXVII, p. 65.
31. Ibid., CIX, p. 215.
32. Ibid., XXVII, p. 66.
33. Bahá'u'lláh, *Kitáb-i-Íqán*, ¶196.
34. 'Abdu'l-Bahá, *Some Answered Questions*, pp. 233–4.
35. Bahá'u'lláh, *Gleanings*, XXI, p. 50.
36. Ibid., XIX, pp. 47–9.
37. Shoghi Effendi, *Unfolding Destiny*, p. 449.
38. 'Abdu'l-Bahá, *Some Answered Questions*, pp. 100–2.
39. Ibid., p. 173.
40. Bahá'u'lláh, quoted in Shoghi Effendi, *God Passes By*, p. 119.
41. Bahá'u'lláh, *Gleanings*, XXII, p. 55.
42. Bahá'u'lláh, quoted in Shoghi Effendi, *World Order*, p. 113.
43. Ibid., p. 115.
44. Ibid.
45. Bahá'u'lláh, quoted in ibid., p. 116.
46. Bahá'u'lláh, *Kitáb-i-Aqdas*, ¶37.

Chapter 3: *LIFE'S LABORATORY*

47. Bahá'u'lláh, *Kitáb-i-Íqán*, ¶14.
48. See 'Abdu'l-Bahá, *Bahá'í World Faith*, p. 383.
49. 'Abdu'l-Bahá, *Promulgation*, p. 227.
50. 'Abdu'l-Bahá, quoted in Shoghi Effendi, *World Order*, pp. 127–8.
51. Hawking, *Brief History of Time*, p. 10.
52. Bahá'u'lláh, *Gleanings*, CLIII, p. 328.

Chapter 4: *BAHÁ'Í PROPHECIES: HISTORICAL EVENTS*

53. Deut. 18:21–2.
54. Bahá'u'lláh, *Tablets*, p. 241.
55. Bahá'u'lláh, *Epistle*, pp. 148–50.
56. Bahá'u'lláh, *Gleanings*, p. 7.
57. Bahá'u'lláh, *Summons*, Súriy-i-Mulúk, ¶12.
58. Shoghi Effendi, *Promised Day*, ¶124.
59. Bahá'u'lláh, *Summons*, Súriy-i-Haykal, ¶138.
60. 'Abdu'l-Bahá, *Some Answered Questions*, p. 33.
61. Ibid.
62. Shoghi Effendi, *Promised Day*, ¶126.
63. Bahá'u'lláh, *Kitáb-i-Aqdas*, ¶86.
64. Ibid., ¶90.
65. 'Abdu'l-Bahá, quoted in Esslemont, *New Era*, p. 244.
66. 'Abdu'l-Bahá, quoted in Shoghi Effendi, *World Order*, p. 30.
67. Ibid., p. 46.
68. Bahá'u'lláh, *Summons*, Súriy-i-Haykal, ¶171, ¶172, ¶173.
69. Shoghi Effendi, *Promised Day*, ¶163.

70. Bahá'u'lláh, *Summons*, Súriy-i-Ra'ís, ¶2.
71. Bahá'u'lláh, *Summons*, Lawḥ-i-Ra'ís, ¶7, ¶9.
72. Bahá'u'lláh, *Summons*, Lawḥ-i-Fu'ád, ¶13.
73. Bahá'u'lláh, *Summons*, Súriy-i-Mulúk, ¶60, ¶61.
74. Bahá'u'lláh, *Summons*, Súriy-i-Ra'ís, ¶5.
75. Bahá'u'lláh, *Kitáb-i-Aqdas*, ¶89.
76. Bahá'u'lláh, *Summons*, Súriy-i-Haykal, ¶221.
77. Bahá'u'lláh, quoted in Shoghi Effendi, *God Passes By*, p. 224.
78. Ibid., p. 225.
79. Ibid.
80. Quoted by Shoghi Effendi, *Promised Day*, ¶169.
81. Bahá'u'lláh, *Kitáb-i-Aqdas*, ¶93.
82. See Shoghi Effendi, *Promised Day*, pp. 68–70.
83. 'Abdu'l-Bahá, quoted in *Diary of Juliet Thompson*, p. 100.
84. See ibid., p. 26.
85. Ibid., p. 101.
86. Bahá'u'lláh, *Gleanings*, p. 216.
87. Bahá'u'lláh, quoted in Shoghi Effendi, *Promised Day*, ¶175.
88. Bahá'u'lláh, *Summons*, Súriy-i-Mulúk, ¶12.
89. Shoghi Effendi, *Promised Day*, ¶118.
90. See Bahá'u'lláh, quoted in ibid., ¶176–¶186.
91. Bahá'u'lláh, *Tablets*, p. 28.
92. Bahá'u'lláh, quoted in Shoghi Effendi, *Promised Day*, ¶201.
93. Bahá'u'lláh, *Summons*, Súriy-i-Haykal, ¶102, ¶103, ¶112.
94. Ibid., ¶112.
95. The Báb, quoted in Shoghi Effendi, *God Passes By*, p. 231.
96. Ibid.
97. Bahá'u'lláh, quoted in Shoghi Effendi, *Promised Day*, ¶154.
98. Shoghi Effendi, *God Passes By*, p. 228.
99. Shoghi Effendi, *Promised Day*, ¶187.
100. See Shoghi Effendi, *World Order*, p. 17.
101. 'Abdu'l-Bahá, quoted in ibid., p. 30.
102. Shoghi Effendi, *Promised Day*, ¶276.
103. 'Abdu'l-Bahá, *Some Answered Questions*, p. 274.
104. Ibid., pp. 65–6.
105. 'Abdu'l-Bahá, *Promulgation*, p. 414.
106. 'Abdu'l-Bahá, quoted in Shoghi Effendi, *Advent*, p. 33.
107. 'Abdu'l-Bahá, letter to Antoinette Crump Cone, *Star of the West*, vol. XXII, 24 June 1921, p. 121.
108. See Morrison, *To Move the World*, pp. 129–30.
109. 'Abdu'l-Bahá, quoted by Zia M. Bagdadi in *Star of the West*, vol. XXII, 24 June 1921, p. 121.
110. Shoghi Effendi, *Citadel*, p. 126.
111. *The New York Times*, article 26 February 1978, cited in "Long Hot Summers of Discontent" (editorial), *World Order*, Summer 1979, p. 2.
112. "Long Hot Summers of Discontent" (editorial), *World Order*, Summer 1979, p. 2.

113. 'Abdu'l-Bahá, quoted in Shoghi Effendi, *Advent*, p. 33.
114. 'Abdu'l-Bahá, quoted by Zia M. Bagdadi in *Star of the West*, vol. XXII, 24 June 1921, p. 120.
115. Bahá'u'lláh, quoted in Shoghi Effendi, *Promised Day*, ¶100.
116. Bahá'u'lláh, quoted in Balyuzi, *'Abdu'l-Bahá*, p. 39.
117. 'Abdu'l-Bahá, quoted in Shoghi Effendi, *God Passes By*, p. 193.
118. Bahá'u'lláh, *Gleanings*, LVII, p. 114.
119. Ibid., LVIII, p. 115.
120. Ibid.
121. Bahá'u'lláh, quoted in Shoghi Effendi, *God Passes By*, p. 99.
122. Ibid.
123. Bahá'u'lláh, quoted in Shoghi Effendi, *World Order*, p. 109.
124. 'Abdu'l-Bahá, quoted in *Messages from the Universal House of Justice*, no. 75.14.
125. Shoghi Effendi, *God Passes By*, p. 326.
126. Shoghi Effendi, *World Order*, p. 23.

Chapter 5: *BAHÁ'Í PROPHECIES: SCIENTIFIC DISCOVERIES*

127. 'Abdu'l-Bahá, *Some Answered Questions*, p. 283.
128. 'Abdu'l-Bahá, *Tablets*, p. 608.
129. 'Abdu'l-Bahá, *Some Answered Questions*, p. 23.
130. Ibid., p. 24.
131. Bahá'u'lláh, *Kitáb-i-Aqdas*, ¶99.
132. Bahá'u'lláh, quoted in Shoghi Effendi, *World Order*, p. 202.
133. Bahá'u'lláh, *Summons*, Súriy-i-Haykal, ¶47.
134. Bahá'u'lláh, *Gleanings*, LXXIV, pp. 141–2.
135. Paraphrased by Adib Taherzadeh in *Revelation of Bahá'u'lláh*, vol. III, p. 137.
136. Bahá'u'lláh, quoted in Shoghi Effendi, *World Order*, p. 125.
137. Ibid., p. 107.
138. Cooper, *Meaning and Structure of Physics*, p. 431.
139. Max Born, quoted in Hawking, *Brief History of Time*, p. 156.
140. Bahá'u'lláh, *Gleanings*, CLXIII, pp. 342–3.
141. Bahá'u'lláh, *Tablets*, p. 69.
142. Blomfield, *Chosen Highway*, p. 184.
143. 'Abdu'l-Bahá, in [National Spiritual Assembly of the Bahá'ís of Japan], *Japan*, p. 30.
144. Bahá'u'lláh, *Gleanings*, XCVII, pp. 197–8.
145. Bahá'u'lláh, *Má'idiy-i-Ásimání*, vol. I, p. 41, quoted in Taherzadeh, *Revelation of Bahá'u'lláh*, vol. II, p. 268.
146. Publisher's foreword to 1964 edition, *Some Answered Questions*, p. xv.
147. 'Abdu'l-Bahá, *Some Answered Questions*, p. 181.
148. Carl Sagan, Introduction to Hawking, *Brief History of Time*, p. x.

NOTES

149. Bahá'u'lláh, *Kitáb-i-Íqán*, ¶165–¶166.
150. Shoghi Effendi's secretary on his behalf, quoted in *Lights of Guidance*, no. 1580, p. 479.
151. Bahá'u'lláh, *Gleanings*, LXXXII, p. 163.
152. Gamow, *Birth and Death*, pp. 200–4.
153. See Ferris, *Coming of Age*, p. 167.
154. Carl Sagan, "So Many Suns, So Many Worlds," *Parade*, 9 June 1996, p. 10.
155. *http://www.washington.edu/newsroom/news/2002archive/11-02archive/k112802.html*
156. Bahá'u'lláh, *Gleanings*, LXXXII, p. 163.
157. 'Abdu'l-Bahá, *Bahá'í World Faith*, p. 338.
158. Shoghi Effendi's secretary on his behalf, quoted in *Lights of Guidance*, no. 1581, p. 479.
159. 'Abdu'l-Bahá, paraphrased in Balyuzi, *'Abdu'l-Bahá*, p. 377.
160. 'Abdu'l-Bahá, *Tablets*, vol. 1, p. 32.
161. Clarke, *Profiles of the Future*, p. 121.
162. 'Abdu'l-Bahá, Tablet to an individual believer, October 1921, in *Lights of Guidance*, no. 603, p. 183.
163. Dulbecco and Ginsberg, *Virology*, p. 335.
164. Ibid.
165. Robbins and Kumar, *Basic Pathology*, p. 205.
166. Ibid., p. 207.
167. Cotran, Kumar and Robbins, *Robbins Pathologic Basis of Disease*, p. 1142.
168. Robbins and Kumar, *Basic Pathology*, p. 207.
169. See *http://www.salk.edu/news/releases/details.php?id=6* for Salk's press release describing its study reported in *Nature*, 17 July 2002. The research was carried out by a team led by Matthew Weitzman, a Salk Institute assistant professor of genetics.
170. 'Abdu'l-Bahá, *Some Answered Questions*, p. 123.
171. Ibid., p. 126.
172. Bahá'u'lláh, *Gleanings*, LXXXII, p. 162; 'Abdu'l-Bahá, *Some Answered Questions*, pp. 180, 202–3, 281.
173. 'Abdu'l-Bahá, *Promulgation*, p. 140.
174. 'Abdu'l-Bahá, *Bahá'í World Faith*, p. 338.
175. 'Abdu'l-Bahá, *Some Answered Questions*, pp. 143–4.
176. Ibid., pp. 185–90.
177. Ibid., p. 177.
178. Ibid., p. 184.
179. 'Abdu'l-Bahá, *Promulgation*, pp. 358–9.
180. C. Owen Lovejoy, "Evolution of Human Walking," *Scientific American*, November 1988, p. 89.
181. Ibid., p. 82.
182. Tim Friend, "Skull Alters Notions of Human Origins," *USA Today*, 11 July 2002, p. 1.
183. Quoted in ibid., p. 1.

184. Carl R. Woese, "On the Evolution of Cells," *Proceedings of the National Academy of Sciences*, 25 June 2002, vol. 99, no. 13, pp. 8742-8747. Woese's findings are summarized at *http://www.news.uiuc.edu/scitips/02/0617evoltion.html* in the official press release by the University of Illinois at Urbana-Champaign.

185. "USF biologists investigate gene-thieving sea slugs," *News at USF* (online), University of South Florida, 1 December 2003, *http://usfnews.usf.edu/page.cfm?link=article&aid=216*.

186. Quoted in a book review by James Gorman, *Discover*, January 1983, pp. 83-4.

187. 'Abdu'l-Bahá, *Some Answered Questions*, p. 183.

188. Ibid., p. 83.

189. Ibid., p. 242.

190. Ibid., pp. 84-5.

191. Ibid., p. 83.

192. Ibid., pp. 83-4.

193. Clark, *Einstein*, p. 141.

194. Ferris, *Coming of Age*, p. 364.

195. Misner, Thorne and Wheeler, *Gravitation*, p. 1202; quoted in Ferris, *Coming of Age*, p. 364.

196. Gardner, *Relativity for the Million*, pp. 34-5.

197. Einstein, *Sidelights on Relativity* (Dover: 1983), p. 23. The full text of his address may be downloaded from the World Wide Web at *http://magna.com.au/~prfbrown/aether_0.html*.

198. Eddington, in Wilbur, *Quantum Questions*, p. 189.

199. Ibid., p. 208.

200. Jeans, in Wilbur, *Quantum Questions*, p. 142.

201. Lederman, *The God Particle*, pp. 101, 375.

202. Williams, "Ether," *The Encyclopedia Americana*, 1989, vol. X, p. 609.

203. Charles Misner, quoted in Yourgrau and Breck, eds., *Cosmology, History, and Theology* (New York: Plenum Press, 1977), p. 95; and Ferris, *Coming of Age*, p. 352.

204. 'Abdu'l-Bahá, *Some Answered Questions*, p. 84.

205. Albert Einstein, quoted in Max Born, *The Born-Einstein Letters* (New York: Walker, 1971), p. 82; and Ferris, *Coming of Age*, p. 290. (Einstein's italics).

206. Wolf, *Taking the Quantum Leap*, p. 201.

207. John A. Wheeler, quoted in ibid., p. 152.

208. Niels Bohr, quoted in Ferris, *Coming of Age*, p. 384.

209. John Clauser, quoted in Wolf, *Taking the Quantum Leap*, p. 206.

210. Jeans, in Wilbur, *Quantum Questions*, p. 144.

Chapter 6: *BAHÁ'Í PROPHECIES:*
UNFINISHED BUSINESS

211. Bahá'u'lláh, *Tablets*, p. 241.

212. Bahá'u'lláh, *Epistle,* p. 150.
213. Bahá'u'lláh, quoted in Shoghi Effendi, *Promised Day,* ¶287.
214. 'Abdu'l-Bahá, quoted in Esslemont, *New Era,* pp. 247–8.
215. 'Abdu'l-Bahá, quoted in Shoghi Effendi, *World Order,* p. 39.
216. 'Abdu'l-Bahá, *Promulgation,* p. 167.
217. Universal House of Justice, *Individual Rights and Freedoms in the World Order of Bahá'u'lláh,* p. 31.
218. Bahá'u'lláh, *Gleanings,* CXVII, p. 249.
219. 'Abdu'l-Bahá, quoted in Shoghi Effendi, *World Order,* pp. 37–8.
220. Ibid., p. 38.
221. Ibid., p. 39.
222. Shoghi Effendi, quoted in *Establishing World Peace,* p. 46.
223. Shoghi Effendi, *Promised Day,* ¶298.
224. 'Abdu'l-Bahá, *Selections,* no. 15.7; the Universal House of Justice, *Messages,* no. 55.5.
225. 'Abdu'l-Bahá, *Selections,* no. 15.7; Shoghi Effendi, *Promised Day,* ¶300.
226. 'Abdu'l-Bahá, *'Abdu'l-Bahá in Canada,* p. 35.
227. Shoghi Effendi, *Messages to the Bahá'í World,* p. 74.
228. Universal House of Justice, letter to the Bahá'ís of the World, April 1990.
229. Shoghi Effendi, *Establishing World Peace,* p. 46.
230. Ibid., p. 48.
231. Universal House of Justice, quoted in ibid., pp. 50–1.
232. Bahá'u'lláh, quoted in Shoghi Effendi, *World Order,* p. 33.
233. Shoghi Effendi, *Messages to the Bahá'í World,* p. 103.
234. Shoghi Effendi, *Citadel,* p. 125.
235. Shoghi Effendi's secretary on his behalf, 21 November 1949, quoted in *Lights of Guidance,* no. 439, p. 131.
236. Bahá'u'lláh, *Hidden Words,* Arabic 51.
237. Shoghi Effendi, *Promised Day,* ¶285.
238. Bahá'u'lláh quoted in ibid., ¶287.
239. Ibid., ¶286.
240. Shoghi Effendi's secretary on his behalf, quoted in *Lights of Guidance,* no. 448, p. 134.
241. Bahá'u'lláh, *Kitáb-i-Aqdas,* ¶88.
242. 'Abdu'l-Bahá, *Tablets of the Divine Plan,* no. 9:3.
243. 'Abdu'l-Bahá, quoted in Shoghi Effendi, *World Order,* , pp. 75–6.
244. Shoghi Effendi, *Citadel,* p. 37.
245. Ibid., pp. 126–7.
246. Bahá'u'lláh, *Kitáb-i-Aqdas,* ¶91.
247. Shoghi Effendi, *God Passes By,* p. 411.
248. Ibid., p. 315.
249. Ibid.
250. Shoghi Effendi, *World Order,* p. 202.

251. 'Abdu'l-Bahá, *Some Answered Questions*, pp. 33–4.

Chapter 7: *THE OBJECT OF ALL KNOWLEDGE*

252. 'Abdu'l-Bahá, *Promulgation*, p. 250.
253. 'Abdu'l-Bahá, *Secret*, p. 7.
254. Ibid., p. 9.
255. Sir Valentine Chirol, *The Middle Eastern Question*, p. 120, quoted in *Appreciations of the Bahá'í Faith*, p. 21.
256. Shoghi Effendi, *God Passes By*, pp. 122–3.
257. Ibid., pp. 123–4.
258. Bahá'u'lláh, *Gleanings*, XLIV, pp. 98–9.
259. Bahá'u'lláh, *Epistle*, p. 39.
260. George Townshend, Introduction to Nabíl-i-A'ẓam, *Dawn-Breakers*, p. xxxvi.
261. George Townshend, in the Introduction to Shoghi Effendi, *God Passes By*, p. ix.
262. For detailed citations from "Pacem in Terris," correlating its highlights with those of Bahá'u'lláh's writings, see Ugo Giachery, "One God, One Truth, One People," *The Bahá'í World*, vol. XV, pp. 612–19.
263. Bahá'u'lláh, *Summons*, Súriy-i-Haykal, ¶192.
264. 'Abdu'l-Bahá, *Some Answered Questions*, p. 34.
265. Phillip K. Hitti, "Arab Civilization," *Encyclopedia Americana*, 1990, vol. II, p. 152.
266. A. F. L. Beeston, "Arabic Language," *Academic American Encyclopedia*, 1989, vol. II, p. 100.
267. G. L. Della Vida, "Arabic Language," *Collier's Encyclopedia*, 1990, vol. II, p. 393.
268. Shoghi Effendi, *God Passes By*, p. 123.
269. Shoghi Effendi, foreword to Bahá'u'lláh, *Kitáb-i-Íqán*, p. vii.
270. Quoted by Marzieh Gail in a letter to the writer.
271. 'Abdu'l-Bahá, *Selections*, no. 4.14.
272. Adib Taherzadeh, "The Station of Bahá'u'lláh" (a tape-recorded talk delivered in 1987 in Brazil).
273. Bahá'u'lláh, quoted in Shoghi Effendi, *God Passes By*, p. 133.
274. Ibid., p. 171.
275. Quoted in Taherzadeh, *Revelation*, vol. I, pp. 35–6.
276. Nabíl-i-A'ẓam, quoted in Shoghi Effendi, *God Passes By*, p. 171.
277. Bahá'u'lláh, quoted in ibid., p. 217.
278. See Gail, *Summon Up Remembrance*, p. 122.

Chapter 8: *THE SUN: ITS OWN PROOF*

279. Bahá'u'lláh, *Gleanings*, XIX, p. 49.
280. John 14:7.

281. 'Abdu'l-Bahá, quoted in Shoghi Effendi, *God Passes By,*
     p. 124.
282. 'Abdu'l-Bahá, *Some Answered Questions,* p. 36.
283. Ḥájí Mírzá Haydar-'Alí, quoted in Taherzadeh, *Revelation,*
     vol. III, pp. 248–9.
284. E. G. Browne, quoted in Taherzadeh, *Revelation,* vol. II,
     pp. 12–13.
285. Shoghi Effendi, *God Passes By,* p. 142.
286. E. G. Browne, quoted in Taherzadeh, *Revelation,* vol. II, p. 12.
287. Ḥájí Mírzá Haydar-'Alí, quoted in Taherzadeh, *Revelation,*
     vol. III, p. 249.
288. T. K. Cheyne, *The Reconciliation of Races and Religions,*
     pp. 8–9, quoted by Shoghi Effendi in Nabíl, *The Dawn-Break-
     ers,* p. 516n.
289. Joseph Arthur le Comte de Gobineau, *Les Religions et les Phi-
     losophies dans l'Asie Centrale* (Paris: Les Éditions G. Crés et Cie.,
     1928), p. 118, quoted by Shoghi Effendi in ibid., pp. 79–80,
     note 4.
290. Gobineau, *Les Religions et les Philosophies dans l'Asie Centrale,*
     pp. 212–13, quoted by Shoghi Effendi in ibid., p. 502n.
291. Gobineau, *Les Religions et les Philosophies dans l'Asie Centrale,*
     pp. 121–122, quoted by Shoghi Effendi in ibid., p. 157n.
292. Bahá'u'lláh, quoted in Shoghi Effendi, *God Passes By,* p. 243.
293. Balyuzi, *'Abdu'l-Bahá,* pp. 70–1.
294. From a Tablet of 'Abdu'l-Bahá translated by Shoghi Effendi
     and transmitted 12 January 1923 to the National Spiritual
     Assembly of the Bahá'ís of the United States, quoted in Elena
     Maria Marcella, *Quest for Eden,* pp. 261–2.
295. Bahá'u'lláh, *Kitáb-i-Íqán,* ¶103.
296. Bahá'u'lláh, *Gleanings,* XXXVII, p. 86.
297. 'Abdu'l-Bahá, *Paris Talks,* no. 47.1.
298. Bahá'u'lláh, *Kitáb-i-Íqán,* ¶61.
299. Bahá'u'lláh, *Epistle,* p. 20.
300. Bahá'u'lláh, quoted in Nabíl, *Dawn-Breakers,* pp. 607–8.
301. Bahá'u'lláh, quoted in Shoghi Effendi, *God Passes By,* p. 101.
302. Bahá'u'lláh, *Epistle,* pp. 93–4.
303. Cheyne, quoted in *Appreciations of the Bahá'í Faith,* p. 18.
304. Alfred W. Martin, quoted in *Appreciations of the Bahá'í Faith,*
     pp. 22–3.
305. E. G. Browne, "The Bábís of Persia," *Journal of the Royal Asiatic
     Society* (1899), p. 933, quoted by Shoghi Effendi in Nabíl, *The
     Dawn-Breakers,* p. 516n.

306. Sir Francis Younghusband, *The Gleam* (London: John Murray, 1923), pp. 183–4, quoted by Shoghi Effendi in ibid., pp. 516–17n.

307. A. L. M. Nicolas, *Siyyid 'Alí-Muḥammad dit le Báb* (Paris: Librairie Critique, 1908), pp. 203–4, 376, quoted by Shoghi Effendi in ibid., p. 515n.

308. Phelps, *Life and Teachings,* pp. 2–10.

309. Blomfield, *Chosen Highway,* p. 220.

310. Matthew 7:16.

311. Bahá'u'lláh, *Epistle,* pp. 42–3.

312. Bahá'u'lláh, *Kitáb-i-Íqán,* ¶226.

313. Bahá'u'lláh, *Gleanings,* CXXXVI, p. 295.

314. Isaiah 55:10–11.

315. John 6:63.

316. Bahá'u'lláh, *Gleanings,* XXVII, p. 68.

317. Ibid., LXXXIX, p. 175.

318. Bahá'u'lláh, *Kitáb-i-Íqán,* ¶226.

319. Ibid., ¶226.

320. Bahá'u'lláh, *Gleanings,* CLIII, p. 326.

321. Ibid., LXX, p. 136.

322. Ibid., CXXXV, p. 293.

323. Bahá'u'lláh, *Prayers and Meditations,* p. 83.

324. Jordan, *Becoming Your True Self,* p. 4.

325. Shoghi Effendi, quoted in Universal House of Justice, *Messages,* no. 35.13.

326. Bahá'u'lláh, *Kitáb-i-Íqán,* ¶267.

327. Bahá'u'lláh, *Gleanings,* CXXV, pp. 266–7.

328. Bahá'u'lláh, *Kitáb-i-Íqán,* ¶118.

329. Bahá'u'lláh, *Tablets,* p. 155.

330. Matthew 5:39.

331. Matthew 26:52.

332. Koran 2:257.

333. Bahá'u'lláh, *Tablets,* p. 173.

334. Toynbee, *Study of History,* VIII, p. 117.

335. Bach, *Strangers,* pp. 75–6.

336. Robert Semple, *British Weekly,* 26 August 1954, quoted in Winston Evans and Marzieh Gail, "The Voice from Inner Space," *World Order,* Summer 1967, p. 40.

337. Shoghi Effendi, *World Order,* pp. 197–201.

Chapter 9: *THE BOOK OF GOD IS OPEN*

338. 'Abdu'l-Bahá, *Bahá'í World Faith,* pp. 383–4.

339. 'Abdu'l-Bahá, *Promulgation,* p. 327.

340. Ibid., p. 227.
341. Shoghi Effendi, *Selected Writings,* p. 7.
342. Bahá'u'lláh, *Epistle,* pp. 148–50.
343. Matthew 7:16.
344. Bahá'u'lláh, *Gleanings,* XXIII, p. 58.
345. Ibid., XCV, p. 195.
346. Ibid., XCII, p. 183.
347. Ibid., LXX, pp. 136–7.

BIBLIOGRAPHY

'Abdu'l-Bahá. *'Abdu'l-Bahá in Canada*. Compiled by the National
    Spiritual Assembly of the Bahá'ís of Canada. Rev. ed.
    Thornhill, Ont.: Bahá'í Canada Publications, 1987.
———. *Memorials of the Faithful*. Translated from the Persian and
    annotated by Marzieh Gail. Wilmette, IL: Bahá'í Publishing
    Trust, 1997.
———. *Paris Talks: Addresses Given by 'Abdu'l-Bahá in 1911*. 12th ed.
    London: Bahá'í Publishing Trust, 1995.
———. *The Promulgation of Universal Peace: Talks Delivered by 'Abdu'l-
    Bahá during His Visit to the United States and Canada in 1912*.
    Compiled by Howard MacNutt. Wilmette, IL: Bahá'í Pub-
    lishing Trust, 1982.
———. *The Secret of Divine Civilization*. Translated from the Persian
    by Marzieh Gail in consultation with Ali-Kuli Khan. 1st
    pocket-size ed. Wilmette, IL: Bahá'í Publishing Trust, 1990.
———. *Selections from the Writings of 'Abdu'l-Bahá*. Compiled by the
    Research Department of the Universal House of Justice.
    Translated by a Committee at the Bahá'í World Center and
    Marzieh Gail. 1st pocket-size ed. Wilmette, IL: Bahá'í Pub-
    lishing Trust, 1996.
———. *Some Answered Questions*. Compiled and translated by Laura
    Clifford Barney. 1st pocket-size ed. Wilmette, IL: Bahá'í
    Publishing Trust, 1984.
———. *Tablets of Abdul-Baha Abbas*. 3 vols. New York: Bahai Publish-
    ing Society, 1909–16.
———. *Tablets of the Divine Plan*. 1st pocket-size ed. Wilmette, IL:
    Bahá'í Publishing Trust, 1993.
———. *A Traveler's Narrative Written to Illustrate the Episode of the
    Báb*. Translated by Edward G. Browne. New and corrected
    ed. Wilmette, IL: Bahá'í Publishing Trust, 1980.
———. *Will and Testament of 'Abdu'l-Bahá*. Wilmette, IL: Bahá'í Pub-
    lishing Trust, 1944.
Appreciations of the Bahá'í Faith. Wilmette, IL: Bahá'í Publishing Com-
    mittee, 1947.
The Báb. *Selections from the Writings of the Báb*. Compiled by the Re-
    search Department of the Universal House of Justice.
    Translated by Habib Taherzadeh et al. Haifa: Bahá'í World
    Centre, 1976.

Bach, Marcus. *Strangers at the Door.* Nashville: Abingdon Press, 1971.

[Bahá'í International Community Office of Public Information.]
    Bahá'u'lláh. Wilmette, IL: Bahá'í Publishing Trust, 1991.

Bahá'u'lláh. *Epistle to the Son of the Wolf.* Translated by Shoghi Ef-
    fendi. 1st pocket-size ed. Wilmette, IL: Bahá'í Publishing
    Trust, 1988.

———. *Gleanings from the Writings of Bahá'u'lláh.* Compiled and
    translated by Shoghi Effendi. 1st pocket-size ed. Wilmette,
    IL: Bahá'í Publishing Trust, 1983.

———. *The Hidden Words.* Translated by Shoghi Effendi. Wilmette,
    IL: Bahá'í Publishing, 2002.

———. *The Kitáb-i-Aqdas: The Most Holy Book.* 1st pocket-size ed.
    Wilmette, IL: Bahá'í Publishing Trust, 1993.

———. *The Kitáb-i-Íqán: The Book of Certitude.* Translated by Shoghi
    Effendi. Wilmette, IL: Bahá'í Publishing, 2003.

———. *Prayers and Meditations.* Translated from the original Persian
    and Arabic by Shoghi Effendi. 1st pocket-size ed. Wilmette,
    IL: Bahá'í Publishing Trust, 1987.

———. *The Seven Valleys and The Four Valleys.* Translated by
    Marzieh Gail with Ali-Kuli Khan. Wilmette, IL: Bahá'í Pub-
    lishing Trust, 1991.

———. *The Summons of the Lord of Hosts: Tablets of Bahá'u'lláh.* Haifa:
    Bahá'í World Centre, 2002.

———. *Tablets of Bahá'u'lláh revealed after the Kitáb-i-Aqdas.* Compiled
    by the Research Department of the Universal House of
    Justice. Translated by Habib Taherzadeh et. al. 1st pocket-
    size ed. Wilmette, IL: Bahá'í Publishing Trust, 1988.

Bahá'u'lláh and 'Abdu'l-Bahá. *Bahá'í World Faith: Selected Writings of
    Bahá'u'lláh and 'Abdu'l-Bahá.* Wilmette, IL: Bahá'í Publishing
    Trust, 1976.

Balyuzi, H. M. *'Abdu'l-Bahá: The Centre of the Covenant of Bahá'u'lláh.*
    London: George Ronald, 1971.

———. *The Báb: The Herald of the Day of Days.* Oxford: George Ron-
    ald, 1973.

———. *Bahá'u'lláh: The King of Glory.* Oxford: George Ronald,
    1980.

Blomfield, Lady (Sitárih Khánum). *The Chosen Highway.* Wilmette,
    IL: Bahá'í Publishing Trust, n.d.; repr. 1975.

Cheyne, T. K. *The Reconciliation of Races and Religions.* London:
    Adam and Charles Black, 1914.

Clark, Ronald W. *Einstein—The Life and Times.* New York: Avon
    Books, 1972.

Clarke, Arthur C. *Profiles of the Future.* London: Victor Gollancz Ltd.,
    1982.

Cooper, L. *An Introduction to the Meaning and Structure of Physics.* New
    York: Harper & Row, 1968.

Cotran, Ramzi S., Vinay Kumar, and Stanley L. Robbins. *Robbins Pathologic Basis of Disease*. Philadelphia: W. B. Saunders: 1989.

Dulbecco, Renato, and Harold S. Ginsberg. *Virology*. Philadelphia: J. B. Lippincott, 1988.

Esslemont, J. E. *Bahá'u'lláh and the New Era: An Introduction to the Bahá'í Faith*. 5th rev. ed. Wilmette, IL: Bahá'í Publishing Trust, 1980.

Establishing World Peace. Compiled by the Research Department of the Universal House of Justice. Haifa: Bahá'í World Centre, 1985.

Ferris, Timothy. *Coming of Age in the Milky Way*. New York: Anchor Books, 1980.

Gail, Marzieh. *Summon Up Remembrance*. Oxford: George Ronald, 1987.

Gardner, Martin. *Relativity for the Million*. New York: MacMillan, 1962.

Gamow, George. *The Birth and Death of the Sun*. New York: Viking Press, 1946.

Giachery, Ugo. "One God, One Truth, One People." *The Bahá'í World: An International Record, Volume XV, 1968–1973*. Compiled by the Universal House of Justice. Haifa: Bahá'í World Centre, 1975.

Hatcher, William S. and J. Douglas Martin. *The Bahá'í Faith: The Emerging Global Religion*. Wilmette, IL: Bahá'í Publishing, 2002.

Hawking, Stephen W. *A Brief History of Time*. New York: Bantam Books, 1988.

Hofman, David. *Bahá'u'lláh, The Prince of Peace: A Portrait*. Oxford: George Ronald, 1992.

Honnold, Annamarie. *Vignettes from the Life of 'Abdu'l-Bahá*. Oxford: George Ronald, 1992.

Jordan, Daniel C. *Becoming Your True Self*. Wilmette, IL: Bahá'í Publishing Trust, 1968.

Lederman, Leon, and Dick Teresi. *The God Particle*. New York: Dell, 1993.

Lights of Guidance: A Bahá'í Reference File. Compiled by Helen Hornby. New Delhi: Bahá'í Publishing Trust, 1988.

Lovejoy, C. Owen. "Evolution of Human Walking." *Scientific American* (November 1988): 89.

Marcella, Elena Maria. *The Quest for Eden*. New York: Philosophical Library, 1966.

Misner, Charles W., Kip S. Thorne, and John A. Wheeler. *Gravitation*. San Francisco: Freeman, 1973.

Motlagh, Hushidar. *I Shall Come Again*. Mt. Pleasant, MI: Global Perspectives, 1992.

Nabíl-i-A'ẓam (Muḥammad-i-Zarandí). *The Dawn-Breakers: Nabíl's Narrative of the Early Days of the Bahá'í Revelation.* Translated from the original Persian and edited by Shoghi Effendi. Wilmette, IL: Bahá'í Publishing Trust, 1932.

[National Spiritual Assembly of the Bahá'ís of Japan, comp.]. *Japan Will Turn Ablaze! Tablets of 'Abdu'l-Bahá, Letters of Shoghi Effendi And Historical Notes About Japan.* Japan: Bahá'í Publishing Trust, 1974.

Phelps, Myron. *Life and Teachings of 'Abbás Effendi.* New York: Knickerbocker Press, 1912.

Rabbani, Rúḥíyyih. *The Desire of the World: Materials for the contemplation of God and His Manifestation for this Day.* Oxford: George Ronald, 1961.

Robbins, Stanley, and Vinay Kumar. *Basic Pathology.* Philadelphia: W. B. Saunders, 1987.

Sears, William. *Thief in the Night: Or The Strange Case of the Missing Millennium.* Oxford: George Ronald, 1961.

Shoghi Effendi. *The Advent of Divine Justice.* 1st pocket-size ed. Wilmette, IL: Bahá'í Publishing Trust, 1990.

———. *Bahá'í Administration: Selected Messages 1922–1932.* 7th ed. Wilmette, IL: Bahá'í Publishing Trust, 1974.

———. *Citadel of Faith: Messages to America, 1947–1957.* Wilmette, IL: Bahá'í Publishing Trust, 1965.

———. *Dawn of a New Day.* New Delhi: Bahá'í Publishing Trust, [1970].

———. *God Passes By.* Wilmette, IL: Bahá'í Publishing Trust, 1944.

———. *High Endeavours: Messages to Alaska.* Compiled by the National Spiritual Assembly of the Bahá'ís of Alaska. N.p.. National Spiritual Assembly of the Bahá'ís of Alaska, 1976.

[———]. *Letters from the Guardian to Australia and New Zealand, 1923–1957.* [Australia]: National Spiritual Assembly of the Bahá'ís of Australia, 1970.

———. *Messages to the Bahá'í World, 1950–1957.* Rev. ed. Wilmette, IL: Bahá'í Publishing Trust, 1971.

———. *Messages to Canada.* N.p.: National Spiritual Assembly of the Bahá'ís of Canada, 1965.

———. *Principles of Bahá'í Administration: A Compilation.* 3d ed. London: Bahá'í Publishing Trust, 1973.

———. *The Promised Day Is Come.* 1st pocket-size ed. Wilmette, IL: Bahá'í Publishing Trust, 1996.

———. *Selected Writings of Shoghi Effendi.* Compiled by the Bahá'í Publishing Committee. 2d ed. Wilmette, IL: Bahá'í Publishing Trust, 1975.

———. *This Decisive Hour: Messages from Shoghi Effendi to the North American Bahá'ís, 1932–1946.* Wilmette, IL: Bahá'í Publishing Trust, 2002.

———. *The Unfolding Destiny of the British Bahá'í Community: The Messages of the Guardian of the Bahá'í Faith to the Bahá'ís of the British Isles.* London: Bahá'í Publishing Trust, 1981.

———. *The World Order of Bahá'u'lláh: Selected Letters.* 1st pocket-size ed. Wilmette, IL: Bahá'í Publishing Trust, 1991.

———, comp. *The Bahá'í Faith 1844–1952.* Wilmette, IL: Bahá'í Publishing Committee, 1953.

Taherzadeh, Adib. *The Revelation of Bahá'u'lláh: Baghdád, 1853–63.* Volume 1. Oxford: George Ronald, 1974.

———. *The Revelation of Bahá'u'lláh: Adrianople, 1863–68.* Volume 2. Oxford: George Ronald, 1977.

———. *The Revelation of Bahá'u'lláh: 'Akká, 1868–77.* Volume 3. Oxford: George Ronald, 1983.

———. *The Revelation of Bahá'u'lláh: Mazra'ih & Bahjí, 1877–92.* Volume 4. Oxford: George Ronald, 1987.

Thompson, Juliet. *The Diary of Juliet Thompson.* Los Angeles: Kalimát Press, 1983.

Toynbee, Arnold. *A Study of History, VIII.* London: Oxford University Press, 1954.

Universal House of Justice. *The Constitution of the Universal House of Justice.* Haifa: Bahá'í World Centre, 1972.

———. *Individual Rights and Freedoms in the World Order of Bahá'u'lláh.* Wilmette, IL: Bahá'í Publishing Trust, 1989.

———. *Messages from the Universal House of Justice, 1963–1986: The Third Epoch of the Formative Age.* Compiled by Geoffry W. Marks. Wilmette, IL: Bahá'í Publishing Trust, 1996.

Wilbur, Ken, ed. *Quantum Questions: Mystical Writings of the World's Great Physicists.* Boulder: Shambhala, 1984.

Wolf, Fred Alan. *Taking the Quantum Leap.* New York: Perennial Library, 1989.

INDEX

For more information about the Bahá'í Faith,
or to contact the Bahá'ís near you, visit
http://www.us.bahai.org/
or call
1-800-22-UNITE

Bahá'í Publishing and the Bahá'í Faith

Bahá'í Publishing produces books based on the teachings of the Bahá'í Faith. Founded nearly 160 years ago, the Bahá'í Faith has spread to some 235 nations and territories and is now accepted by more than five million people. The word "Bahá'í" means "follower of Bahá'u'lláh." Bahá'u'lláh, the Founder of the Bahá'í Faith, asserted that He is the Messenger of God for all of humanity in this day. The cornerstone of His teachings is the establishment of the spiritual unity of humankind, which will be achieved by personal transformation and the application of clearly identified spiritual principles. Bahá'ís also believe that there is but one religion and that all the Messengers of God—among them Abraham, Zoroaster, Moses, Krishna, Buddha, Jesus, and Muḥammad—have progressively revealed its nature. Together, the world's great religions are expressions of a single, unfolding divine plan. Human beings, not God's Messengers, are the source of religious divisions, prejudices, and hatreds.

The Bahá'í Faith is not a sect or denomination of another religion, nor is it a cult or a social movement. Rather, it is a globally recognized independent world religion founded on new books of scripture revealed by Bahá'u'lláh.

Bahá'í Publishing is an imprint of the National Spiritual Assembly of the Bahá'ís of the United States.

Other Books Available
from Bahá'í Publishing

The Hidden Words
by Bahá'u'lláh

A collection of lyrical, gem-like verses of scripture that convey timeless spiritual wisdom "clothed in the garment of brevity," the Hidden Words is one of the most important and cherished scriptural works of the Bahá'í Faith.

Revealed by Bahá'u'lláh, the founder of the religion, the verses are a perfect guidebook to walking a spiritual path and drawing closer to God. They address themes such as turning to God, humility, detachment, and love, to name but a few. These verses are among Bahá'u'lláh's earliest and best-known works, having been translated into more than seventy languages and read by millions worldwide. This edition will offer many American readers their first introduction to the vast collection of Bahá'í scripture.

The Kitáb-i-Íqán: The Book of Certitude
by Bahá'u'lláh

The Book of Certitude is one of the most important scriptural works in all of religious history. In it Bahá'u'lláh gives a sweeping overview of religious truth, explaining the underlying unity of the world's religions, describing the universality of the revelations humankind has received from the Prophets of God, illuminating their fundamental teachings, and elucidating allegorical passages from the New Testament and the Koran that have given rise to misunderstandings among religious leaders, practitioners, and the public. Revealed in the span of two days and two nights, the work is, in the words of its translator, Shoghi Effendi, "the most important book written on the spiritual significance" of the Bahá'í Faith.

Advancement of Women: A Bahá'í Perspective
by Janet A. Khan and Peter J. Khan

Advancement of Women presents the Bahá'í Faith's global perspective on the equality of the sexes, including:
- The meaning of equality
- The education of women and the need for their participation in the world at large
- The profound effects of equality on the family and family relationships
- The intimate relationship between equality of the sexes and global peace
- Chastity, modesty, sexual harassment, and rape

240

The equality of women and men is one of the basic tenets of the Bahá'í Faith, and much is said on the subject in Bahá'í writings. Until now, however, no single volume created for a general audience has provided comprehensive coverage of the Bahá'í teachings on this topic. In this broad survey, husband-and-wife team Janet and Peter Khan address even those aspects of equality of the sexes that are usually ignored or glossed over in the existing literature.

Tactfully treating a subject that often provokes argumentation, contention, polarization of attitudes, and accusations, the authors elevate the discussion to a new level that challenges all while offending none.

The Bahá'í Faith: The Emerging Global Religion
by William S. Hatcher and J. Douglas Martin
Explore the history, teachings, structure, and community life of the worldwide Bahá'í community—what may well be the most diverse organized body of people on earth—through this revised and updated comprehensive introduction (2002).

Named by the *Encylopaedia Britannica* as a book that has made "significant contributions to knowledge and understanding" of religious thought, *The Bahá'í Faith* covers the most recent developments in a Faith that, in just over 150 years, has grown to become the second most widespread of the independent world religions.

"An excellent introduction. *[The Bahá'í Faith]* offers a clear analysis of the religious and ethical values on which Bahá'ism is based (such as all-embracing peace, world harmony, the important role of women, to mention only a few)."—Annemarie Schimmel, past president, International Association for the History of Religions

"Provide[s] non-Bahá'í readers with an excellent introduction to the history, beliefs, and sociopolitical structure of a religion that originated in Persia in the mid-1800s and has since blossomed into an international organization with . . . adherents from almost every country on earth."
—Montreal Gazette

Close Connections:
The Bridge between Spiritual and Physical Reality
by John S. Hatcher
Examines the bonds between spiritual and physical reality and their implications for science.

Close Connections will appeal to anyone interested in spirituality and its link to everyday life. For more than twenty-five years John Hatcher has studied the nature and purpose of physical reality by exploring the theological and philosophical implications of the authoritative Bahá'í texts. His latest book explains how the gap between physical and spiritual reality is routinely crossed, and describes the profound implications that result from the interplay of both worlds.

God Speaks Again:
An Introduction to the Bahá'í Faith
by Kenneth E. Bowers
Written by an internationally known member of the Bahá'í community, *God Speaks Again* is the first comprehensive introduction to the Bahá'í Faith written for general readers that includes many important and beautiful

passages of Bahá'í scripture to both illustrate and explain the Faith's history, teachings, and distinctive relevance for life on our planet today. The book contains 30 chapters covering all aspects of the religion, as well as notes, a glossary, a bibliography, and a suggested reading list. The history and teachings of the Bahá'í Faith center around the inspiring person of its Prophet and Founder, Bahá'u'lláh (1817–1892). The extraordinary qualities that Bahá'u'lláh displayed throughout the course of His life, the voluminous and comprehensive body of His written works, and the impact they continue to have around the globe undeniably qualify Him as a major figure in world religious history.

It's Not Your Fault:
How Healing Relationships Change Your Brain
& Can Help You Overcome a Painful Past
by Patricia Romano McGraw

Simply put, you can't think your way to happiness if you're suffering the effects of trauma or abuse. Yet every day, millions receive this message from a multi-billion-dollar self-help industry. As a result, many think it's their fault when their efforts to heal themselves fail. Far too many sincere, intelligent, and highly motivated people who have followed popular advice for self-healing still feel depressed, anxious, unloved, and unlovable. Why is this? If popular pathways for self-healing don't work, what does? How can those who suffer begin to find relief, function better, and feel genuinely optimistic, relaxed, loved, and lovable? This engaging and highly readable book, based on the author's professional experience in treating those who suffer from the devastating effects of emotional trauma, offers hope for those who suffer and those who care about them. McGraw describes how trauma affects the brain and, therefore, one's ability to carry out "good advice"; explains the subtle and largely hidden processes of attunement and attachment that take place between parents and children, examining their impact on all future relationships; tells what is needed for healing to occur; discusses the profound health benefits of spirituality and a relationship with God in assisting and accelerating the healing process; and suggests how members of the helping professions can begin to tap the deepest, most authentic parts of themselves to touch the hearts of those they seek to help.

Marriage beyond Black and White:
An Interracial Family Portrait
by David Douglas and Barbara Douglas

A powerful story about the marriage of a Black man and a White woman, *Marriage beyond Black and White* offers a poignant and sometimes painful look at what it was like to be an interracial couple in the United States from the early 1940s to the mid-1990s. Breaking one of the strongest taboos in American society at the time, Barbara Wilson Tinker and Carlyle Douglas met, fell in love, married, and began raising a family. At the time of their wedding, interracial marriage was outlawed in twenty-seven states and was regarded as an anathema in the rest.

Barbara began writing their story to record both the triumphs and hardships of interracial marriage. Her son David completed the family chronicle. The result will uplift and inspire any reader whose life is touched by injustice, offering an invaluable perspective on the roles of faith and spiritual transformation in combating prejudice and racism.

Prophet's Daughter:
The Life and Legacy of Bahíyyih Khánum, Outstanding Heroine of the Bahá'í Faith
by Janet A. Khan

The first full-length biography of a member of Bahá'u'lláh's family, an important woman in world religious history.

A biography of a largely unknown yet important woman in world religious history—the eldest daughter of Bahá'u'lláh, founder of the Bahá'í religion—who faithfully served her family and the early followers of a then completely new faith through nearly seven decades of extreme hardship. During the mid-nineteenth and early twentieth centuries, when women in the Middle East were largely invisible, deprived of education, and without status in their communities, she was an active participant in the religion's turbulent early years and contributed significantly to its emergence as an independent world religion. The example of her life and her remarkable personal qualities have special relevance to issues confronting society today.

The Reality of Man
compiled by Terry J. Cassiday, Christopher J. Martin, and Bahhaj Taherzadeh

An important new collection of Bahá'í writings on the spiritual nature of human beings.

This compilation provides a sample of the Bahá'í religion's vast teachings on the nature of man. Topics include God's love for humanity, the purpose of life, our spiritual reality, the nature of the soul, how human beings develop spiritually, and immortality and life hereafter. The writings are from Bahá'u'lláh and His appointed successor, 'Abdu'l-Bahá.

"Men at all times and under all conditions stand in need of one to exhort them, guide them and to instruct and teach them. Therefore He hath sent forth His Messengers, His Prophets, and chosen ones that they might acquaint the people with the divine purpose underlying the revelation of Books and the raising up of messengers, and that everyone may become aware of the trust of God, which is latent in the reality of every soul."—Bahá'u'lláh

"The mission of the Prophets, the revelation of the Holy Books, the manifestation of the heavenly teachers and the purpose of divine philosophy all center in the training of the human realities so that they may become clear and pure as mirrors and reflect the light and love of [God]. . . . Otherwise, by simple development along material lines man is not perfected. At most, the physical aspect of man, his natural or material conditions, may become stabilized and improved, but he will remain deprived of the spiritual or divine bestowal. He is then like a body without a spirit, a lamp without the light. . . ."— 'Abdu'l-Bahá

Refresh and Gladden My Spirit:
Prayers and Meditations from Bahá'í Scripture
Introduction by Pamela Brode

Discover the Bahá'í approach to prayer with this uplifting collection of prayers and short, inspirational extracts from Bahá'í scripture. More than 120 prayers in *Refresh and Gladden My Spirit* offer solace and inspiration on themes including spiritual growth, nearness to God, comfort, contentment, happiness, difficult times, healing, material needs, praise and gratitude, and strength, to name only a few. An introduction by Pamela Brode examines the powerful effects of prayer and meditation in daily life, outlines the Bahá'í approach to prayer, and considers questions such as "What is prayer?" "Why pray?" "Are our prayers answered?" and "Does prayer benefit the world?"

Release the Sun
by William Sears

Millennial fervor gripped many people around the world in the early nineteenth century. While Christians anticipated the return of Jesus Christ, a wave of expectation swept through Islam that the "Lord of the Age" would soon appear. In Persia, this reached a dramatic climax on May 23, 1844, when a twenty-five-year-old merchant from S͟híráz named Siyyid 'Alí-Muḥammad, later titled "the Báb," announced that he was the bearer of a divine Revelation destined to transform the spiritual life of the human race. Furthermore, he claimed that he was but the herald of another Messenger, who would soon bring a far greater Revelation that would usher in an age of universal peace. Against a backdrop of wide-scale moral decay in Persian society, this declaration aroused hope and excitement among all classes. The Báb quickly attracted tens of thousands of followers, including influential members of the clergy—and the brutal hand of a fearful government bent on destroying this movement that threatened to rock the established order.

Release the Sun tells the extraordinary story of the Báb, the Prophet-Herald of the Bahá'í Faith. Drawing on contemporary accounts, William Sears vividly describes one of the most significant but little-known periods in religious history since the rise of Christianity and Islam.

Seeking Faith:
Is Religion Really What You Think It Is?
by Nathan Rutstein

What's your concept of religion? A 2001 Gallup Poll on religion in America found that while nearly two out of three Americans claim to be a member of a church or synagogue, more than half of those polled believe that religion is losing its influence on society. Seeking Faith examines today's concepts of religion and the various reasons why people are searching in new directions for hope and spiritual guidance. Author Nathan Rutstein explores the need for a sense of purpose, direction, and meaning in life, and the need for spiritual solutions to global problems in the social, economic, environmental, and political realms. Rutstein also discusses the concept of the Spiritual Guide, or Divine Educator, and introduces the teachings of Bahá'u'lláh and the beliefs of the Bahá'í Faith.

The Story of Bahá'u'lláh:
Promised One of All Religions
by Druzelle Cederquist

An easy-to-read introduction to the Prophet and Founder of the Bahá'í Faith.

The Story of Bahá'u'lláh presents in a clear narrative style the life of the prophet from His birth into a wealthy merchant family, through His transforming spiritual experience while incarcerated in the infamous Black Pit of Tehran, and over the decades of harsh and increasingly remote exile that followed. Woven into the story are Bahá'u'lláh's principal teachings and references to historical events and persons that place the development of the new religion in a global perspective. This book chronologically follows the story told in *Release the Sun* (Bahá'í Publishing, 2003).

As explained in such resources as *The Oxford Dictionary of World Religions* and the *Encyclopaedia Britannica,* members of the Bahá'í Faith believe that all the founders of the world's great religions have been Messengers of God and agents of a progressive divine plan for the education of the human race. According to Bahá'u'lláh (1819–1892), the Prophet and Founder of the Bahá'í religion, the teachings of the divine Messengers—including Abraham, Moses, Buddha, Christ, Muḥammad—vary with the receptivity and maturity of the people of their era, but all represent one single "religion of God." Bahá'u'lláh, whom Bahá'ís accept as the divine Messenger for the present age, taught that the unity of all the peoples of the earth is the spiritual destiny of this period in human history.

A Wayfarer's Guide to Bringing the Sacred Home
by Joseph Sheppherd

What's the spiritual connection between self, family, and community? Why is it so important that we understand and cultivate these key relationships? *A Wayfarer's Guide to Bringing the Sacred Home* offers a Bahá'í perspective on issues that shape our lives and the lives of those around us: the vital role of spirituality in personal transformation, the divine nature of child-rearing and unity in the family, and the importance of overcoming barriers to building strong communities—each offering joy, hope, and confidence to a challenged world. Inspiring extracts and prayers from Bahá'í scripture are included. This is an enlightening read for anyone seeking to bring spirituality into their daily lives.

VISIT YOUR FAVORITE BOOKSTORE TODAY
TO FIND OR REQUEST THESE TITLES
FROM BAHÁ'Í PUBLISHING.